Fire In My Bones

BOOKS BY RABBI ROLAND B. GITTELSOHN

Fire In My Bones
Wings of the Morning
My Beloved Is Mine
Consecrated Unto Me
Man's Best Hope
Little Lower than the Angels
Modern Jewish Problems

Roland B. Gittelsohn

Fire In My Bones

Essays on Judaism in a
Time of Crisis

BLOCH PUBLISHING COMPANY
New York

And if I say: "I will not make mention of Him,
Nor speak any more in His name,"
Then there is in my heart as it were a burning fire
Shut up in my bones,
And I weary myself to hold it in,
But cannot.

–Jeremiah 20:9

Introduction

Let me begin, gentle reader, with a necessary confession and a warning. The confession is: I probably ought not be the writer of this Introduction, because I am not without a strong (but completely defensible and justifiable) bias toward the author of this volume. The warning is, therefore, read these introductory words with a measure of cautious evaluation, but with the solid assurance, nonetheless, that they are valid and true.

You see, the author of these sermon essays is my dearest friend in the rabbinate and the affection and friendship which bind us grow stronger and more precious through the years. Indeed, if I were not myself a rabbi, I would move to where Rabbi Gittelsohn is, become a member of his congregation and so guarantee myself the unfailing refreshment of spirit which his preachment offers Sabbath after Sabbath.

But I am grateful for this collection, a revivifying draught drawn from the well of living waters which Rabbi Gittelsohn has managed unfailingly to tap across the rich, contributing years of his brilliant ministry.

So, having issued fair warning, I can proceed with clear conscience.

Rabbi Gittelsohn calls these writings "sermon essays," and I would not quarrel with such a description. Nevertheless, these essays are clearly the written record of what is manifestly intended, in the first place, for delivery from the pulpit. As indeed these "sermon essays" have been. For aside from some minor changes, chiefly to give greater contemporaneity, and the combining of some material from several "essays" into one, it is obvious from structure and style that we are dealing with public, pulpit utterance. Then let me use the term "sermon" instead of "sermon essays."

Now a sermon is a literary art form of a delicate and specialized nature. It must have inner unity and balance, true to itself, and it must have outer relevance, true to the world to which it seeks to add meaning.

At its very best, a sermon combines a challenge to the mind an exaltation to the spirit. If it merely challenges the mind, then it is only the brave exploration of some theme which engages the interest of the preacher and which he hopes will likewise arrest the attention of the listener. What the preacher is saying may be well said and worthy, but he is walking the fertile meadows of the mind only; and his gaze is level and his words horizontal, as it were. The world may be very much present in what he is saying, but the mountain peaks and the upreaching heights are beyond the scope of his vision.

On the other hand, there are sermons which derive in large measure from the heart rather than from the head. They can have passion, and the words fly upward; and the preacher's vision may be lifted to the mountains; and still these qualities are not enough to shape that kind of sermon into a true work of art.

The heart-words may be lambent flame, and each one a fire burning bright. But the fire dies quickly, and grey, cold ash on the creative hearth is all that remains. The heart-words by themselves bring into being only a partial sermon, just as do the mind-words by themselves.

But let the preacher take the mind-words that challenge him to struggle with the insecurities of the world and the inequities in human relationships. Let him declare what has seized hold upon his mind. Let him combine these with the heart-words in which the divine fire glows, adding moral passion's flame to the mind's light. When a preacher fashions this harmony, this indivisible fusion of intellect and spirit, then there is an authentic sermon, a preacher's creation that makes outreach and upreach a singularity, that unites heart and mind in a marriage which is nothing less than a binding together of earth and heaven.

In the pages of this volume, Rabbi Gittelsohn has given us such a harvest of creative sermons.

But even a volume of creative sermons, rich in their fulfillment, suffers from certain inherent disabilities. A sermon needs the preacher, his voice, his gesture, the authority of his presence. It also needs a listening congregation. In other words, a preacher needs the immediacy of congregational contact; the members of the congregation need the sermon as a living, present urgency, meant for each worshipper and spoken, as it were, directly to him.

A printed sermon is under double handicap. Firstly, the preacher's words are there, but not the preacher. What does he look like? How is he saying the words? What is there in his heart which fails to come through in the printed speech? What is in his mind that cold print cannot enkindle into glowing completeness?

Secondly, the preacher's words are there, but the congregation is only a congregation of one: you. The sense of sharing, of community with others is absent. Consequently you, the reader, need to bring your own creative imagination to the sermon. You have to add yourself to the words; and only as you succeed in the difficult but essential task of becoming both preacher and listener does the printed word fly from the page, and the paper text becomes the robut vitality of the living word.

Everything I have said to this point is germaine to this collection of sermons which are, according to the standards set forth, the work of a genuinely superior and imaginative preacher. I have heard him many times. I have been held by the driving power of his mind and heart. By which I do not mean that Rabbi Gittelsohn is a kind of pulpit hypnotist, a grandiloquent sermonizer, given to the broad and dramatic gesture; nor is he the histrionic performer, delighting in words for their own sake, nor the pedant who speaks in footnotes.

On the contrary, Rabbi Gittelsohn eschews such devices. They are remote from his thinking and from his style. He has a clear, incisive mind. He preaches clear, incisive sermons. He cares about people from the depth of a compassionate heart. He preaches compassionate sermons. You will never, good friend, meditate upon sermons that bear a cleaner seal of honesty, nor are filled with a more resolute passion for the creation of a good world.

These are the sermons of a courageous fighter against iniquity. They are the utterance of a dedicated believer in the fraternity of man, of one who believes in the perfectibility of man. He believes in the possibility of creating a decent world. He believes in the rights which all men must ultimately share in this imperfect, indecent, unrighteous world of ours. In him, the mind and the heart find noble union. In his preaching, the mind-words and the heart-words are one.

The man who can write the sermon, "Between Man and

His Conscience," is a brave and fearless man. The man who can write the sermon, "What Every Christian Should Know About Judaism," has a proud sense of his Jewishness and an equally proud sense of the meaning of Jewish peoplehood. The man who can write the sermon, "The Two Faces of Israel," is a man who cares deeply and passionately about his people's fate and destiny. The man who can write the sermon, "I Believe in Miracles," is a man immovably faithful to the Divinity in Whom he believes; to the God in Whom his trust unshakably abides.

It is sometimes said of a preacher that his vision, his courage and his forthrightness place him in the line of the prophets. I am not always certain what that expression means. If, with reference to this book, it is supposed to mean that Rabbi Gittelsohn is another Amos or is to be added to the Biblical prophetic company, I would say that it is an assertion better left unsaid. But if one means by "the line of the prophets" a man of penetrating, orderly mind, one who never gets lost in an undisciplined tangle of words and ideas; if one means a leader who leads, a fighter who fights, a visionary who refuses to deny the world's reality, a realist who refuses to give up the vision, then Rabbi Gittelsohn is one of those in the generations of our history who have known the fire burning in their bones, the fire that will not be quenched until evil shall have been removed from the face of the earth.

In this company of the valiant and the incorruptible, Rabbi Gittelsohn most assuredly belongs; and these sermons testify why.

JACOB P. RUDIN

Foreword

In terms of both content and intent, these sermon-essays should speak for themselves, without preface from my pen.

Yet I cannot allow them to see the light of day without expressing my deepest gratitude to those who made this volume possible. When four former pulpit associates— Harvey J. Fields, Leon A. Jick, Charles A. Kroloff and Robert W. Shapiro—decided to publish a collection of sermons to mark the thirtieth anniversary of my ordination, they touched my heart profoundly. Because they are all creatively busy rabbis, the gestation period of selection, editorial preparation and publication lasted longer than they had anticipated.

I am inexpressibly grateful to them, to the many friends who provided the financial means of issuing these chapters, and to my beloved friend, Jacob Philip Rudin, for his gracious words of introduction. May the messages which follow at least partially repay them for their efforts and affection.

ROLAND B. GITTELSOHN

Boston, Massachusetts

Contents

BETWEEN MAN
AND HIS
CONSCIENCE

1
Answer to an Anonymous Letter

Like every person in public life, I have received my
share of anonymous correspondence. Usually I ignore it, on
the theory that any individual who declines to accept responsibility for his views deserves neither the courtesy nor
the dignity of being recognized. Why, then, do I make an
exception of the anonymous letter which elicits this response? Plainly and simply, because I believe that profound
and pervasive issues are raised by it, issues which involve
the proper role of a rabbi, the relationship between a rabbi
and his congregants, between a rabbi and his conscience. I
hope my unidentified correspondent is present tonight.
Whether he is or not, however, there are others in our
midst who feel as he does and who therefore are entitled to
the kind of explanation I now propose to offer.

When I decided to preach on Rosh Hashanah about
Vietnam, I was aware of the fact that some of you would
take exception to my message. I knew in advance that such
a sermon would invite a substantial volume of mail. It did.
My only surprise—a very pleasant one, I confess—was to
discover that by a margin of about five-to-one these letters
supported my position. In view of the well-known truth
that most people take to typewriter or pen only in angry

opposition, this response speaks most favorably for the social and spiritual maturity of our congregation. All but two
of the letters I received—whether in opposition or agreement—were courteous and polite. The anonymous letter,
as you will see in a moment, was different.

It contained as an enclosure the lead article in the November *Reader's Digest*, a piece called *A Hero Comes
Home*, relating the tragic story of Captain Christopher
O'Sullivan's death in Vietnam just before his scheduled
return to his wife and two sons. Let me read the letter in its
entirety, not even correcting its grammatical errors, lest I
be accused of doctoring it to my own advantage. Here it is:

October 31st 1965
*One of the chief factors which brought you as a Rabbi to the
attention of the world and the Jewish community was the
very fine statement you made while you were a United States
Chaplain in World War 2. This was printed in newspapers and
I am sure was one of the deciding things in choosing you for
your present position at Temple Israel.*

*I am taking the liberty of asking you to read the enclosed
article and searching your own heart to see whether your
former attitude to war and its results was just a means to an
end in order to gain you publicity and "fame" or Captain
Sullivan's idea of the present conflict in Viet Nam and his
sacrifice in death for a cause he really believed in.*

*I am not signing my name to this letter because I believe its
sentiment is that of a great many of your Temple members,
both friends and detractors.*

*Our parents, our teachers and our ministers are supposed to
be our examples to live by. When I see the burning of draft
cards, the sudden increase in the number of conscientious objectors and statements by young men that they would like to*

*see the Viet Cong lick the United States, I feel that part of this
behavior must be attributed to men like you and I feel a little
ashamed of you!*

The letter ends with an exclamation mark, but without
signature.

Before commencing my formal—and I hope restrained
—reply, let me assure you that I do not want the Vietcong
or anyone else to "lick the United States," and that I do not
approve the empty, vain gesture of burning draft cards. I
do admire honest objectors to war on grounds of conscience; even though I haven't entirely agreed with them
for many years, I am convinced from personal experience
of both kinds that it sometimes requires a higher order of
personal courage to be a conscientious objector than to
participate in combat. The intent of this somewhat paren-
thetical paragraph is that I be criticized or credited—as the
case may be—for the things I actually believe, not for those
created by someone else's fertile imagination.

Very well, then, suppose we turn to the substantive
issues. Other letters state explicitly what this one only implies. There are, it appears, three grounds for the discomfort some of you experienced after listening to me on Rosh
Hashanah. First, you felt that my theme was not appropriate for the High Holy Days because it wasn't spiritual.
Second, you objected that Vietnam isn't the rabbi's public
business because he does not qualify as an expert in diplomatic or political matters; his expertise is in the spheres of
theology and religion. And third, you resented my criticism of American policy as a threat to your patriotism and
love of country. One correspondent admonished me to
follow the advice of Stephen Decatur: "Our country in her
intercourse with foreign nations, may she always be in the

right; but our country, right or wrong." Let me deal now
with each of these objections in sequence.

Whether or not a sermon on Vietnam—or, for that matter, on any public issue—is spiritual, becomes a matter of
semantics. To get anywhere, we must first arrive at a definition of the word *spiritual*. For me it denotes the trans-
physical aspect of human experience, anything and everything about man which transcends his physical anatomy as
an animal. To be at once more specific, every attitude or
action of man which is aimed at the creation or appreciation of truth, of beauty or of moral goodness is spiritual. If,
therefore, I seek in a sermon to discover and disclose the
truth about Vietnam, that immediately qualifies as a spiritual message. If, moreover, I strive to apply the ethical
insights of my faith to American foreign policy, that—
clearly and unmistakably—is spiritual. The trouble with
many of us is that we have grown accustomed to using the
word *spiritual* for things which are vague, amorphous and
abstract—and are therefore undisturbing and comfortable.
Once we understand the word accurately, the ground is cut
out from the first objection to such a sermon.

Up to this point, everything I have said applies to all
religious leaders or groups. There is a special emphasis,
however, which must be addressed specifically to Jews. We
cannot determine what is or is not spiritually appropriate
for us as Jews unless first we decide who we are and what
destiny demands of us.

We are history's most obstinate and persistent rebels
against conformity. We are the descendants of Abraham,
who smashed his father's precious idols; of Nathan, who
dared point even to the King himself and say: "You are the
man!" We are the heirs of Jeremiah, who decried pretenders for shouting "peace, peace, when there is no peace."

We spring from the loins of Zechariah, who—in a time no less obsessed with militarism than our own—proclaimed: "Not by might, and not by power, but by My spirit, saith the Lord." We are, in short, a people that has always insisted on applying its moral imperatives to every individual and communal aspect of life. We are that, or we are nothing. And it is, I submit, only in the light of what we really, truly are that we Jews can decide what is spiritual and what belongs in our pulpits.

This brings us to our second objection, that rabbis should refrain from public pronouncement in such areas as political and diplomatic matters, where they are not experts. I am nearly the last person in this congregation to pose as a political or diplomatic specialist, though I don't think I am as ignorant and naive in these fields as some of my critics apparently believe me to be. But I am an expert on ethics. If not, I have no right to wear this robe or occupy this place. And especially in Judaism ethics cannot and must not be isolated from the warp and woof of practical life. The notion that individuals should strive to be righteous in their personal lives but that societies and nations need not, is just about as utterly un-Jewish as anything could be. When you ask whether the rabbi has a right to speak on the ethics of foreign policy, you ask the wrong question. This isn't a matter of right but of obligation—of solemn, ineluctable duty.

The Central Conference of American Rabbis spoke what should be the last word on this subject. Let me read you a small section of its statement on *The Rabbi and the Political Process:* "We hereby reaffirm the rabbi's right and obligation to exercise political responsibility as a citizen and as a moral teacher . . . the rabbi who seeks to affect the character of his congregants must seek to affect the charac-

ter of the environment in which they live . . . Therefore,
the rabbi must bring to bear the insights of his faith and
experience to aid his congregants to discern the moral dimensions of contemporary problems."

Does anyone here doubt that there are moral dimensions
to the conduct of American foreign policy? Then let me
share with such doubters the following devastating exchange, published in the New York Herald-Tribune of 17
November 1965 under the by-line of David Wise, Washington Bureau Chief. On 24 February of the same year
Secretary General U Thant of the United Nations said: "I
have presented certain ideas on my own to some of the
principal parties directly involved in the question of Vietnam. I have even presented concrete ideas and proposals
. . ." The very next day George Reedy, White House
Press Secretary, said: "The President has received no proposal from U Thant." At a press conference on 15 November this question was asked: "Did U Thant in late summer
and/or fall of 1964 on one or more occasions advise the
U.S. Government that the North Vietnamese government
was prepared for talks of some kind?" Answer, by Robert
J. McCloskey of the State Department: "Yes."

I love my nation. I love it enough to have volunteered
for duty as a chaplain when no power other than my own
conscience could have compelled me to do so. But my
government has lied to me and the world, and that's a moral
issue. My government lied to me and the world not only
about Hanoi's readiness to negotiate peace, but also in the
incident involving the U2 plane shot down over Russia. My
government lied about its training of Cuban guerrillas preparing to invade their homeland. My government lied
about its attempt to bribe the premier of Singapore. Each
of these deliberate lies was exposed by the alert conscience

of someone who refused to be brainwashed and was only then admitted by officials. When my government lies, that's a moral issue. So long as God gives me strength and you give me the privilege of this pulpit, I intend to talk about moral issues, be they pleasant or painful.

My anonymous correspondent is ashamed of me for the wrong reason. If I ever desist from preaching truth as I see it, from castigating immorality as I understand it, I shall then have deserved shame from him and from all of you.

That leaves us with only the last of the objections to sermons such as mine on Rosh Hashanah, the idea that as a molder of public opinion, I should uphold my nation, right or wrong. Well, I'm afraid that my unidentified pen-pal and I have diametrically different notions on what constitutes true patriotism. What troubles me here most, however, is something else. The claim that one must always support his government, that it is dangerous and subversive to criticize one's government, smacks much more of dictatorship than of democracy. This is the psychology of "Heil Hitler," not of "I pledge allegiance." This was the rationale for millions of Germans to close their eyes and ears and hearts to the painful plight of cremated Jews! No, I don't buy this notion. I won't hold my government always right, any more than I honestly believe that my children or my wife or I myself can always be right. There are times when honest, even trenchant complaint is the most genuine token of love.

Are you aware of what has already begun in American life? We are headed full-speed into a period of neo-McCarthyism. One of the most precious of our democratic privileges—the right to dissent—is being disastrously corroded. Increasingly those who have the honest courage to criticize are being branded as communists. Demonstrations

against the war in Vietnam have been countered by the
cheapest, shabbiest, most maudlin kind of propaganda: by
inciting soldiers to express contempt for all critics; by television screens which show us night after night only the
bearded beatniks among the protestors, and only the most
handsome and clean-cut of administration defenders. Intelligent criticism is being met not with rational response but
with the kind of long T.V. sequence I saw Wednesday
night, showing a tearful young widow, a tiny infant in her
arms, reading the last letter she received from her husband
before he was killed in combat.

Letters of protest against policy in Vietnam are now
being officially answered by the Internal Security Division
of the Justice Department, the division charged with responsibility to prosecute communists and spies. You don't
really think that's a simple coincidence, do you?

We who deplore current American policy are accused of
letting our soldiers down. Far from it! I wouldn't deliberately let any American in combat down. I know his fear in
my own gut. The people who are really betraying him are
those who encourage our government to sacrifice his life in
vain for a purpose of most dubious morality.

Here, then, is my reply—to my anonymous correspondent and to those who had the decency to sign their commu-
nications. I must respectfully reject all three of their premises. I must insist that my theme on Rosh Hashanah was
both spiritual and appropriate; that it is precisely my responsibility as a rabbi to subject American policy to the
microscope of moral judgment: that he is most patriotic
and loyal who most consistently challenges his nation toward truth.

The writer of this letter implies that I have betrayed the
ideals of my Iwo Jima sermon. I wonder when he last read

it, or if he truly understood it. I am satisfied that my views on Vietnam are in direct fulfillment of the ideals I cherished and the promise I voiced in March of 1945. Listen, will you not?—and judge for yourselves. Perhaps as you do, you will understand why I speak on Vietnam as I have, why anything else would be a gross betrayal of my conscience and my God:

We shall not foolishly suppose, as did the last generation of America's fighting men, that victory on the battle-field will automatically guarantee the triumph of democracy at home. This war, with all its frightful heartache and suffering, is but the beginning of our generation's struggle for democracy . . . . We promise you who lie here . . . . We will join hands with Britain, China, Russia—in peace, even as we have in war, to build the kind of world for which you died. . . . .

Thus do we memorialize those who, having ceased living with us, now live within us. Thus do we consecrate ourselves, the living, to carry on the struggle they began. Too much blood has gone into this soil for us to let it lie barren. Too much pain and heartache have fertilized the earth on which we stand. We here solemnly swear: this shall not be in vain. Out of this, and from the suffering and sorrow of those who mourn this, will come—we promise—the birth of a new freedom for the sons of men everywhere.

2

"We Cry to Them in God's Name!"

Tonight is the third time in fourteen months that I have addressed this congregation on the subject of Vietnam. There is, I believe, a grim appropriateness in the fact that my third discourse on the subject is dated eleven November, a day set aside to memorialize and honor our military heroes. Some of us fear that everything decent for which they allegedly fought, all the noble ideals which have made the United States a different kind of nation, are in imminent danger of gross betrayal. What better time than Veterans' Day to reassess our moral status in southeast Asia?

Every conversation on Vietnam to which I have been party in the last eight months has ended on the same note. After few or many minutes devoted to how we became involved there in the first place, after vigorous accusation and defense on the degree of our culpability in that unhappy little land, someone has invariably said: "All right, let's grant, at least for the sake of argument, that we have been guilty of many mistakes. But we cannot retrace our steps. We're there. You have no right to criticize the State Department and Pentagon unless you have viable alternatives to propose."

More often than not, before I have scarcely commenced

my reply to this challenge, the argument is resumed, as a result of which I have never yet had an opportunity to spell out the whole of my alternative without interruption. To-night, protected by the etiquette and ethic of the pulpit-pew relationship, I shall have that opportunity for the first time. Much more is involved here, however, than just my desire to complete a train of thought free from intrusion. There is no short or simple way to extricate ourselves from the insidious morass in which we have become entrapped. No one of the five steps I am about to suggest will suffice. In all likelihood no two or three of them together would be enough. Only a massive effort, a cumulative program con-sisting of all five measures at least, announced at one time as an organic national intent and backed at each juncture by impressive action—only such an effort stands the slightest chance of averting disaster. I bid you, therefore, to consider the whole proposal as such, and to judge each suggestion only within a context which includes all the others.

I urge you also to adopt the mood projected by Pope Paul VI in his memorable encyclical of 19 September. Speaking to the adversaries in Vietnam, he said: "We cry to them in God's name to stop! . . . A settlement should be reached now, even at the expense of some inconveniences or loss, or it may have to be made later in the train of bitter slaughter and involve great loss." So tonight, I cry to us in God's name to stop! On what basis, in what stages and degrees, *can* we stop?

First, by putting an end to our bombing of North Viet-nam. That bombing has failed to accomplish a single one of the aims for which it was begun. It has not terminated the infiltration of either men or supplies from North to South Vietnam. It has not destroyed or even damaged enemy morale; if anything, the incredible punishment we have meted out has strengthened Hanoi's determination to fight. It has not inclined our adversary to approach the conference table; no one who understands anything about human dynamics ever thought it would. Just as the bombings of Rotterdam and London in World War II stiffened the will of the Dutch and British to fight, so each ton of napalm dropped on the Vietcong moves them farther away from any tendency to talk peace.

Our war in Vietnam is a guerrilla war. Guerrilla wars are not won by saturation bombing. No one has expressed this truth more effectively than Eric Sevareid on his CBS newscast of 21 June. He said: "We are using giant sledgehammers to kill hornets. . . . The enemy needs an estimated eighty-seven tons of supplies each day; the American establishment alone needs about twenty thousand tons a day." So the first essential step—if we would improve the prospect for peace, and not just feed our national paranoia—is to stop the bombing.

The second is to propose a cease-fire in military activity on the ground. This, of course, requires reciprocity. We can terminate the bombing by air unilaterally because we are the only ones who have been indulging in it. A cease-fire on the ground would have to be by mutual agreement. But we should be the first to advocate it. Our proposal should include the barring of further escalation during the suspension of fighting and of course there must be effective international machinery to police a cease-fire. International supervision and inspection might well be provided by such nations as India, Pakistan, Indonesia and Japan—all of them anti-Communist but militarily unaligned Asians, all of them nations which have successfully repelled the threat of Communism without our "help."

Observe also, please, that none of these nations was represented at the recent Manila Conference. That's what made the Manila meeting just about the most ludicrous farce ever perpetrated on a gullible world. For President Johnson to travel to Manila to confer pretentiously only with our own lackies makes about as much sense as for Chile and Panama and France to confer on the future of the total American continent, without inviting the participation of Canada, Mexico or the United States. Manila was an insult to the intelligence and integrity of every American whose I.Q. is above 90. To be effective, a Vietnamese cease-fire must be implemented and policed by a body which will include the independent and important nations of Asia, not just those bought and supported by us.

Step three should be our announced desire—I said *desire*, not just reluctant willingness—to participate in an immediate and truly unconditional peace conference. This implies, of course, that we are ready to accept and help effect the decisions of such a conference, however unpalatable they may be to our preference or taste. We cannot continue presumptuously to play God in the lives of others.

The peace conference obviously cannot be held under the auspices of the United Nations, for neither Vietnam nor Red China belongs to the U.N. The most likely sponsorship would be a continuation of the Geneva Conference. On this score Washington is fond of reminding us that Russia was one of the two co-chairmen at Geneva and that Russia has refused to go along with any proposal that the conference be reconvened. What Washington conveniently forgets is that on the twenty-fifth of July 1964 Russia urgently suggested a resumption of the Geneva Conference and our President's reaction the same day was: "We do not believe in conferences called to ratify terror, so our policy is unchanged." Again in February of 1965 the

Soviet Government proposed a meeting at Geneva; this time we didn't even deign to reply.

If this were a conversation, not a pulpit monologue, someone would be sure to inject at this point: "But rabbi, what about the dozens of times that Johnson and Goldberg and Rusk have appealed for peace negotiations?" Very well, what about them? By the weirdest concatenation of coincidences, the record shows that every time our government calls for peace talks, without exception at the same time—usually the very same day!—we announce an escalation of our belligerence. When Arthur Goldberg made his otherwise impressive plea this fall at the U.N., several times in a statement calculated to induce peace he referred to the North Vietnamese as "aggressors." We send 400,000 men nearly half-way round the world to intervene in another nation's civil war, then call one of their factions—fighting on their own soil—aggressors! And apparently we expect them to accept an invitation, thus phrased, to discuss reconciliation. Within hours of Goldberg's statement, moreover, Secretary McNamara announced a 30% increase in our bomber production. On the very day of President Johnson's most recent peace plea in Manila our navy sent its ships closer to Vietnam than ever before to shell shore batteries.

Each time we have ostensibly pleaded for peace, simultaneously we have acted toward escalated war. When I suggest that our third step must be a call for discussions aiming at peace, I mean words and actions which will cohere with at least reasonable consistency. I mean also a peace conference in which our principal adversary, the National Liberation Front, will participate fully.

We still, at this inexcusably late date, have never explicitly declared our willingness to negotiate with the NLF.

Nor have we even once repudiated or criticized Premier
Ky's frequently repeated assertion that he would under no
circumstances ever sit down with them. On this point we
must make ourselves immediately and incontrovertibly
clear.

This brings us to my fourth proposal. We must agree, as
the international police force already described becomes
able to assume its duties, gradually to withdraw all our
forces; then, together with the whole international community, to guarantee the neutrality of Vietnam, its freedom
from outside military interference by any nation. Such
neutrality is imperative not only for the Vietnamese themselves, but also to allay China's fear that in our plans Vietnam is only a stepping stone for attack on her. A few years
back we grew fearfully disturbed—and properly so—over
Russian missiles embedded in Cuba. Those Russian weapons were as toy pistols compared to the armaments we have
already massed on China's borders.

Are China's fears unrealistic? Not if we remember that
in 1965 Peking proposed an agreement that neither we nor
they would be the first to use atomic weaponry against the
other. Our State Department summarily rejected the offer,
saying that it did not represent "a constructive step toward
the paramount problem of controlled disarmament." Are
China's fears unrealistic? On 25 July 1966 Premier Ky
publicly called for an armed confrontation with Commu-
nist China. In the words of the following day's *New York
Times* dispatch, "The State Department press officer, Robert J. McCloskey, said that the department had no official
comment." *Are* China's fears unrealistic?

If not, then the withdrawal of our troops and the guarantee of neutrality must apply not merely to Vietnam itself,
but to all of southeast Asia. We already have 35,000 or

more troops in neighboring Thailand, with huge bases under construction there or completed. What good would it do to withdraw from Vietnam if these forces be left as a continuing threat to China?

I know the usual rejoinder at this point; you don't have to remind me. It has been popularized as the so-called domino theory. If we don't actively resist Communism in Vietnam, the litany goes, one by one all the nations of the sub-continent will fall. The only trouble with this neat hypothesis is that it doesn't happen to square with reality. It completely ignores the fact that we did "stop Communism" in Korea, but apparently that didn't avert the threat in Vietnam, did it? Since 1948, moreover, Communist-sponsored "wars of liberation" have been successfully repulsed by Burma, Indonesia, the Philippines and Malaya—all without our intervention or interference.

Communism will be a threat—with or without the United States' presence—wherever rank poverty and injustice prevail and all other avenues of reform are blocked. The truth of the matter is that our military policy in Vietnam has done more to boost the prospect of Communism there than anything the most fiendish minds in Peking could have devised. We have made it appear that only Communists are genuinely interested in the welfare of the impoverished Vietnamese peasants. We have obliterated a thousand years of bitter enmity between the Vietnamese and Chinese, driving the leaders of Hanoi, against their own instincts and history, into the arms of Red China. For us to postulate a domino theory is ridiculous.

If Communism is to be turned back in Vietnam, it will be not by military means but by our fifth and final step. We must draw up and announce now the most massive plan of reconstruction ever designed by any nation on earth for another. Except for a glib and rather meaningless reference to such aid, mentioned by President Johnson almost in passing a year-and-a-half ago, nothing effective has been done. Whatever monies we have thus far ostensibly dispatched for this purpose have only fed the greed and nourished the contamination and corruption of the fattened few who rule in Vietnam. The rest of the world should be invited to participate with us in the humanitarian restoration of this bruised and battered people; but with or without others, we're the ones who have brutalized them beyond endurance. We therefore face an inescapable moral obligation to repair what we have nearly ruined.

Here, then, is the syndrome I promised. First: an end to the bombing of North Vietnam. Second: an internationally-policed cease-fire in the ground war. Third: a peace conference without preconditions or counteractions, one in which the NLF is to participate and the decisions of which we promise to accept. Fourth: at the proper time and pace, withdrawal of our military forces and genuine neutralization of southeast Asia. Fifth: the most heroic plan of reconstruction mankind has ever seen or dreamed.

Would even so ambitious an effort as this succeed? There are no guarantees. Surely nothing less than this has a chance. Fourteen years of error piled on error, of stupid mistake compounded with inexcusable blunder, must now be rectified. The patient is desperately sick. For a long time the disease wasn't even diagnosed; then it was woefully mistreated by a succession of inadequate therapists. No one can promise now that even the most intelligently skilled medical genius can prevail. But the alternatives are too horrible to contemplate. They range from the United

States' becoming the most bitterly hated nation on earth—
at best!—to universal nuclear catastrophe, at worst.

And between these possibilities is the price we are already paying for our mistakes in Vietnam. That price
includes gross deterioration of our relations with Russia at a
time when we seemed almost on the threshold of rap-
prochement . . . defeat of the Civilian Review Board in
New York after a most nauseatingly and lavishly financed
campaign of propaganda by extremists . . . election of such
illustrious Americans as Lurleen Wallace and Ronald Re-
agan as governors . . . the corrosion of our Great Society
into sardonic fiction . . . the contamination of our right to
dissent to the point where the President of the United
States contemptuously refers to those who disagree with
him as "Nervous Nellies" who "turn on their own leaders,
their own country, and their own fighting men." All this is
the price we have already paid for Vietnam; and while I
cannot in good conscience promise the success of my proposals, I can absolutely guarantee that the alternative will
be further drastic inflation of the price on every level just
enumerated.

Far from defeating Communism, we stand in grave peril
of destroying Americanism. This is the heart of our moral
crisis. No one has articulated it with more sensitive eloquence than Neil Sheehan a few weeks ago in the *New
York Times Magazine*. Mr. Sheehan is not a dove; in fact,
he began his journalistic tour of duty in Vietnam as a hawk.
Now he writes: "I simply cannot help worrying that, in the
process of waging this war, we are corrupting ourselves. I
wonder, when I look at the bombed-out peasant hamlets,
the orphans begging and stealing on the streets of Saigon,
and the women and children with napalm burns lying on
the hospital cots, whether the United States or any nation

has the right to inflict this suffering and degradation on another people for its own ends."

I wonder too. It is against a background of this wondering, this unutterable torment and agony, that I cry to us in God's name to stop!

3

When Is It Right to Break the Law?

Tomorrow's Torah portion has for many years intrigued and haunted me. Most of you need no reminder that it tells the unforgettably poignant tale of Abraham and Isaac, of the Patriarch's willingness to sacrifice his beloved son at God's behest. The first High Holy Day sermon I ever preached—thirty-three years ago as a student rabbi in Davenport, Iowa—was in explication of this story. Since then, every three or four years I revert to it, almost as if by hypnotic compulsion. And each time unfailingly I find in it a new insight, a new twist or turn of truth which had never occurred to me before. So, tonight again: a sermon about Abraham and Isaac.

The narrative itself requires no lengthy review. At God's command Abraham has taken Isaac—his only son by Sarah, the blessed fulfillment of his past and sole presage of his future—Abraham has taken this Isaac to the top of the mountain and has tied him there on an altar. Then, with anguish and torment that any parent can easily imagine, he has raised his knife perilously over the bound body of his son. In another split second the dread weapon would commence its precipitous and irrevocable plunge into Isaac's heart. At the last melodramatic instant an angel's

voice calls out the words which Abraham had despaired of
hearing: "Do not raise your hand against the boy!" The
suspense has been almost beyond bearing. The angel's intervention leaves us now nearly faint with relief. Isaac has
been saved.

As I reached this point in re-reading the story last month,
a question arose which had never come to me before. Suppose the angel had not interceded? Suppose Abraham had
gone through with his murderous intention, actually slay-
ing his beloved son because he believed this to be God's
will? Would we then applaud him for obeying divine law,
no matter what the personal cost to himself?

Many men would. To Soren Kierkegaard, prototype and
progenitor of Christian existentialism, Abraham's readiness
to kill his son was humanity's most exemplary instance of
unqualified religious devotion. Kierkegaard approvingly
called this "the teleological suspension of the ethical." He
left no doubt that for him unswerving obedience to divine
law was more important than adherence to ethical impulse.
Other commentators disagree with Kierkegaard. They hold
that Abraham would have been a higher and finer kind of
man had he followed his own keenest ethical intuition
rather than God's voice from outside himself.

Does all this seem like an excursion into biblical semantics, an exercise in abstruse theology—of interest, no doubt,
to a certain type of academic mind but of no real concern
to ordinary, practical people like ourselves? Don't decide
too hastily! If you will shift gears with me a moment,
transposing this problem from the dimension of divine law
to that of human law, at once the matter becomes compel-
lingly urgent. Abraham's dilemma—had the angel not appeared—is precisely the practical problem you and I must
confront today: when, if ever, is it right deliberately to

break the law? In a society founded on respect for law, is civil disobedience ever justified?

One Friday night last April I preached at The Temple in Nashville. The following morning I addressed the members of that congregation's Confirmation Class. Though my topic was Jewish theology, the youngsters— perhaps with some suspicion of my past positions and statements—began to ask me questions about civil rights. The problem of civil disobedience was raised. I remarked that most Americans hold Henry David Thoreau to be something of a hero, precisely because he had propounded and implemented the doctrine that there are times when man's highest duty is to disobey the law.

Several parents of confirmands were present. A deeply-distressed father rose to his feet at this point and voiced his apprehension: "Rabbi," he said—not in anger but with a gently-chiding southern drawl—"how can we parents teach our children to respect the law when a religious leader stands on the pulpit of this chapel, telling them that sometimes laws should be broken?"

That was a good question. I told him so. It's an excruciatingly difficult question to answer, but that doesn't justify ducking it. When Martin Luther King, Jr. or Jim Reeb or Arthur Lelyveld breaks a local discriminatory law, we who call ourselves liberal approve and applaud. When George Wallace or Louise Day Hicks defies the law, we howl with indignation and dismay. Surely it won't do just to say that laws with which I and my friends agree must be obeyed, while those which are repugnant to us may with impunity be broken. Assuming that there will be no voices from heaven—neither of angels nor of God—to guide us, how is our dilemma to be resolved? When is it right to break the law?

Allow me to propose three criteria. No one of them by itself will suffice; indeed, not even all three together will give us a decisive answer in every instance. But the combination of these criteria will, I believe, offer us the only sound counsel we have a right to expect.

The first question to be asked is: how many human beings will be helped by observing a given law in a specific setting, and how many by defying it? Under other circumstances and in different contexts, many of you have heard me state it as one of nature's inexorable laws that smaller particles and components always exist for the sake of larger units. Electrons and protons must maintain the right relationship with each other, performing but never exceeding their proper functions, in order to make atoms possible. Unless atoms, in turn, cohere in a purposeful pattern, molecules are out of the question. So with molecules forming cells, then cells functioning within organs, then organs within organisms, then individuals within flocks and clans and tribes and nations. Always laws are obeyed by smaller components, not just for their own sake, not just for the sake of law as such—but in order that larger, more meaningful wholes may develop and survive! Indeed, the philosophy of science leads us to suspect increasingly that the very nature of the smaller component is determined by its relationship to other components and to the larger whole of which it forms a part.

Have I forgotten my theme? All appearance to the contrary notwithstanding, no. What may have seemed to be the irrelevant excursion of the last three minutes was meant only to establish that nature itself supplies us with a paradigm by which to approach our question of civil disobedience. A fundamental purpose of law in human affairs—as in nature—must be to serve the welfare of larger numbers of individual particles—in this case, persons—and thereby to make possible the development of more complex and meaningful wholes. Hence my first criterial question: how many human beings will be helped by observing a given law in a specific setting, and how many by defying it?

Let's try to be more concrete. Just what is ultimately involved when we weigh the civil disobedience of George Wallace against that of Martin Luther King, Jr.? On Governor Wallace's side of the scale is a tiny, nasty, contemptible group of bigots and a power structure which is insatiable in its voracious demands. When Wallace defies the law, he serves the interests only of these. On Dr. King's side of the scale are not only all the Negroes of this nation, plus the newly-emerged Negro polities of Africa, plus all the yellow-brown-black-tan-red-skinned peoples of earth—but also the possibility of peace in the world. Which means to say, under current conditions of nuclear development, the very possibility of elemental human survival. When King defies the law, he serves the interests of all these. This gives his defiance a dimension altogether beyond that of Wallace. It illustrates at once the validity of my first criterion and leads us directly to the second.

What effect will the observance or defiance of a given law have on the freedom of individuals to be themselves? There is an intriguing paradox involved in the relationship between smaller components and larger units as we observe them through physics and biology. The electron must, in a sense, limit itself for the sake, so to speak, of the atom, but only thus does it gain the freedom, as it were, to be an electron. True, without electrons there can be no atoms; but no less true, without atoms there can be no electrons. Without specialized, individualized cells there is no organism; but without an organism there are no specialized, indi-

vidualized cells. If, God forbid, cells within my body so far
reject the welfare of the whole as to become cancer, they
destroy not just my body as such but also themselves.

Another point is crucial here. Not only does nature
demand that its larger units guarantee a degree of freedom
to their smaller components, it also insists, as it were, on
individuality and uniqueness among these smaller particles.
A hydrogen atom does not duplicate an oxygen atom. A
molecule of inorganic rock is not the same as a molecule of
living protoplasm. A liver cell does not function exactly as
does a brain cell. In short, nature requires on the one hand
that components serve the interests of larger units, and on
the other that larger units allow for uniqueness and difference among their components. Now back again, from nature to civil disobedience.

What has just been said explains why we must ask, in the
second place, whether the proposed defiance of a man-
made law is calculated to increase or decrease the freedom
of individuals to be and develop themselves. A law which
prevents men of a certain color or creed from living on my
street or working by my side or sending their children to
school with mine, obviously impairs their individual freedom painfully. But the opposite is not true. A law which
guarantees their rights in these respects does not restrict my
freedom to be uniquely myself. It does reduce my right to
be bigoted. It does diminish my special class or caste privileges. But it does not in any way preclude me from discovering and then developing to their utmost those capacities and talents which are individually and uniquely my
own. Thus laws are not by any means equal in their effect
on the freedom of the individual. A law which in fact pre-
serves and protects such freedom deserves to be obeyed. A
law which corrodes and denies such freedom—if it cannot

be changed in a reasonable period of time by the ordinary processes of amendment—may call for outright defiance and contempt.

So, we have covered the first two of my criteria. Will the welfare of more men be served by respecting a particular law or by deliberately breaking it? And which alternative will maximize freedom for the greater number of individuals? But the matter is far from being completely settled. There is a third question: what are the means proposed for disobedience, and do those means enhance or inhibit the larger ends we would serve? The relationship between means and ends has preoccupied the best philosophic minds for centuries. I don't propose to enter these murky waters now, except to say that means and ends are inextricably intertwined. They can never be divorced without doing massive violence both to logic and to life. Hence the question of whether a specific law in a given context should or should not be broken cannot be resolved without inquiring into the contemplated means. The non-violent defiance of certain laws by southern Negroes who refused to move to the back of the bus, or who marched *en masse* to Selma, or who sat stubbornly at restaurant counters until they were served, unquestionably aided the over-all cause of human freedom. The burning of draft cards and blocking of troop trains, on the other hand, most probably did not improve the prospect for peace in the world; they may even have had the opposite effect. The means employed must be consistent with and conducive to the final end desired.

Not all examples of means are as easily judged as those just enumerated. Take, for example, recent Negro riots in Harlem and Watts and the Hough area of Cleveland. I received my elementary education in Cleveland's Hough Avenue School. Last month, while in my native city to attend my mother's funeral, I spent a nostalgic hour driving through the several neighborhoods in which I had lived as a child. On Hough Avenue, near my former school, I saw buildings burned, businesses destroyed, innumerable looted stores desolately boarded up. A stretch of main road almost a mile in length—along which I walked to school each day as a child—looked like a military combat zone. Surely no reasonable person can as a matter of policy recommend or approve this kind of civil disobedience.

Yet can it honestly be said that the Cleveland riots served no useful purpose in the cause of Negro freedom? A week or two after they had ended, three Roxbury legislators addressed to Mayor Collins a set of demands for cleaning up the slum district they represent. I would like to believe that the Mayor responded with favorable dispatch just because he knew in his heart that their demands were just. But wouldn't it be more than slightly naive to pretend that he didn't also have in mind the possibility that Hough might be repeated in Roxbury if he failed to act?

Bayard Rustin is one of the most intelligently dynamic Negro leaders in the United States today. In a late August address to the American Federation of Teachers he summarized tersely the point I'm emphasizing here. He said: "Any Negro youngster who doesn't believe now that the way to get something is through violence obviously is not intelligent." If this is the lesson painfully learned by bright Negro youngsters, we—the white world—have taught it. Sometimes even the wrong means of defiance must be blamed not on those who embrace them but on a power structure which refuses to heed the right methods. Wherever the blame belongs, however, the stark truth is that violence begets only more violence, in a vicious, self-defeating, unending circle. Those who would disobey laws in the cause of ethical goals must, as far as possible, employ means which are consistent with those goals.

Of course we must have law and respect for law. Without them, civilization and society are impossible. The only person who is entitled even to contemplate civil disobedience is he who in general respects and obeys the law. But let us not forget that man-made law is the product of fallible men. As such, it can be either good or bad. Rigid adherence to all man-made laws can become a form of idolatry. No one obeyed the laws of his government with more compulsively scrupulous zeal than Adolf Eichmann! After every reasonable effort has been made to abrogate or amend laws which are bad, and when all such efforts have failed, there comes a time when the highest duty of the most ethical man or woman is to disobey and to accept the consequences.

We began with Abraham. Let us conclude with him too, specifically with the question which precipitated this sermon. Can there be any serious doubt now what he should have done had the angel not interceded? Isn't it obvious that by refusing to kill his son—if necessary, even in defiance of the highest law he knew, he would have contributed to the welfare not only of his own generation but of the multitudes destined to follow? And that, by such refusal, the right of free men to be unique individuals would have been immeasurably reinforced?

We are less fortunate than Abraham. For one thing we can be less sure than he that the voice we hear is really God's. Then too, there will be no angels to give us guidance. We must ask instead, in each case; does this law do the greatest good for the largest number of our fellowmen? . . . does it enlarge the prospect for individual freedom?

. . . are the means by which we propose to disobey consistent with the ends we seek to serve?

Our speculation about Abraham can be of immense help in determining when it may be right to break the law. So can further thought about Thoreau. There is a story, perhaps apocryphal but trenchant nonetheless, that when he was in jail for defying what he believed to be an unjust law, his friend Emerson visited him. "Henry," the great essayist is alleged to have asked, "what are you doing in here?" To which the prisoner is said to have responded: "Ralph, what are you doing out there?"

Let us not be too prone to criticize everyone who defies the law. There are times when the man who languishes in prison is more ethically commendable by far than we who are free.

4

Fallacies of Our Time—
Concerning American Free
Enterprise

Because so much of what I propose to say here will be
critical, it is important that I begin with an open statement
of my position vis-a-vis our American economic system.
Like most intellectuals whose college years spanned the
depression of 1929, I lived through a period when I believed that socialism was the most promising economic and
political structure for an industrial society. In so far as the
United States is concerned, I am no longer thus persuaded.
While I am still convinced that some form of democratic
socialism will be needed for most of the emergent and
as-yet-undeveloped nations of the world, for us in this
country I strongly favor a democratically controlled and
regulated form of capitalism.

The adjectives just used—controlled and regulated—will
probably disturb some of you. My only rejoinder for the
moment is that uncontrolled capitalism in today's world
makes no better sense than uncontrolled traffic on today's
highways. In an ideal world, one in which each individual

governed himself according to the greatest good for the greatest number of his fellow-men, perhaps no such supervision or surveillance would be needed. But this, needless to say, is not an ideal world. To pretend that what is immediately best in the short-run for each American corporation will automatically add up in the long-run to what will be best for our nation as a whole is as unrealistic as to assume that the immediate decisions of unregulated drivers will in the aggregate serve the purposes of highway safety. In both cases the whole is considerably more than the sum total of its separate parts. In both cases, the more complicated life becomes, the more desperately is intelligent control required. Let there be no mistake, however, as to my own orientation or objective. I favor the continuation of capitalism in this nation. I speak now not out of the desire to destroy it, but rather to improve and preserve it. With this, then, as background, let me proceed to a consideration of as many of our economy's fallacies as time will permit.

The first is the very notion that our system is one of unadulterated free enterprise. Nothing could be farther from the truth. In point of fact, we live under a mixed economy, some sectors of which are assuredly forms of private enterprise while others are no less clearly types of socialism. If socialism be defined as public ownership—and of course that's precisely what it is—then our public schools are examples of socialism. So is our network of publicly built and administered roads. If this were in fact purely private enterprise, our inter-urban roads would be built and financed entirely by private construction firms, then operated by them as toll roads maintained for private profit. For additional examples of socialism, integrally fused into a context of private enterprise, one need mention only public housing, publicly-owned transportation systems,

Veterans Administration life insurance, Social Security or
the Tennessee Valley Authority.

The division under our system between public and private enterprise is, moreover, by no means always logical.
Why, for example, in terms of rigid logic, should the delivery of letters be under public, socialistic auspices and that
of telegrams be by a private corporation? While there is no
really rational answer to that question, there is a plausible
practical explanation. It is easy to make money out of the
one and hard not to lose money from the other. American
businessmen have rather consistently followed the principle
that where there is a good possibility of profit, they try to
retain that possibility for corporate operation; where there
is a likelihood of loss, they turn willingly, sometimes even
eagerly, toward the government. When a New Haven
Railroad can operate profitably, it resents and rejects the
least semblance of government interference. When it
reaches the brink of bankruptcy, it rushes to that same
government in a panicked plea for help and even entertains
the possibility of public ownership.

Perhaps the most interesting combination of public and
private enterprise in this country today is to be found in the
field of housing. Not only do private builders and Uncle
Sam work side-by-side in the construction industry; even
the private sectors of housing are dependent on public
enterprise. Between 1945 and 1955 something like ten million houses were built in the United States, the overwhelming majority of them by private builders. Of that number,
however, more than four million were financed with mortgages guaranteed by a Federal Government agency. No
economy which operates that way can without qualifica-
tion call itself free enterprise. Max Lerner has described the
true nature of our economy with his usual cogency and

conciseness: ". . . the American economy is today an example neither of pure 'capitalism' (as so many Europeans and Asians still seem to think) nor of 'creeping socialism' (as some of the more frightened American Tories seem to think). It is becoming a mixed economy, with large areas of freedom and varied techniques of regulation, control, and some forms of planning."* So much for our first fallacy.

The second is the notion that prices of the products we buy are determined in our economy by the so-called law of supply and demand. In a truly free enterprise system this would be true. When the supply of a given item exceeded the demand, prices would decline. When the demand was greater than the supply, prices would rise. Thus would a kind of balance be maintained. To suppose that this is how prices are determined in our economy today, particularly in those major industries which are the backbone of all production, is to be guilty of incredible and inexcusable naiveté. One doesn't have to be an economist to recognize something more than either coincidence or supply and demand in the fact that in a given area all major oil companies charge exactly the same price for their respective grades of gasoline; all major steel manufacturers list precisely the same prices for each ton of steel as does United States Steel; and the Big Three among automobile firms vary only minutely, if at all, on the prices of comparable models.

A limited number of more specific examples will have to suffice. Near the end of 1956, the Ford Motor Company was the first to announce its prices on new models for 1957. Increases ranging from $1 to $104 per car were posted, with the public explanation that they reflected "our actual costs for materials and labor." Two weeks later General

---

* M. Lerner: *America As A Civilization,* p. 341 Simon and Schuster, 1957.

Motors issued its new price list for Chevrolet, showing increases of $50 to $166 per car. Now if this were in fact a system of free enterprise, with prices determined by supply and demand, that would have placed Ford in a competitive position of great advantage. But apparently Ford did not desire such an advantage. One week after the General Motors announcement, Ford revised its list, raising its prices an additional notch to match those of Chevrolet. Walter Reuther didn't increase his popularity with the manufacturers but he certainly came close to the truth when he wryly remarked: "This is the first time in the history of a free-enterprise economy where a company raised the price of their products in order to be competitive."

Professor Vernon A. Mund cites several dozen similar examples in the *Journal of Political Economy* for April 1960. The Bureau of Reclamation in Washington advertised bids for transformers. Three companies responded: Westinghouse, General Electric and Allis Chalmers. Their bids? Exactly $2,695—all three of them right on the nose! The United States Army solicited bids for yeast. The four concerns which responded offered their products for exactly 14½ cents per pound, not a fraction more nor less. The State of Virginia needed a large quantity of paper cups. Eight allegedly competing companies offered them at precisely $6.18 per thousand—not $6.17, not $6.19, but eight identical bids of $6.18! Anyone who wants to believe that this kind of thing happens as often as it does purely by coincidence or because cost-accounting is so exact a science, is entitled to his folly. The rest of us will reach the inescapable conclusion that these are instances of administered prices, quite the opposite of supply and demand.

One further word needs to be said on this point. It may

well be that in some areas of our economy the competition which attends supply and demand is outmoded and destructive. I for one am scarcely competent to judge that. But I am competent, I believe, to insist that American industrialists cannot have it both ways. If they are ready to concede, in whole or in part, that administered prices are necessary, then they must also concede that the consumer has an interest in such prices too and that only the government can properly represent consumer interest. Industry cannot retreat from supply and demand in practice, then invoke the sanctity of supply and demand in theory when government steps in to protect the public concern. Here, in distilled essence, is our second fallacy.

The third is that poverty is being eliminated in our economy today, that the wide gap between the very rich and the very poor is being dramatically narrowed, so that we are well on the road toward becoming a middle-class society. That there has been some improvement along this line, no one would deny. That the improvement is anywhere near that which is frequently alleged, is our third fallacy.

The plight which still afflicts great masses of Americans was humorously illustrated only this past week by a delightful cartoon. A man is shown seated at a desk strewn with the most impossible accumulation of documents and papers. He looks up—pencil in hand and a look bordering between anguish and triumph on his face—as he says to his wife: "Well, that balances our budget for this year, provided we win the Irish Sweepstakes." One doesn't prove a point by a cartoon, however, so let's look at evidence of greater substance.

Are we in fact as close as our propagandists claim to the elimination of poverty? According to the United States

Department of Labor, a city family of four in 1958 required $4,800 to achieve a "modest but adequate standard
of living." According to the United States Bureau of Cen-
sus in the same year, one-third of American families of four
or more fell below this level. According to figures released
by economists of the AFL-CIO for the same year, five-
and-a-half million Americans in households of two or more
persons were receiving aggregate gross incomes—gross incomes; that's before taxes!—of under $1500 a year. An-
other thirty-six million persons were receiving less than
$3,000 per year. That adds up to something like 41½
million persons, 24% of the population in the wealthiest
nation on earth, with annual income far below a decent
minimum. That doesn't sound like the threshold of Utopia,
does it?

How about the opposite end of the spectrum? Is it true,
as we so frequently are told, that sizable profits and the
accumulation of great wealth are things of the past in this
country? There are so many reliable statistics which answer this question in the negative that one scarcely knows
where to commence in citing them. Between 1953 and
1959, the profits of our eight largest steel producers rose on
the average from $9.07 to $17.46 per ton shipped. Calculated as a percentage either of net worth or of sales, the
proportionate increase is almost exactly the same.

The most reliable and exhaustive study on this question
that has come to my attention is one published by Dr.
Robert Lampman, an economist formerly on the Faculty
of the University of Wisconsin, now a member of President Kennedy's Council of Economic Advisers. It covers
the period 1922 to 1956 and shows that while the proportion of American income received by the top fifth of our
population in wealth indeed declined from 1929 to 1945,

since that time it has again begun appreciably to increase. Lampman discloses, moreover, that in 1944 there were 13,297 Americans who owned one million dollars or more in wealth; but by 1953, the number had more than doubled to 27,502. Even after allowing for shrinkage in the purchasing power of the dollar during this interval of nine years, the number had increased to 17,611. It was the *Wall Street Journal*—not the *Daily Worker* but the *Wall Street Journal*—which reported in 1960 that "more individuals have become millionaires since World War II than in any comparable earlier period."

One more significant fact disclosed by the Lampman study completes the picture. It shows that in 1929, the top one percent of our population in wealth owned 65.6% of all corporate stock. By 1953, the proportion owned by this same group had risen to 70% and most estimates would place the percentage still higher today. I am not arguing tonight the morality of abject poverty and almost immeasurable wealth existing side-by-side. That will have to remain as a topic for another occasion. What I do say now is a simple statement of fact: It is not true that we have eliminated poverty; it is not true that we have made profit impossible or wealth less attainable; it is not true that we are becoming a nation limited to the middle-class.

Here, then, in my judgment are the three fallacies about our economic system which need most to be exposed: that it is or can be a system of unadulterated free enterprise . . . that prices are determined by the simple operation of supply and demand . . . that both poverty and extreme wealth are being eliminated.

Let me return now at the end to the place where I began. By and large, American capitalism has served our nation well. With all its deficiencies and defects, it is highly doubtful whether any other system could have done as much for us as a people during the nineteenth and early twentieth centuries. But American capitalism will continue to serve us well, indeed it will continue to exist at all, only if it faces facts honestly and adjusts with courage to changing needs.

I would have to be stupid in the extreme not to know that this sermon will not sit well with some of you. I have no hesitation in asserting, however, that I may prove in the long-run to be a more effective friend of capitalism than those who seek to defend it by denying the truth. No economic system is sacrosanct. Only human life and human needs are sacred. And only that economic system which enhances human life and equitably satisfies human needs will endure. I have spoken tonight out of profound conviction that for the United States a democratically oriented and democratically regulated capitalism can succeed—better than any other system yet devised—in providing the American people with the two essentials of democracy: bread plus liberty.

Max Lerner has come about as close as anyone to a fair, objective evaluation of our economic system. I subscribe to his verdict: "This, then, would be a rough trial balance of American capitalism as a going concern: that it has done brilliantly in productivity and national product; that it has done less well with the swings of the business cycle and with boom and bust, but that substantial steps have been taken to meet this; . . . . . . that in its income distribution it is a good deal better than its opponents would admit but not nearly as good as its apologists claim, good enough to retain the faith of those who are fulfilled by it but not good enough to exact the loyalty of those who feel left out; that it allows for creativeness but within a limited sense of that word; that as a whole it is an economy which has wrested from the world its envy along with a grudging respect, but not its imitation."*

* M. Lerner: Ibid., p. 273 f.

5

Negro and Jew—Friends or Foes?

The problem of Negro-Jewish relationships in the United States is one of increasing aggravation. It was propelled most disgustingly into public attention by a recent David Susskind telecast. Three Negroes on that program ventilated as vicious and vitriolic a brand of anti-Semitism as anything broadcast since the Nazi period in Germany. They made more than a few Jews sit up, take notice, and reassess their previous attitudes toward civil rights.

They induced one cherished friend—a member of my congregation's Board—to write me a long and troubled letter. His key question read: "Are Jews now being blackmailed by Negroes into continuing their hitherto magnificent support . . . of causes that are genuinely striving to eradicate the . . . injustices suffered by most Negroes?" It is in the hope of shedding light on his question and your doubts that I have chosen this topic.

I propose that we begin by eschewing illusions, by recognizing and accepting even the most painful of truths. And the plainest, most ineluctable truth is that in the Negro-Jewish equation considerable antagonism exists in both directions. Substantial anti-Semitism is to be found among Negroes; strains of anti-Negro prejudice are discernible among Jews. A New York study made as long ago as 1946 revealed that 60% of the Jews queried held unfavorable stereotypes regarding Negroes, while 70% of the Negroes harbored similar stereotypes about Jews. It can be reasonably assumed that any change—certainly in the last year or two—has not been for the better.

The facts should not be exaggerated. In the struggle for Negro equality no other segment of the American population has contributed anything remotely equal to our Jewish effort. The names of Julius Rosenwald and Arthur Spingarn, of Alan Gartner and Kivie Kaplan, attest to that. More than two decades ago Gordon Allport at Harvard summarized his own investigations and those of others by writing: ". . . studies of prejudice show that the average Jewish attitude seems to be significantly more tolerant than the average attitude in Catholic or Protestant groups." Yet the indisputable truth remains that all too frequently in recent months the ugly voice of anti-Negro sentiment has been raised among Jews.

A similar ambivalence is evident on the other side of the coin. Samplings taken nationally in an on-going study sponsored by the Anti-Defamation League indicate that 24% of Negro respondents said Jewish landlords are superior to other white landlords, while only 7% felt they were worse. Twenty percent reported that in their judgment Jewish store owners are better than other white merchants; again, 7% reflected the opposite conclusion. So there is a reservoir of good-will for which we must be grateful.

But there is virulent anti-Semitism too. Nor is all of it a product of recent frustration. As long ago as when he wrote *Native Son*, James Baldwin confessed: "I remember meeting no Negro in the years of growing up who would

really trust a Jew, and few who did not, indeed, exhibit for
them the blackest contempt." Richard Wright recorded the
same kind of experience from his youth: "All of us black
people who lived in the neighborhood hated Jews . . . To
hold an attitude of antagonism or distrust toward Jews was
bred into us from childhood . . ."

There is, then, and for a considerable time has been,
overt anti-Semitism among Negroes. How shall we explain
it? I think on several grounds. For many American Negroes the Jew happens to be the most proximate white man.
Of all whites, he is most often present and visible—either as
local merchant or as landlord. He is therefore the most
immediately available target for whatever diffused resentment is felt against white people generally. This is true but
it is far from a complete explanation. At least two additional factors contribute to the special virulence of anti-
Jewish sentiment among some Negroes.

The first is the fact that anti-Semitism is perhaps the only
sociological phenomenon through which the Negro can
identify with the white majority, can himself become part
of the establishment, which ordinarily excludes and victim-
izes him. By virtue of his black rather than white skin, the
Negro feels inferior. By virtue of his Christian rather than
Jewish faith, in a predominantly Christian nation he ac-
quires an illusion of superiority.

A second factor—too often either ignored or minimized
—emerges from the theological rather than the psychological component of the Negro's religious identification. Most
dark-skinned Americans have been not only Christians, but
adherents of one or another of the Protestant fundamentalist sects. They have thus been inclined to accept a literal,
not a liberal interpretation of those Christian doctrines
which have been the seminal causes of anti-Semitism: that

Jews as such killed Christ . . . that they were therefore rejected by God as an accursed people . . . that they are condemned to wander homelessly until they agree to accept Christian dogma. In short, most Negroes with whom we deal today are products of a Christian creed which induces them toward anti-Semitism. Thus psychological and theological motives conspire to encourage antagonism against Jews.

Now what of anti-Negro prejudice among Jews? It too can be explained on several levels. Among Jews, as well as others, prejudice does serve certain psychological functions, even if pathologically. It enables the person who feels inferior in every other way to achieve a spurious status vis-a-vis someone who is even less prestigious. A recent *Nubbins* cartoon illustrates the point memorably. In the first frame Nubbins is shown declaiming to someone not in the picture: "I'm smarter than you are! I'm better lookin' than you are!" In the second frame, the object of his comparison still unidentified, he declares with even greater emphasis: "An' I got more money than you got!" In the third and final frame at last we discover that the target of all this braggadocio has been a scarecrow. Nubbins, as he slinks away, is muttering to himself: "A fella's got to feel superior *once* in a while!" The humor scarcely disguises a grim psychological truth, one which unfortunately operates occasionally in Jews, as it does in all men.

In our long, lugubrious history we have not often been able to indulge in the luxury of sublimating our own pains by directing hostility against others. For the most part, we still reject such cheap psychological satisfactions. But it would be idle to deny that there are some in our midst who have taken refuge in an anti-Negro stance from the inadequacies and disadvantages they would otherwise find it

difficult to tolerate. We have already observed that for
many Negroes the Jew is the only white man against whom
they can vent hostility without fear of paying too extrava-
gant a penalty. By the reverse of the very same psychology,
there are some Jews who can with impunity voice their
resentment of all Christians only against the most helpless
of them in this country, Negroes.

This is apt to be true especially among those lower-mid-
dle-class Jews who live in areas which have either already
been largely taken over for Negro occupancy or are immediately contiguous to such areas. Their attitudes are sometimes not too unlike those of other immigrant groups—the
Irish, Poles, Italians, et al—who inhabit similar neighborhoods. They are the ones against whom the expansion of
Negro rights poses the greatest threat, in terms both of
physical proximity and of social status.

They are the ones also who are most immediately endangered by the changing character of neighborhoods in
which they have lived and worked for decades. It is no
small thing to have one's store repeatedly looted, to be
beaten physically for the sake of a few miserable dollars in
one's purse, to fear leaving one's apartment or home after
dark. My own father—then a physician already in his
eighties—was brutally assaulted once in an all-Negro
neighborhood while providing medical care to Negro patients. A member of my congregation was killed, his wife
mercilessly pummeled, by black assailants in the store they
had owned and operated for years.

It is not easy for such victims—especially if they themselves have worked diligently on behalf of equal rights—to
place the blame for Negro truculence and violence where it
primarily belongs: on the insensitivity of the white world
to Negro needs, on the rank hypocrisy with which white

America has promised and pretended a solicitude for black America that was never really meant. Yet the difficulty of maintaining proper perspective must not be used, especially by Jews, as an excuse for reneging on our responsibilities. We of all peoples know the injustice of branding the group with the guilt of the individual, of blaming a minority for the very traits forced upon it by the majority. We must not forget that we have been strangers in many Egypts.

So we have both latent and overt prejudice among both Negroes and Jews; and we have at least some little under-standing of the dynamics which are responsible for it. Which brings us to the real heart of the matter: what kind of program can be projected for dealing with the situation as it in fact exists?

Suppose we begin with ourselves. Let us admit—openly and honestly—that there *are* Jewish slumlords and unscru-pulous merchants. The facts that most Jewish owners of property and business in the Negro ghetto are decent and honest . . . that there may well be more Gentile than Jewish landlords who abuse their tenants . . . that, indeed, some Negro owners are among the very worst offenders: none of these patent truths should be permitted to camou-flage or protect those Jews whose behavior toward Negro tenants or customers is reprehensible. Such Jews are the responsibility of the entire Jewish community. In the ab-sence of operative communal authority, they will not be easy to control or even to influence, but this difficulty does not exonerate us from the effort.

Individual Jews who are remiss in these respects must be confronted by their rabbis, by the officers of Jewish Com-munity Councils and Federations, by their peers in the country clubs to which they belong—in short, by any and every authority-figure in the Jewish community who could conceivably bring pressure to bear. And yes, why not learn a lesson from our fund-raising experts? Let them be approached if necessary also by those on whom they are economically dependent! Above all, let the Jewish community as such rise up in righteous indignation against the miserable self-abasement of paying obeisance and rendering public honor to those whose tainted contributions to organizations within our own household come from the ill-gotten gain of exploited slum properties.

Will such action, even if it be successful, substantially alleviate Negro anti-Semitism? It should have some effect. I would guess that the mere knowledge among Negroes that the Jewish community is moving along this line would be impressive and effective. But the most efficacious use of communal discipline will probably make no more than minor inroads on the incidence of anti-Semitism. Our own defense, however important it be to us and the community, is not the most persuasive motive for the program here recommended. We need to embark upon such action not in terms of a *quid-pro-quo* but, plainly and simply, because it is right!

Have I made it appear that only we Jews are obliged to change some of our ways? This would obviously be neither accurate nor fair. The main thrust of my argument has been in that direction simply because I am addressing my fellow-Jews. No use in dwelling for them on what others should be doing.

The Negro does share our responsibility, of course he does. He is the only one who can analyze and, as a consequence, significantly remedy those psychological and theological distortions which may predispose him to anti-Semitism. In addition, if there is to be continuing and meaningful dialogue between him and ourselves, he must take steps to establish a responsible Negro community with identifiable leaders. As disorganized and elusive as our Jewish community can be, for understandable historic reasons the Negro community is often non-existent. In Boston there have been occasions when we Jews have been utterly frustrated in attempting to locate our Negro counterparts for honest confrontation.

Both Negro and Jew need to learn more about each other and about their respective histories. It would be particularly constructive for the Negro to know more about Israel's contribution to the development of the African nations, especially since he is now becoming more aware of his own cultural affinity with them.

Finally, responsible Negro leadership has the same obligation to discipline and disavow the anti-Semites in their group as we have to deal harshly with the racists among ourselves. There is no room for repetition of the reluctance and reservation with which the national office of CORE repudiated a vicious expression of prejudice by one of its Westchester County leaders in 1966. If any Negro organizations or leaders have publicly decried the noxious anti-Semitism expressed on the Susskind show, their protest has escaped my attention. It is dialogue we need, not monologue; and dialogue, by very definition, demands the participation of two. The Negro cannot evade his share of obligation.

But in the end, for a Jew addressing other Jews, our own responsibility takes precedence. To be a Jew means to be a special kind of human being, a kind committed under all circumstances to the pursuit of justice. Our dedication to what is right must be unconditional. It cannot be contingent on reciprocity. Either the chosenness of which tradition speaks means this, or it means nothing. I like the way my colleague Harold Schulweis puts this point. He writes: "I do not practice Judaism by looking over my shoulder to see how it will impress the other. I do not care what the Negro expects of me. I care what my child expects of me, what my people expect of me, what God expects of me."

Which leaves just time enough for one final plea, addressed equally to Negroes and Jews. Despite any temporary animosity or frustration, our fate in America will be a common fate. In his memorable book, *Blood Accusation*, Maurice Samuel reminds us how easy it has always been for an evil power structure to delude its victims by diverting their attention to another oppressed minority. Both Negroes and Jews have played this tragic role too often in history. What bitter irony it would be—how the Klansmen and Birchites would howl with laughter!—if either of us be trapped now into abusing the other as a decoy. How did Rabbi David Polish put it? Addressing himself to Negro anti-Semites, he said: "They should know that when scapegoats look for other scapegoats, the wolves rejoice."

Let us give the wolves no occasion for such joy. Let us instead unite our efforts and zeal to build the only kind of society in which both our peoples can be secure. Let us recognize that we are endangered by common enemies and must be sustained by a common hope. Let us understand that our destinies are indivisible, that there will be room in this nation for both of us or for neither. Let us join hands and minds and hearts, as we say in chorus to those of narrow vision and nasty spirit: "Let my people go!"

6

Another White Look at Black Power

This is not the first time I have approached the subject of black power. It is not likely to be the last. The new militancy so characteristic of Negro attitudes and behavior is a phenomenon which will remain with us through the foreseeable future. It will demand our continued attention.

I suppose the place to begin is with definition. Since my prime purpose here is to induce a more sympathetic understanding of black power, and since rabbis are more vulnerable than anyone to misunderstanding and misquotation, let me assure you at the outset explicitly that I do not condone rioting, burning or looting. I deplore violence, whether it be instigated by the rabble or the police. So do all responsible Negro militants. But it is not enough just to condemn the tactics of those who resort to extremes, any more than it will suffice merely to pass resolutions against cancer or to threaten punitive measures against the victim of cancer. Both cancer and urban turbulence are diseases. The intelligent procedure on both is to search for the underlying causes in the hope that prevention and cure may become possible.

The black power of which I speak is not that which causes mass destruction of property and life. It is that which encourages the Negro in this country to throw off the shackles of intramural colonialism, to reject selection of his values and goals by the white community, to assert a large measure of control over his own life. More specifically, it is the new militant mood which demands Negro teachers and principals in ghetto schools, Negro policemen on ghetto streets, Negro owners and managers in ghetto stores.

Unless we blind ourselves with self-deception, these new expectations are not at all difficult to understand. They are the black man's reaction to the agonizingly slow rate of progress he has experienced. No one in his right mind would deny that there has been some progress. A black man represents our nation in the highest councils of the U.N., another sits with distinction on the Supreme Court, a third serves in the Senate of the United States. There has been measurable improvement in job advancement, in median income, in the legal status of the Negro. But these indices of progress have accomplished little or nothing for the hapless inhabitant of our slums.

Despite Ralph Bunche and Thurgood Marshall and Edward Brooke, in 1967 the national rate of unemployment among Negroes was more than twice that of whites. Even that comparison is deceptive. The overall rate of unemployment in the City of Cleveland was 3.5%; in the Negro Hough area it was 15.6%. The proportion is typical of most other large cities. In the words of the Kerner Commission, nearly two-thirds of all Negroes in our central cities "live in neighborhoods marked with substandard housing and general urban blight."

In 1967—thirteen years after the Supreme Court school decision—only 14% of black students in eleven southern states were enrolled in desegregated schools. Near the end of 1968 the Southern Regional Council summarized our progress in school desegregation as "a terrifying story of the object lesson in dishonesty and hypocrisy our Government and our society have provided for a whole generation of young Americans." The American Negro is three times more likely to be poor than the white man; his wife or daughter is four times more likely to be raped than your wife or daughter.

Even more important than these stark statistics is how the black man feels within himself. The Harris poll checked the response of American Negroes over a two-year period to the statement: "The people running the country don't really care what happens to people like ourselves." In 1966 32% reacted to that assertion affirmatively; by 1968 the proportion had reached 52%!

Sometimes a single incident, especially if it be typical, can be more illuminating than voluminous accumulations of statistical evidence. Such an incident was reported in July 1967 by a Roman Catholic priest in Newark. It occured after the riots had ended and the National Guard had been withdrawn. The priest saw two Negroes walking down the street, carrying a case of soda water and two bags of groceries. Five policemen drove up in an unmarked car. Two white officers, asking no questions, in possession of no evidence, accused the Negroes of looting and forced them to put their groceries on the ground. They then kicked the bags open, scattered the contents all over the street, commanded the two black men to get going, and sped off in their car. When the priest crossed the street to help gather up the groceries, one of the men said: "I've just been back from Vietnam two days. I feel like going home, getting a rifle, and shooting the cops."

To the genuine shame of every United States citizen, this kind of thing has happened enough times, in enough cities, to help us considerably in understanding the growth of black power. When the Negro sees this, when he hears George Wallace say our progress in civil rights has proceeded too rapidly and Richard Nixon insist that the federal government should not withhold funds in protection of justice on his behalf—no great mystery remains as to why he turns an increasingly attentive ear to the advocates of black power.

But there is more here than just the black man's justifiable disappointment with his own treatment. He has also become totally disenchanted with the values of white society which he hitherto sought to emulate. Stirred at first by the Black Muslims, then by a variety of Negro nationalists, he now asks what is so superior about our way of life that he should beat out his brains to gain admission into it. He is accused of sexual promiscuity but has reason to suspect the chief distinction between the races on this score is that more whites than blacks can afford abortions. He is charged with looting but discovers increasingly that his looting is petty compared to the tax evasions and embezzlements and devious business trickeries practiced by the white world. He is told he must sacrifice himself for law and order by the very white men who have been contemptuous of law and defiant of order in suppressing him. He is blamed for violence but is aware that Mayor Daley and General LeMay are whites; that the fictionalized violence on our television screens and the all-too-realistic violence in Vietnam are products of white civilization; that the assassins of the two Kennedys and Martin Luther King, Jr. were not Negroes. So he asks: why should I clamor for admission to a house so decadent and corrupt as this? Why not build my own house instead?

Black power, then, is a two-edged reaction: against promises made endlessly but never meant seriously; against the implicit premise that white society is superior. These, however, are both negatives. The positive aspect of black power is its search for ethnic identity. This, we Jews of all peoples should be able to understand and approve. The American Negro today is in this respect retracing precisely the experience of American Jews a generation or two ago. We too had our assimilationists, our Uncle Toms—or should I say, Uncle Davids?—to whom everything Gentile seemed superior to everything Jewish, who were eager to sell their souls for admission into mainstream culture. And we too, thank God, had our survivalists, those who cherished and nourished the values of Judaism, who were bold enough to believe that perhaps non-Jewish Americans had at least as much to learn from us as we from them.

This is exactly the crisis brewing in the Negro community today. Some of us Jews, unfortunately, mis-read the analogy. We are fond of holding up to the Negro—either in chastisement or challenge—our own example of self-help. The implication is: if we could lift ourselves up so dramatically in two or three generations by our own boot-straps, why can't they do the same?

The parallel is spurious; the inducement is insulting. We Jews came to America because we wanted to—freely, hopefully, passionately. Negroes first set foot on this soil as captive slaves. We brought with us a sophisticated tradition and culture. They came rootless and lost, cruelly ruptured from the civilization to which they had been indigenous, rudely excluded from that which was emerging here. The Negro today, moreover, is struggling for advancement in an economy whose unskilled sector is drastically shrinking under the impact of automation; he lacks the advantage we had of getting his initial start in an expanding frontier economy which provided considerable opportunity for advancement even at its less lucrative fringes.

We should observe also that when the Negro takes seriously the example of self-help by which he is goaded, with the result that he withdraws from the white world and resorts to Black Power, the very people who have challenged him in this respect often become his most vociferous critics.

Last year I was privileged to participate at the Harvard Club in an all-day meeting of blacks and whites, of religious and business leaders, convened at the behest of Dana Greeley, President of the American Unitarian-Universalist Association. There I listened and watched as an eloquent leader of the Roxbury community explained his people's goals. He concluded with a most memorable statement: "A man who doesn't know who he is or where he came from, will never be able to decide where he wants to go." Elma Lewis expressed the same sentiment last week. Her words: "A man without a past is a man without a future." Either of these sentences would make an ideal motto for Jewish education. The American Negro today is trying to discover his past in order to insure for himself a future. Not his past as a slave, as the butt of discrimination and oppression. Rather his past as a free man, creator of a solid civilization which has produced some values superior to those regnant in the United States today.

Only thus can we understand the wearing of dashikis and other African garb. Only thus can we evaluate what it meant to self-respecting black men in Boston when a small group of Jewish leaders made it possible for the combined Jewish philanthropies, in the most statesmanlike act of any Jewish community in the country, to give the former Mishkan Tefila building to the Elma Lewis School as a gift. The trend to African costume by American Negroes is to some degree comparable to the placing of a mezuzah on the doorpost of a Jewish home. Either can be an empty motion, a gesture of chauvinistic pride. Or either can symbolize a healthy return to the roots of one's cultural past.

The Black Power advocate is the Negro's Zionist. Africa is his Israel. That should not be at all difficult for us to accept and approve.

When I hear my black friends insist that they want to choose their own leaders, not have leaders thrust upon them by well-meaning whites, their challenge strikes a responsive chord in me. I have quarrelled with the editor of the Catholic *Pilot*—also a friend—more than once, when he has presumed to tell us who the authentic spokesmen of the Jewish community should be. We Jews reserve the right to decide among ourselves who shall speak for us and represent us. We don't always choose wisely, but are entitled to make our own mistakes. Black power means the insistence of Negroes on the same right for themselves. The citizens of Brookline and Newton and Scarsdale and every other suburban community control the policies of their children's schools. Black Power means that Negro parents want no less authority and privilege for themselves.

Some years ago Erik Erikson described the pathetic plight of a little Negro schoolgirl who stood at the sink for an hour, soaping and scouring herself, trying desperately to wash off her blackness, to become white. Later, when an art teacher asked the class to paint the most beautiful thing they could think of, that same child painted her paper solid white. Thus had our civilization scarred her with the stupidity that white is aesthetically preferable to black. It is for the mental health and emotional balance of such children that Negro leaders are insisting today: *Black is Beautiful*.

No one has articulated the essential meaning of Black Power more eloquently than James Farmer. He writes: ". . . the black nationalists tell the Negro that he is somebody and that his salvation depends upon the proud acceptance of his own blackness. White civilization, say the nationalists, taught the Negro to hate himself . . . Stripped of a sense of history, deprived of his majesty, brain-washed by a white man's religion, without a name or any claim to fame, The Negro was a man without suitable memories and a suitable self-definition. Therefore, as the first order of business, before economic or social reforms, the nationalists say we must mend black souls and replace shame with pride."*

Does the effort to accomplish this sometimes lead to lamentable excesses? Of course it does. Black racism is no more praiseworthy than white racism. But let us not forget: we Jews have had our extremists too, our chauvinists who repudiated all non-Jews, our Irgunists who blew up the King David Hotel and assassinated Bernadotte. The responsibility for these acts of excess rested in large part on the British, for their tactics of heartless repression. In no less measure the responsibility for ghetto violence must be shared by white America, which has been much too insensitive for a century to Negro anguish and need.

A word of caution must be directed here to the Negro anti-Semite and the anti-Negro Jew. Prejudice is conta-

* J. Farmer: (*Freedom—When?*, p. 93) Random House, 1965.

gious; democracy is indivisible. Scratch the bigot who gives top priority to his hatred of Jews and in the very first drop of blood you will find the virus of equal animosity against black men. Give the man who ostensibly hates only Negroes one hour of power and he will reveal the anti-Semitism he had previously camouflaged. The Negro who hates Jews or the Jew who is prejudiced against Negroes is, in each case, looping a lynch rope around his own neck. The Negro who associates himself with Nasser's insensate sadism against Israel is preparing the way for his own destruction. Negroes and Jews will win this battle together or they will inhabit the next round of concentration camps together.

Does Black Power mean the end of the integrationist dream? Does it condemn our nation to two separate societies? In the short run, I fear the answer to both questions may be affirmative. In the long run, it need not be so. The possibility of integration will become viable again when two preconditions have been fulfilled: when the black American succeeds in discovering with pride who he is; and when the white American, rather than reluctantly allowing integration, eagerly seeks it because he is convinced that he has as much to gain from it as the Negro. Meanwhile, at least for the next decade, perhaps for a lot longer, consummate patience will be required of those whose skins are white. The black man has had to endure with boundless patience for more than two centuries; now it is our turn.

What does Black Power mean? Robert Browne answered effectively in the *New York Times Magazine* two months ago: "It marks the end of an era in which black men devoted themselves to pathetic attempts to be white men and inaugurates an era in which black people will set their own standards of beauty, conduct and accomplishment."

7

The Most Dangerous Sin

What would you list as the most dangerous sin of which man is capable? My guess is that, whatever your response, it would not be the same as mine.

I do not propose to deal here with such lurid offenses as murder or massacre or rape or even the most monstrous of all modern immoralities, the waging of war. Instead, I plan to talk about a far less spectacular kind of sin which, precisely because of its inconspicuousness, makes all these others possible—the sin of moral neutrality. Let me turn at once to the two most frequent forms of moral neutrality in our civilization.

The first is the theory of ethical relativism: the idea that there are no objective criteria by which to distinguish right from wrong; the most we can say is that societies and civilizations differ in their moral tastes. The responsibility of the individual, according to this view, is to conform to the ethical fashions of his society rather than to search for universal ethical truths, which don't exist.

The protagonist of this view usually reminds us by way of example that among the Eskimos it is considered highly ethical to do away with one's elders when they have reached a certain age, while in our society we try to pro-

vide them with the best available care and rest. The implication is, of course, that neither method can be called more
or less ethical than the other; each is right for the society in
which it prevails.

No one who is familiar with the facts would deny that
there is indeed an element of relativity in our pursuit of
ethics. Often it becomes necessary to hold one ideal in
abeyance for the moment in order to achieve another
which, in that particular circumstance, is more pressing. So
there is admittedly an element of relativity involved; but to
broaden this into the generalized assertion that all ethical
values are subjective and none therefore can be considered
superior to others, is to compound our confusion and to
seek easy excuses for our deficiencies.

How true this is will at once become apparent by way of
analogy. There are also vast differences among social
groups in their comprehension of scientific fact. There are
societies in the remote corners of civilization which still
believe that the earth is flat or that magic rites of one kind
or another are necessary to coax the sun into continued
shining. The fact that some men believe these things doesn't
make them true; it simply demonstrates that some civilizations have developed farther than others and therefore
come closer to an understanding of certain objective and
demonstrable facts.

Another helpful analogy may be found in the area of
aesthetics. One man can enjoy Beethoven's music more
than Mozart's or the poetry of Wordsworth more than that
of Keats, while another reverses the preference in both
cases, and neither can be labelled right or wrong. But if one
were to claim that the music of the Beatles is superior to
that of either Mozart or Beethoven or the poetry of Edgar
Guest more beautiful than that of Wordsworth or Keats,

this is no longer a matter of legitimate subjective preference but rather of aesthetic illiteracy. The aborigine in the jungle isn't to be blamed for preferring the rhythm of the tom-tom to superb symphony; his experience and taste are simply on a lower level of aesthetic development than other societies have reached. But neither can we justifiably pretend there isn't a valid objective difference between these levels.

Do I make myself and my position clear? In science and aesthetics we admit the legitimacy of subjective judgments but we also recognize the existence of objective and universal criteria by which one level of fact or art is understood to be superior to another. The same thing is true in ethics. Here too some individuals and groups have developed to higher levels of perfection and attainment than others. Those of us who are privileged to partake of the benefits of such higher civilization, to enjoy its conveniences and comforts, must also be prepared to meet the greater measure of ethical responsibility it imposes on us.

There isn't time in this context for a complete or extended discussion of what the objective ethical criteria are which ought to govern all men everywhere. Allow me to suggest, merely as a rubric to be elaborated on a later occasion, the following. Whatever, in a given circumstance or setting, helps the individual man or woman to grow, whatever assists him to fulfill his highest human potential, whatever maximizes his freedom together with that of his fellows, whatever encourages him to develop and express his human margin of superiority over all other known forms of life—is good. Whatever restricts or inhibits or constrains him in these respects—is evil. Here are criteria, I submit, which can serve for all men, at all times, in all places. They are valid objectively and universally. They dispense, once and for all, with the first form of moral neutrality: the foolish notion that all morality is relative.

The second manifestation of moral neutrality is the idea that it is possible to be indifferent in matters of ethics, that there are three basic positions in ethics, corresponding to the three positions in shifting the gears of an automobile: forward, reverse and neutral. He who isn't moving either forward or backward can be presumed not to be moving at all. This is obviously true with reference to a car. It is a hopeless delusion with reference to ethics. So long as a human being remains conscious and alive, there are only two positions open to him ethically: he moves in one direction or the other—there is no standing still. He who, in any given situation, is not moving forward toward ethical improvement is thereby of necessity moving backward toward ethical regression. It is no more possible to stand still morally than for the pilot of a plane to remain motionless in mid-air. In one case as in the other, we move forward or we crash.

I remember the exact circumstance in which this truth impressed itself upon me most indelibly. It was on the ship which brought me back from the battle of Iwo Jima to the Hawaiian Islands. No doubt the indescribably horrible experience through which I had just lived increased my emotional receptivity for a novel I read on the trip from hell back to earth. It was entitled *The Cross and the Arrow*. It told the story of an ordinary, average German in the 1930's, a man whose instincts were basically decent, who was not a Nazi, who was disgusted and sickened by much of what he saw the Nazis doing. But he was also a man who enjoyed his evening pipe and slippers; and after a hard day's work he didn't want to be bothered by matters of politics. So he lived in a limbo of moral neutrality during the whole period of Hitler's rise to power and his fiendish persecution of Jews and the onset of World War II. Until finally, when his beloved pipe and slippers had been taken from him, along with his freedom and self-respect, he rose to a climactic moment of self-destructive heroism by igniting a huge arrow of haystacks to guide a squadron of British bombers toward their German military target.

Whose was the most dangerous sin? That of the relatively few fanatics and psychotics who terrorized the entire world? Or of the vast number whose moral neutrality made such terrorization possible? My own personal answer is by this time obvious. The moral neutrality, moreover, which to me is the most dangerous of all sins, can be found here in our own civilization no less than in that of Germany a generation ago.

It manifests itself most vividly and fearfully in the current controversy over segregation. I have enough confidence in the American people to believe that even in Alabama and Mississippi there are substantial numbers of people who are ready to accept racial integration as inevitable. Their preference, to be sure, may well be for a continuation of the *status quo*, but they recognize in their hearts that the destruction of American democracy is too high a price to pay for such a luxury. Yet they do nothing. The unspeakable tragedy in our land today—North and South —is not the extremist; it is the many decent men and women who, by their inaction and silence, make the extremist possible. They confirm, more than any group I know in contemporary America, the judgment of Edmund Burke, who said: "For the triumph of evil it is only necessary that good men shall do nothing."

Harry Golden once wrote of his visit to the home of Dorothy Counts, the first Negro girl who was admitted to a white school in Charlotte, North Carolina, then forced to withdraw by the harassment of white hooligans. Dorothy's father was a minister and a university professor. He showed Harry a list containing the names of people, among them some of the leading citizens of the community, who had called him to express their indignation over the treatment his daughter had received. Harry was moved by their expressions of sympathy, but then he asked a question which should burn indelibly into the conscience of every person on that list: "Why didn't these people call the school board instead, or the principal of Dorothy's school, or why didn't they write a letter to the editor?" Why indeed! Because they were guilty of moral neutrality—the most dangerous of all sins.

Is it necessary to remind you that no one has in recent weeks given a more deplorable demonstration of this sin than the President of the United States?* You remember the press conference at which he refused to express an opinion pro or con on the substantive issue of segregation. When asked whether or not he personally endorsed the Supreme Court decision calling for public school integration he replied: "I think it makes no difference whether or not I endorse it." The most trenchant comment I have seen on the President's statement was written by Walter Lippmann: "The integration of the public schools of the deep south poses the most difficult internal problem which has appeared in this century, and the President's conception of his role in dealing with this problem is so abstract, so generalized, and so unrealistic that he will not even say whether he believes in the principle which he has used Federal troops to enforce. . . . This is a weird view of his

* Dwight D. Eisenhower in 1958.

own office." To which it is only necessary to add: this is a weird view also of moral leadership, an abject surrender to moral neutrality.

It would be soothing and comfortable to let the matter rest where it is now, to use only the citizens of the South and President Eisenhower as our examples, and by implication at least to exonerate ourselves. But it would also be dishonest. So let's have a look at ourselves too before we conclude. How do we stand on the matter of moral neutrality?

As Northerners and particularly as Jews, we're all on the side of the angels with reference to desegregation, aren't we? We deplore discrimination and prejudice. We ourselves have never lifted a single finger to deny the Negro opportunity. But how many affirmative fingers have we raised to assure him opportunity? That's the real question. How many of us have ever taken a positive step toward helping a Negro family purchase property in our neighborhood or on our street? How many of us have ever hired a Negro in office or factory or store—not just in the usual menial capacities, but as a salesman or secretary or executive? There are a few, thank God, who can answer these questions affirmatively. The rest of us would do well to memorize the words of Martin Luther King, Jr.: "It may well be that the greatest tragedy of this period of social transition is not the glaring noisiness of the so-called bad people, but the appalling silence of the so-called good people. It may be that our generation will have to repent not only for the diabolical actions and vitriolic words of the children of darkness, but also for the crippling fears and tragic apathy of the children of light."

Here is something for each of us to think about with impeccable honesty on this sacred day. Most of us during the past year have not been guilty of any spectacular sin which would bring our names to public print. Most of us are decent, responsible people who want to do the best we can. But having said that, we haven't said enough. Our self-appraisal will be neither faithful nor complete until we have searched within ourselves for the most dangerous sin of all: moral neutrality. And the validity of our atonement tonight will be directly proportionate to our efforts in this new year to move off the dead center of moral neutrality.

Let me close with an example which each of us might well seek to emulate. When I lived on Long Island, among my casual Jewish acquaintances was a man named Morris Milgram. In 1947 when Morris was married he was invited into his father-in-law's construction firm. He accepted with a clear understanding that he wasn't interested in building houses only for white purchasers and that after a reasonable time to learn the business he would be allowed to initiate new policies. It was 1952 before Morris was able to begin implementing his intentions. By that time his father-in-law had died and Morris himself was directing the family business.

If Morris Milgram had been like most of us, he would have convinced himself that discrimination in housing wasn't his personal responsibility. He would have appeased his conscience by saying that he hadn't made the unwritten rules by which a Negro could almost never purchase a home in a white neighborhood and he didn't discriminate against minorities himself. And anyway he was a new young builder whose primary obligation was to make a living. Had he done this, no one would have accused him of being a wicked man. But he would have known himself that he was guilty of moral neutrality.

Morris did not want to build a Negro ghetto either. His

goal was an integrated community where Negroes and Whites could live together. He was warned that it couldn't be done: that no bank would advance money for mortgages, that no whites would buy houses in such developments, that he would lose his shirt. It was true that banks didn't rush to provide the necessary financing. So Morris found himself a Quaker named George Otto who headed a large construction company and together they raised the necessary capital from sixty-five individuals. Within three years they completed two large-scale integrated suburban housing developments near Philadelphia. The proportion of families in each was about fifty-five percent white, forty-five percent Negro. Despite the inevitable mistakes of beginners, the Quaker and the Jew who refused to remain morally neutral made nine-percent profit on their investment. Morris subsequently organized several national enterprises through which capital can be raised for loans to other builders willing to follow his example.

This is what it means to avoid moral neutrality. This is the effect which Kol Nidre and our atonement prayers should have on all of us. Anything less than this is deception of ourselves and betrayal of what Judaism must mean. I think our ancient rabbis would have had deep respect for a man like Morris Milgram. For it was they who said, long centuries ago in the Talmud: "A man who retires to his house and says, 'What have I to do with the burden of the community . . . why should I listen to their voices? . . . Peace to thee, O my soul'—such a man destroys the world!"

8

Man's Flight From Himself

Some years ago, Dr. Rollo May wrote a penetrating and perceptive study of human behavior called *Man's Search for Himself*. I deliberately invert his title now to form my own, *Man's Flight from Himself*.

My text is the *haftara* reading for tomorrow afternoon, the Book of Jonah. Let me begin by approaching the mystery of why this little book should ever have been assigned by Jewish tradition to so exalted a place in our people's liturgy. It consists of only four short chapters containing forty-eight verses in all. The whole thing is compressed into just over 2 pages out of 1136 in our Jewish Publication Society English Bible. Why should such a story —really more a pamphlet or tract than a book—have been chosen by our rabbis to be read on the most sacred afternoon of the Jewish year? I think we can assume, by way of immediate answer, that they must have sensed in it something more than the mere surface narrative itself. My hope is that we too may be able to mine precious meaning from the crude ore of the anecdote.

Jonah, you will remember, was a prophet directed by God to preach to the Babylonian inhabitants of Nineveh, to remind them of their sins and warn them that unless they

repented and improved, they would be punished. In order
to evade this responsibility—which was distasteful to him
for reasons we shall shortly explore—Jonah tried to "flee
. . . from the presence of the Lord" by boarding a ship
bound for Tarshish. After the ship had sailed, with Jonah as
one of its passengers, a violent storm broke out. When the
efforts of the sailors seemed insufficient to insure the ship's
safety, they cast lots to discover whose iniquity had in-
voked the wrath of God and the lot fell on Jonah. He then
proposed that in order to save themselves they cast him into
the sea. When they did this, the storm at once abated.

It should almost be unnecessary to remind you that
Jonah was then swallowed by an enormous fish, spent the
next three days in its belly, and was finally regurgitated by
the fish on dry land. God then redirected him to prophesy
in Nineveh. This time he complied. The people and King
of Nineveh were so impressed by his warning that at once
they turned from their evil ways and the city was spared.
At this point one might have expected the prophet to be
delighted that his mission had succeeded. Instead, to quote
the words of the author, "it displeased Jonah exceedingly
and he was angry." He went out into the desert to the east
of Nineveh, where God caused a tree to grow over him,
shading him from the hot sun. The next day when the tree
was destroyed and the shade was gone, Jonah was dis-
tressed. The book ends most peculiarly with God saying to
him: "Thou hast had pity on the gourd, for which thou
hast not labored, neither madest it grow, which came up in
the night, and perished in the night; and should not I have
pity on Nineveh, that great city, wherein are more than six
score thousand persons that cannot discern between their
right hand and their left hand, and also much cattle?"

So much for the story. We can safely assume there isn't a

single person here who believes that Jonah or any other human being was ever swallowed by a fish and vomited up alive three days later. Why, then, do we retain the story both in the Bible and in our prayerbook? What does it mean? What was its author attempting to say which gives his narrative a special relevance for the Day of Atonement? I believe he was trying to tell us at least two things.

The first is the simpler and easier to understand, though not for that reason less important. The voice of God from which Jonah attempts to flee is clearly meant to represent his conscience. In purchasing his passage on a ship bound for Tarshish, Jonah is trying to avoid the dictates of his conscience. He knows full well what his responsibility is; but he doesn't want to assume it. He wants an easy way out. He wants to be shielded, protected, coddled, soothed by religion—not stimulated or challenged.

Erich Fromm has illuminated the true meaning of the symbols used in this story. Notice: Jonah goes "down into the innermost parts of the ship" . . . he "lay and was fast asleep there" . . . he "was in the belly of the fish three days and three nights." One doesn't have to be a psychoanalyst, as Erich Fromm is, to understand the significance of all this, though it helps to hear it expressed in Dr. Fromm's words: "All these symbols stand for the same inner experience: for a condition of being protected and isolated, of safe withdrawal from communication with other human beings. They represent what could be represented in another symbol, the fetus in the mother's womb."

So this is what the story of Jonah really means to say. Did you think ten minutes ago that Jonah's life had nothing to do with yours? It has everything to do with you and your life. You are Jonah—you and I, each of us without exception. There isn't a single one of us who doesn't fre-

quently hear the clear voice of conscience or who doesn't,
almost as frequently, seek to flee from it. We explain, we
rationalize, we justify ourselves; we argue and maneuver
and squirm and sometimes we almost convince ourselves.
Almost, but not quite. For when we evade the voice of
conscience, in the bottommost depths of our hearts we
know it. The first great truth enunciated by the Book of
Jonah is that in the end there is no escape from conscience.

There are those among us who know so little about
psychiatry as to believe that its primary purpose is to absolve us entirely from every trace of guilt. I don't deny that
in some instances and for some individuals psychotherapy
does seem to accomplish that end. Where it has, however, it
has failed, not succeeded. A skilled and perceptive psychiatrist once said to me: "The purpose of our science is to
keep people from feeling guilty over the wrong things,
while helping them to experience reasonable guilt over the
right things." What he meant was that when people hold
themselves liable for evils they never in fact committed or
feel excessively accountable way out of proportion to the
extent of a sin actually perpetrated, they become ill. And
that when we have really done evil, we must learn not to
erase our guilt but to understand it, to handle it construc-
tively and to avoid the same guilt-producing action in the
future.

This business of when to feel guilty and when not—of
how much guilt is good for us and at what point it becomes
dangerous—is one of the most delicately balanced dilemmas
in human experience. Our rabbis approached it centuries
ago with uncanny acuity. They said the prayer known as
Al Chayt, the crucial confession of sin which we and all
Jews recite together on this holiday—is arranged alphabeti-
cally in order for men to know the proper limit to be

placed on confession and guilt. Were it not so arranged, they said, on this soul-searching occasion there might be no end to man's acknowledgment of guilt. But because there is an end to the alphabet, there must also be an end to our communal confession. After a Jew has conceded as many varieties of sin as there are letters in the Hebrew alphabet, it is time to stop facing the past with remorse and begin facing the future with hope.

No man can permanently evade the voice of conscience without immense peril to his integrity and health. Many of you know that. Some of you have come here with heavy hearts, knowing that for too long you have attempted to circumvent your consciences and that it just won't work. Some of you have discovered this in your psychiatrist's office and some in my study and some have yet to discover it in the future. You may be able for a time to fool everyone else in the world—to camouflage the ache of conscience with all the clever disguises of wealth or popularity or power or communal activity or social success. But you can't fool yourself forever! Like Jonah, sooner or later every one of us must confront his conscience with impeccable honesty and answer in the nakedness of his own soul.

A mature conscience is a crystallization of mankind's millennial experience. Just as men have learned through the ages that certain physical actions are conducive to their welfare while others are productive of distress, so the wise among us recognize the same things to be true morally. Hygiene is our guide in distinguishing the beneficial from the harmful physically. Conscience is our guide toward accomplishing the same end morally. The man who consistently ignores the directives of hygiene is likely to suffer for his negligence. The man who makes a practice of ignoring his conscience—in family life, with his friends, in business, in his sexual relationships, anywhere!—such a man is apt to end up in the belly of tragedy and to stay there far longer than three days. Jonah had to learn this the hard way. Perhaps at least some few of us will learn it more easily. Thus far the first message of the book.

To appreciate its second meaning we must ask why Jonah was so reluctant to preach God's word. He was far from the first prophet to be reticent about undertaking his appointed mission; indeed, such hesitancy was characteristic of nearly all the prophets. But the key to this man is understanding that his reason for at first refusing to preach was exactly the opposite of that felt by the others. Moses demurred in the beginning because, he said: "Who am I, that I should go unto Pharaoh? . . . I am not a man of words . . . I am slow of speech and of a slow tongue." Jeremiah balked at becoming God's spokesman because, he said: "I cannot speak for I am a child." These men remonstrated at first for fear of failing. Jonah protested out of fear that he would succeed! Here is the crucial difference; here is a second key to the reading of this book on our holiest day.

In the end, after the people of Nineveh have repented and God has decided not to punish them, Jonah says in effect: "This is why I ran away the first time You ordered me to preach. I was afraid they would repent; and I knew that if they did, You would forgive them. I didn't want them to be saved; I wanted them to be destroyed!"

The usual explanation given for this strange behavior is that Jonah was a chauvinistic Jew who wanted only Jews to be forgiven and saved. Because the inhabitants of Nineveh were Babylonians, he wanted no part in their repentance. The Book of Jonah is said to be a protest against such narrow views. Together with the Book of Ruth, it is accepted as a classic biblical expression of the wide universalism characteristic of our faith even in ancient days. Without denying for a moment that this is indeed a valid interpretation of the book before us, I think there is another explanation which gives it even deeper meaning.

We have already noted one vast difference between Jonah and the other prophets in terms of their respective reasons for approaching their missions with diffidence. There is a second difference of consequence. The others preached because they loved their fellow men and wanted to help them. Jonah preached because he hated his fellow men and desired them to suffer. When Noah learned of God's intention to destroy the world, tradition tells us that even while building the Ark he tried to dissuade his contemporaries from sinning in the hope that God would relent. When Abraham was informed of the impending doom of Sodom and Gomorrah, he bargained with God to save the wicked cities if only ten righteous men could be found in them. When Jonah was ordered to preach repentance to the people of Nineveh, he refused lest they listen!

Can we account for Jonah's conduct? I think we can. Jonah hated his fellowmen because in them he saw himself. Or more accurately: in them he saw a reflection of that which he unconsciously despised in himself. This is the essential nature of sick human beings. Instead of facing up honestly to their own deficiencies, they become ultra-sensitive to the same or similar inadequacies in others. By concentrating their crusading zeal fanatically outward rather than inward, they divert attention from their own intolerable failings.

The worst thing that can happen to such crusaders is to succeed. If the targets of their attacks indeed repent and reform, they are then stripped of their most effective defense and left only with the alternative of facing themselves honestly. This is what Jonah couldn't bear; this is why he ran away to Tarshish and, when that failed, sulked in the desert at the threat of success.

Here again, as in the first instance, Jonah symbolizes a human propensity to be found in many of us. Whenever crusading zeal turns to fanaticism, you can bet your bottom dollar someone is trying to choke himself to death, using his neighbor's neck. The prohibitionist who practically foams at the mouth in decrying the evils of drink is very apt to be afraid of his own unconscious desire for drink. The celibate who in lurid detail depicts the sinfulness of sex is most probably a man or woman who can't cope with the intensity of his own sexual urges. The white man who fulminates flamboyantly about the Negro's sexual designs against white women is the very one who fears his own desire for Negro women. The individual who proclaims that Jews are out to conquer and rule the world is precisely the one who would like to vanquish the world himself. Witness Hitler! The man who argues for capital punishment with purple vehemence is struggling to eradicate in others the criminal tendencies he doesn't dare face in himself. Over and over again, in every generation and century—Jonah!

Have I exaggerated or erred in thus interpreting the fanaticism of Jonah? If there were time, I could quote from the writings of a dozen eminent experts to prove that my analysis is sound. Since time at the moment is a precious commodity, let me just read you three selected sentences from *Christ and Freud*, a partly illuminating, partly aggravating book by the British psychiatrist, Dr. Arthur Guirdham: "To rid oneself of guilt by punishing others is one of the most clearly established psychiatric mechanisms . . . It is a truism that we condemn in others those failings against which we ourselves have our hardest struggle . . . Men tend to condemn most ferociously in others the active expression of those tendencies which are latent in themselves."

This, I submit, is exactly the mechanism which operated in the case of Jonah. What he and the fanatic of every kind does so grossly, each of us does in his own lesser way. We too would rather attack our own deficiencies in others than face them openly in ourselves. May I propose a valid rule of thumb for every single one of us to follow? When you grow angriest at the malfeasance or dereliction of others— be they your children, your husband or wife, or anyone else—look sharply within yourself! When your criticism of others goes beyond the point of reason, when you are ready to attack or strike—be careful: make sure you aren't your own target!

Wise indeed were the rabbis who assigned the reading of Jonah to the most sacred day in the Jewish year. They knew how prone every one of us is, first to flee from the strictures of conscience and, secondly, to avoid facing himself by attacking others. They knew too that the Day of Atonement can have no real meaning of consequence unless we learn the lessons so skillfully symbolized in the story of Jonah.

We need to learn them—you no less than I—I no less than you. The person who leaves this place tonight without reminding himself of specific instances during the past year when he fled from his conscience, when he criticized in others faults which he was unable or unwilling to recognize in himself—that person has vitiated the meaning of Yom Kippur. The person who stops fleeing from himself tonight —who faces himself honestly—who begins now, immediately, to correct and improve himself—that man or woman has used the occasion of Kol Nidre as it was meant to be used. For him the ancient promise is in truth fulfilled: *"Ki vayom hazeh y'chapare alaychem*—On this day God will grant you atonement—*lifnay Adonoy tit-haw-ru*—Before the Lord shall you be cleansed."

BETWEEN MAN
AND GOD

9

Religion and Its Substitutes

Ours is an age in which religion must compete with an increasing number of spurious substitutes. That such substitutes exist should surprise none of us. No human being who is both intelligent and mature can live without some ultimate object of devotion, which means to say, without some form of religion. A man—if he is to be a man, not just a more complicated, more ingenious kind of animal—must have something in which to believe, something to give direction and meaning and purpose to his fleeting years on earth. If, either by his own choice or at the enforced direction of others, he be deprived of real religion, he quickly finds that nature abhors a vacuum spiritually no less than physically. This is as true of mankind collectively as of human beings individually. The individual bereft of devotion to God is likely to find his life's energy polarized around the quest for wealth or prestige or power. The nation so denied ends up devoted either to a dictator or a dialectic. In either case those who have lost religion are likely to take refuge in one of its substitutes.

Let us inquire here into the nature and sufficiency of two such substitutes, of two philosophies or faiths which millions of modern people have enthroned in place of religion, to see whether either is really adequate to replace religion. I choose deliberately to make our task more difficult by selecting not the lesser and more easily demolished substitutes like personal ambition or political idolatry, but instead two of the most highly respected and intellectually honest substitutes for religion, namely, humanism and psychiatry.

There are probably almost as many definitions of humanism as there are individuals who consider themselves humanists. What distinguishes all of them is that they dispense relentlessly with any motive for human behavior which goes beyond the observable nature of man himself. Beginning with a conviction that the individual human personality is the most precious thing on earth, they then set up as the guiding goal of their lives the principle of the greatest good to the greatest number. They admit, to be sure, that in the past it was quite necessary for men to invoke divine, super-human sanctions for the sake of decent behavior. Now, however, they insist we have advanced beyond the need of a cosmic taskmaster. The belief in God has served its historic purpose. All we need now is a belief in man: in his dignity and value, in his greatest good as the highest, worthiest goal of human endeavor.

This hasty summary does less than complete justice to all the shadings and nuances to be found among those who call themselves humanists. For the purpose of our present analysis, however, it should suffice to distinguish, from those of us who believe in God, that group of thoughtful men and women who have arrived at what may fairly be labeled a religion without God.

Let me now begin my analysis of this first substitute for religion by acknowledging that so far as it goes, there is little in it with which to quarrel. The only trouble is it doesn't go far enough. The twin doctrines of man's infinite worth and of the greatest good for the greatest number are altogether acceptable to religionists as well as humanists. But religion insists that these doctrines, however acceptable, are not sufficient to stand by themselves; they become adequate as motives for man's behavior only to the extent that they flower forth from fundamental convictions about the universe of which man is a part. Let me pursue this distinction a step further.

Humanism proclaims as a dogma that man's welfare is the greatest good on earth . . . period! It offers no convincing, compelling reasons for that doctrine. It leaves us to accept or reject it purely as a matter of choice. Religion, on the other hand, goes significantly beyond the *period* of humanism when it explains that man's welfare is the greatest good on earth only because each human person is created in the image of God. Because deeply imbedded within us, inextricably interwoven throughout us, is a great, creative, emergent dynamic Power called God, which keeps our universe from being just a cosmic accident or joke.

This is an altogether different thing from humanism—different both in theory and in practical consequence. A belief that man is important for his own sake, just because he is man, leads sooner or later to one little group of men proclaiming themselves superior to all other men, which is the beginning of what used to be called slavery, the modern name for which is totalitarianism. An impudent faith that man, by and for himself, is the greatest good in life, is what turned a movement like Communism—in its beginnings a true form of idealism—into an ugly, festering, ingrown abscess that poisons the very values it professes.

This is where religion and humanism part company, despite any superficial similarity. Religion teaches that man is important, that his welfare and development are the highest, most legitimate aims of society, not just for his own sake, but because he is a reflection of God. Religion proclaims the individual human personality at its best to be important and precious because it is, so to speak, a sample of God. Humanism unadorned is in essence the boldest, baldest kind of conceit. Religion, properly understood, is the profoundest sort of humility. Between these two there is as vast a difference as between brightest day and deepest, blackest night.

There is another reason why humanism *per se* cannot suffice. It is based on the obvious truth that the whole is not only greater than any of its parts, but that it also determines the specific nature of its parts. An apple tree cannot bear the leaf of an orange. The fact that it is an apple tree presupposes or predetermines that its leaf, its stem, its texture, everything about it must be consistent with the nature of the whole, namely, of a tree that produces apples.

In like manner, we human beings are essential, integral components of the universe in which we live and to which we belong. We are to the universe what the leaf is to the tree. Our specific nature is therefore limited by the nature of the universe as a whole. We cannot be one kind of creature if the total picture around us is the opposite of that creature. We cannot be individuals of precious value and worth if the universe in which we live is a setting of little value and of no worth. In short, there cannot possibly be any meaning or purpose in human life if there is neither meaning nor purpose in the whole existence of our universe.

So humanism, however noble in intent or eloquent in expression, is simply not enough. Before we can believe in human personality as a goal or human welfare as a value, we must first believe certain things about the meaning of the universe and of life at large. Which is another way of saying that to make our humanism more than an unfounded premise, we must subscribe to genuine religion.

William Ernest Hocking, Professor-Emeritus of Philosophy at Harvard, summarized this need perhaps as well as anyone: ". . . no man can have worth unless there is a worthful totality in which he devotedly participates; worth passes from the whole to the part. If the whole is worthless, no man can derive value from that direction. In a worthless world, no man has intrinsic value. . . . The ultimate question cannot be evaded: Is the world worth our devotion? If you say 'no' the whole system of values is in for a slow collapse."

So much, then, for humanism. A second and even more popular proposed substitute for religion is psychiatry. There are vast numbers of men and women today who would enthrone psychiatry in place of religion. Their argument runs that the way to salvation and grace is in the proper understanding of man's unconscious mind. We do not need God any more. Our only requirement is a skilled technique for manipulating and massaging man's anxieties and complexes, his frustrations and fears.

It is so easy to be misunderstood in talking about psychiatry that I want to make myself unmistakably clear. This is not an attack on psychiatry as an invaluable tool for the enhancement of human happiness. I believe in the efficacy of psychiatry. I believe in it as a direction of enormous future hope in our struggle both for personal adjustment and social stability. Often in my counselling of congregants I make referrals to psychiatrists. But I believe with equal fervor and conviction that psychiatry, like humanism, is by itself not enough.

My basic reason is very much the same as it was in the

case of humanism. Mental health—or, if you prefer, personal happiness, which means very much the same thing—can be briefly defined as the proper adjustment of the individual to all the circumstances and environments of his life. That means proper adjustment, first, to his own self, both the conscious and unconscious parts of him; second, to his fellow men and his society; third, and most important for our present purpose, adjustment to the universe in which he lives. To be mentally healthy, in other words, a man must accept not only himself and his fellows, he must also accept his universe. To me it is inconceivable that a person who perceives no purpose or sense in life at large could manage nevertheless to adjust himself to life on his own small personal level.

People can be sick, fearful and neurotic not only because of conflicts within themselves or conflicts between themselves and other individuals, but also because of conflicts between themselves and their ideas about the elementary meaning of human life. How can a person be either happy or mentally secure if he really believes what the late Clarence Darrow so often professed to believe: that human life is a grim, ghastly, irredeemably tragic joke? How can a man perform the daily motions of his life with confidence and assurance if he has no conviction that in the long run all those daily motions add up to something with meaning and sense? The answer, of course, is that he cannot. The man who believes with Macbeth that "life is a tale told by an idiot, full of sound and fury, signifying nothing"—that man, with or without the tools of psychiatry, cannot be mentally healthy or sound.

Psychiatry and religion are, therefore, inseparable partners. Neither is sufficient without the other. Only a person who gains from psychiatry a measure of insight into the conscious and unconscious motives of his own conduct can be completely religious; and only a person of intelligent faith, who believes in a meaning and purpose behind all of life, can be well-adjusted and thus happy. Paul Lushheimer, a New York psychiatrist under whom I had the privilege of studying some years ago, has said: "A psychotherapist cannot be an atheist or an agnostic and at the same time do good work." Professor Hocking cast the same thought in the perspective of philosophy rather than psychology when he wrote: "It is in the end a man's religion which must finish what psycho-analysis begins."

What we found to be true of humanism, then, is no less true of psychiatry. As undeniably valuable as each unquestionably is, by themselves they are not enough. Indispensable as adjuncts *of* religion, neither is sufficient to be a substitute *for* religion. If we are to live by a sustaining faith in human values, we must go back to religion which tells us: *You shall be holy, for I the Lord your God am holy*. And if we are to be healthy and sound, we must temper the profound insights of psychiatry with the exalted wisdom of religion.

I remember from my senior year in high school a lecture given at one of our assemblies by Admiral Richard Byrd. What impressed me most was his description of the method used by explorers to keep from getting lost in the Arctic wastes. Whenever they were about to leave their base for an excursion of exploration, he said, first they would hoist a flag high on a pole firmly implanted in the ice. The flag could be seen for miles. Wherever they were, in whatever direction they traveled, so long as they remained in sight of the flag which oriented them in the frozen vastness, they could find their way back. They needed their sleds and dogs as the techniques of travel. But even more they needed their flag for direction, for safety, for hope.

Humanism and psychiatry are among the indispensable techniques of modern living. None of us would willingly choose to live without them. Yet they are not enough. It is only when we have what Ibsen called "a fixed point outside ourselves," it is only when we have a flag to point our direction, that we are safe. That flag is religion. For that flag, there is no substitute.

10

Three Who Found God

I was first moved toward preaching this sermon several years ago while reading a Midrashic passage which told of three mortal men who were able to perceive God through their own consciousness. The three who were thus identified were Abraham, Job and King Hezekiah. Each found God in a manner uniquely his own.

As so frequently happens in the life of most preachers, I made a few notes on the subject at the time, filed them in their proper place, and promptly proceeded to forget the whole thing. What brought it back to memory recently was the number of people who have remarked in conversation that they genuinely wish they could believe in God but thus far, at any rate, such faith has evaded them. In one way or another, each has asked the same question: how does a man find God through the experiences of his own life? In facing their doubt and search, I thought again of Abraham, Job and Hezekiah, resting comfortably in my files. Tonight I exhume them in the hope that their success in finding God may be of help to many of us.

Turning first to Abraham, the Bible is not explicit in telling us the avenue through which he discovered divinity. Rabbinic literature, however, is more helpful by far. It

embellishes the bare narrative of the Torah with embroi-
dery rich and rewarding. Abraham, according to the rabbis, found God through nature. The story of his search is
surely known to every Religious School pupil. At first, you
remember, he was so dazzled by the sun that he thought it
was God. When the sun disappeared at dusk he decided the
moon must be God. When the moon had passed its fullness
and vanished, he suspected the stars to be God. But when
the stars too disappeared in the returning light of day,
Abraham became aware for the first time that none of these
was God; that all of them were but the visible evidence of
God, who was an ineffable, intangible Spirit, to be found in
nature but not identified exactly with nature.

There are those in our midst today who, while acknowledging that the story of Abraham retains a certain charm,
insist that it is far too naive and unsophisticated to point the
way to God for us. When our earth was believed to be the
center of the universe, they say, and man was envisaged as
the exclusive and final climax of the cosmic creative effort,
it was well and wise to think in terms of a God who
fashioned the whole of this planet and its biological cargo
in six days before resting on the seventh. But how does that
simple picture fit what we know of the universe now?

The answer is that it doesn't. If our comprehension of
the universe has radically changed, then our concept of
God must change correspondingly. But that does not mean
that our new knowledge of nature makes God less necessary or real. The universe with which we are acquainted
now is immeasurably more complicated and wondrous than
that of Abraham. He knew of only one sun; we are aware
of millions. He—or those who wrote of him—believed our
planet to be less than 6,000 years old as of now. We know
that this earth is five billion years of age and the universe at

large is probably twice as old. He conceived the outermost extremities of the universe to be earth and sun. We have established that it takes eight minutes for light rays to reach us from the sun, but eight billion years for them to travel from one end of the universe to the other. That is, if, indeed, the universe has ends! He took it for granted that our earth was the sole bearer of life. Scientists assure us now that there are probably millions of planets in the cosmos capable of sustaining life.

The scope of the universe we know is almost beyond the power of the ordinary person to comprehend. Perhaps a simple comparison will help. If our earth were reduced to the size of the period punctuating this sentence—which means to say, to a diameter measuring one-fiftieth of an inch—the sun would be 21 feet away; the nearest star would be removed by 1,100 miles; the farthest known galaxy of stars would be 350,000,000 miles away. All this, remember, on a scale which measures the diameter of the earth at one-fiftieth of an inch!

Ours is indeed a universe incomparably different from that of Abraham. Where is the logic, however, of those who say that we can therefore dispense with God? To the contrary, we need to postulate the existence of God in nature far more than did Abraham. If a simple, static, self-contained, cozy little universe consisting of earth, sun, moon and a few stars was impossible to understand as a cosmic accident, how much more a universe of today's complexity. If a Cosmic Power was needed to explain the emergence of life on one planet, how much the more when life has probably made its appearance on innumerable planets.

Our trouble today is not that nature no longer can lead us to God, but that we no longer have time for nature.

Many of you have visited the Cathedral of the Pines in southern New Hampshire. I defy any person of reasonably normal intelligence and sensitivity to sit under the trees there on a clear day—looking out across valleys and forests and lakes to the rocky peak of Mt. Monadnock, the oldest known geological formation in continental United States —and not to feel in all of this and within himself the same creative impulse which came to Abraham. For those with eyes to see, with minds to think, with hearts to feel—nature still is one avenue to God.

Then there was Job, with his way toward the discovery of divinity. Job found God through sorrow. While things went well and life was good for him, Job knew God only as philosophy or theory. When his wealth had been dissipated and his property destroyed, when his children had perished and his health had been ruined, only then was Job able to say *"L'shayma ozen sh'ma-tee-cha; v'ata aynee ra-at-cha*—I had heard of Thee by the hearing of the ear; But now mine eye sees Thee."

This is quite the opposite of how many of us feel. We are more inclined to acknowledge God—at least in terms of hasty, passing recognition—at the height of prosperity and comfort, while doubting or even denying Him when adversity afflicts us. I recall a heavy midnight hour when I walked into the home of parents who had just been bereft of a son in his twenties. I knew them well enough to come not merely as their rabbi, but equally as their friend. The mother greeted me as I entered with words that seared their way unforgettably into my memory. Out of uncontrollable anguish and tears, and without even the amenities of welcome, she almost shrieked at me: "This is why I can't believe in God! If something like this can happen, there is no God!"

The last thing in the world I want to do—now or ever
—is to minimize that poor woman's grief or to criticize
anything she might do or say under the immediate impact
of the tragedy from which she suffered. I am aware, moreover, of the fact that more of us would probably react in
her direction than in that of Job, who felt that he had first
begun really to experience God only after a multitude of
oppressive burdens had been laid upon him.

But isn't this really one of our best ways of distinguishing
the mature from the immature in religion? And isn't the
situation here similar in more ways than one to the relationship between parents and children? The youngest, most
immature child is apt to feel that his parents love him only
so long as his every wish is granted. Punishment or denial to
such a child means withdrawal of the love he needs. Only
as he grows older in years and wiser in understanding does
he perceive that sometimes the rejection of his requests
bespeaks more love than would the granting of them. Some
of us, to be sure, never reach that level of understanding
toward our parents or, later in life, toward parent substitutes. And precisely those who fall short of such maturity
in their relationship with parents are likely to exhibit a
similar immaturity in their attitudes toward God.

Much the same thing is true in the partnership between
husband and wife. There are more than a few among us
who equate marital love with the granting of their every
wish, who are driven away from each other in marriage
when adversity strikes. And there are others whose strong-
est, most imperishable bonds of love are forged on the anvil
of the anxiety and sorrow they must endure together.
These last are the mature partners in marriage.

Even so, Job was mature in his recognition of God.
What might he have meant when, rising from the ashes of

destruction and death, he said: "Now mine eye sees Thee"? These are impressively poetic words, but unless we translate them into the specifics of our own lives, they will have little value in our search for God. So what might Job have meant? First, that he recognized the existence of law and order, no less in the tragic moments of life than in its times of exultation. Second, that he did not expect the universe to cater only to his personal needs, that, indeed, there might be occasions when the ultimate purpose of the universe could be served only if his individual needs were rebuffed.

Maimonides understood that. In the greatest of his philosophic works, *The Guide to the Perplexed*, he wrote: ". . . every fool thinks that life is there for his sake alone, and as though nothing existed but he. And so, when anything happens that opposes his wishes, he concludes that the whole universe is evil. . . . It is of great advantage that man recognize the measure of his worth, so that he may not fall into the error of believing that the universe exists only because of him. . . . Most of the evil that befalls individuals comes from the imperfections within themselves. Out of these imperfections of ours we cry out demands. The evil we inflict upon ourselves, of our own volition, and which pains us, this evil we ascribe to God."

What else might Job have had in mind and heart? That he as a human being had been endowed with intelligence enough to discover the laws by which the universe operates, and, by utilizing those laws, materially to reduce—not to eliminate entirely, but materially to reduce—the amount of suffering by which he and his fellowmen were to be afflicted. And finally, that—once more in accordance with the laws of life—there was a Power in the universe and in himself which could enable him to surmount the moment's sorrow; to grow because of it into a finer specimen of humanity; to use his tragedy as a means of fulfilling the purpose of evolution, by leading the way toward a higher and nobler kind of life on this earth.

Is all this just poetic theory, pleasant to hear but divorced from the realities of life? A few weeks ago I officiated at the funeral of a woman who died in her early forties, after several years of agonizing illness. Some of you were there and will know of whom I speak. Her identity, however, is far less important than the fact that all through the time of her incapacity, during the many months that her family physically had to carry her from bed to wheel-chair and back again, she was in fact carrying them. Carrying them with some of the most robust strength and precious sweetness and confident faith I have ever seen or known. She too was saying, in her way, "now mine eye sees Thee." You ask the wrong question, friend, when you want to know how we can explain so much sorrow in the world if there is God. The real puzzle is: how can there be so much sweetness and goodness in the world if there is not God? This was Job's way.

Then finally, according to the Midrash, there was King Hezekiah, who ruled over Judah in the time of the prophet Isaiah. His road to God is identified in the following brief description given him by the prophet: "Butter and honey shall he eat, when he knows to refuse the evil and choose the good." Hezekiah found God through his own inner nature, most notably through his conscience, his ability "to refuse the evil and choose the good." Here it becomes necessary to revert for a moment to my earlier reference regarding law and order in the universe. My treatment of this topic then was intentionally incomplete. I knew the rest of it would fit more persuasively at this point. There are those who say that order is a characteristic not of the

universe but of man's mind. They would add that the same
thing is true of beauty, of truth and of moral goodness. It is
our human propensity, they insist, to think in such terms as
these, and then to impose them upon the universe, to read
them into rather than out of the world of nature.

Suppose, for the sake of argument, we grant that truth,
beauty and goodness are postulates of the human mind.
From whence did the human mind come? Is it a novelty, a
break from the past, a rude intrusion into the natural order
of things which preceded it? Or has it evolved—slowly,
imperceptibly but surely—out of everything which anticipated it on earth? The only possible answer is the second.
Man's mind and creativity and conscience are just as much
products of the universe—hence just as consistent with the
nature of the universe—as his hand or spine or brain.
Which means to say: if you want truly, accurately to
know the inherent characteristics or qualities of the universe, one route to discovery is the study of man. If man
possesses a mind, then mind must be a potential, if not a
quality, of the universe at large. If man has developed a
conscience, then moral values must be potentially present in
the universe. In every respect man is a response to that
which existed before his first appearance. His hunger is a
response to the pre-existence of food. His sight is a response
to light waves. His hearing is a response to sound waves. In
the same way—though of course not physically demonstrable—his capacity for beauty, for goodness, for truth is a
response to something ineffable in the very structure and
substance of the universe. We have grown accustomed to
calling that something God.

Rabbi Robert Gordis has understood and expressed this
thought with admirable clarity. Concerning the matters

under immediate discussion, he has written: "These attributes of man's nature reveal something about the universe,
just as an apple discloses the nature of the tree upon which
it has ripened, and it itself in turn was present in the seed
from which the tree grew." What Dr. Gordis is clearly
attempting to say here is that beauty, goodness and truth
could no more appear in man if the universe itself is devoid
of them than an apple could grow on a cactus tree.

Here, then, are our three ways to God. Abraham found
Him through nature, Job through suffering, Hezekiah
through conscience. Each of us can find God in these same
ways. But we will not find Him just for wanting it, any
more than the cure for cancer or the mysteries of space or
the secret of life's origin will be discovered just by waiting.
God is not likely to appear by miraculous revelation to any
member of this congregation who merely sits and wants
and waits. God will not search for us; we must actively
seek Him. Amos understood this. It was he who said:
"Dir-shu-et Adonai vi-ch'yu—seek ye the Lord and live."
Jeremiah understood also. He put these words, as it were,
into the mouth of God: ". . . seek Me, and you shall find
Me; when you seek for Me with all your heart, I will reveal
Myself to you."

God is nigh. God is discoverable for us, as he was for
Abraham, for Job, for Hezekiah. He will be found only by
those who zealously seek. They, and they alone, will arrive
at the sublime perception of the poet:

> ". . . . .*And I have felt*
> *A presence that disturbs me with the joy*
> *Of elevated thoughts; a sense sublime*
> *Of something far more deeply interfused,*

Whose dwelling is the light of setting suns,
And the round ocean and the living air,
And the blue sky, and in the mind of man;
A motion and a spirit that impels
All thinking things, all objects of all thought,
And rolls through all things."

11
Watchword or Rote?

The most important words in Judaism—if indeed not in the entire religious experience of mankind—are the six Hebrew words of the *Shema*. They constitute the central theme and core of every Jewish worship Service. In addition to being prominently recited near the beginning of each, they are, as you know, repeated when the Torah is removed from its Ark. In most cases they are the first Hebrew words a very young Jew learns to lisp and the last that an old Jew gasps before he dies. Throughout the ages these have been the valedictory words with which multitudes of Jewish martyrs have sealed their earthly existence.

Tradition embellishes the *Shema* with all the accoutrements of immense importance. Each word, we are enjoined, nay each syllable is to be enunciated with impeccable clarity. We are told in the Talmud not to interrupt our recitation of the *Shema* even for the purpose of greeting a king. The Jew who happens to be out walking at the time the *Shema* is to be recited is ordered to stop for this purpose, in order that every ounce of his energy and attention may be concentrated without dilution on this most essential religious obligation.

Kaufman Kohler—perhaps the greatest, certainly one of

the two or three most eminent Jewish theologians thus far in American history—has summarized the impressive role of the *Shema* in these words: "Throughout the entire realm of literature, secular or sacred, there is probably no utterance to be found that can be compared in its intrinsic intellectual and spiritual force, or in the influence it exerted upon the whole thinking and feeling of civilized mankind, with the six words which have become the battle-cry of the Jewish people for more than twenty-five centuries."

There is grave danger, however, that we in our time will come to take these words for granted. As is the case with all such formulae of faith, frequent repetition by rote is not conducive to reflection on intrinsic meaning. Some of us, moreover, are tempted to assume that the *Shema* is no longer as urgently important as it once was because, nominally at least, all of civilized mankind seems to have accepted the idea of one God. We today are no longer confronted by the polytheistic religions of the Canaanites or Babylonians or Egyptians. Even the dualism of the Zoroastrians, with their twin-gods of good and evil, is for all practical purposes extinct. Why, then, get excessively excited over a battle-cry which no longer seems necessary because the battle has been won?

The thesis undergirding this sermon is that our *Shema* is no less necessary or meaningful now than it was at any time in the past. That is, not if we attend with due emphasis and concentration to its deepest meanings. In this instance, as in so many others, our ancient rabbis—perhaps only through instinct or intuition—discovered certain truths about the universe and themselves which subsequent centuries of scientific exploration and discovery have shown to be even more valid than those rabbis could have suspected. What are these truths? What are we really saying—tonight and on all such occasions—when we recite the *Shema?* In the lexicon of today, what does it mean to proclaim and insist that our God is One God?

First, that man and his universe are one. By reminding myself and my people that God is One, I mean, to begin with, that the universe is one, and I am part of its oneness. We know this today in a far more concrete and convincing manner than the ancient rabbis could have imagined. We know that matter and energy are one: matter is, in a manner of speaking, energy at rest, while energy is matter in motion. *Adonai elohaynu Adonai Echod*—the Ultimate Essence of the universe is one!

The organic and the inorganic are one. No longer do chemists divide their studies into the two branches which prevailed when I was a college student, one branch for inert matter such as minerals and rocks, another for living molecules and cells. Today they recognize that there is no specific point at which it is possible to say: precisely here is where lifeless matter becomes life. Instead, our scientists understand now that life was potentially present even in the inorganic and gradually evolved from the inorganic. *Adonai elohaynu Adonai Echod!*

We know, moreover, that exactly the physical laws which govern the earth, the sun, the planets and all the galaxies govern man's body. The movement of protons, electrons and neutrons within the atom—in this book, in that wall, in our very bodies—corresponds amazingly to the movement of the planets in each solar system around their sun. The arrangement of chromosomes within living cells are precisely the same in number and function in a celery stalk or a toad or a man. Each piece of protoplasm, no matter where or in what form it appears, anywhere on this earth—or if life exists on other planets, everywhere in the universe—is physically and chemically exactly like all pieces of protoplasm. At least one eminent scientist has gone so far as to suggest that the universe itself is evolving or expanding in precisely the way that an egg or a blossom expands from its earliest beginnings.

The evidence is impressive and exhaustless. This whole vast breath-taking universe of ours consists of one ultimate basic reality. And I as a human being am not a detached observer, standing outside it; I am one of its products, made of the same stuff, governed by the same laws, evolved through the same processes.

Is this just a matter of academic concern? If it were, it would scarcely belong here. What gives it a unique religious significance as an expression of the *Shema* is its practical application. Like every other form of life, man is a product of nature. Unlike all other forms, man has the capacity to alienate himself from nature. A tree or a virus or a horse has no problem of alienation. It can never divorce itself from what it is, never pretend to be what it is not. Man alone has that choice. This is at once his glory and his peril. Man can deny the nature of his own reality. But he does so only at the frightful risk of losing himself.

Erich Fromm sees in this the root-cause of much mental and emotional illness. He has emphasized again and again, in volume after volume, that as man allows himself to become divorced from nature, to forget that he is ineluctably a part of nature, subject whether he likes it or not to the rules of nature, he becomes ill. The beginning of mental health, then,—and I would add here also of religious understanding and growth—is for man to learn more about his nature as an integral part of the universe and to conform to what he discovers. Here are two short sentences out of scores in which Dr. Fromm has said something very much like this: "Mental health is achieved if man develops into full maturity according to the characteristics and laws of human nature. Mental illness consists in the failure of such development."

Hear, O Israel—hear, O man—you and the universe are one! This is our first application of the *Shema.*

The second is that man within himself must also be one. On the most elementary level this is true beyond man's accepting or rejecting it. All the cells in our bodies, all the corpuscles and organs and glands are coordinated into a marvelously unified whole—each part working together with all others in fantastically wondrous ways for the survival and health of the whole. In this sense obviously each of us is one. In a more significant sense, our bodies and minds are one, our bodies and souls are one. This is the primary truth of psychosomatic medicine. There is no affliction or disease in human experience which is altogether physical or entirely emotional. Often we cannot even determine which area was responsible for the initial onset of a given malfunction. But we know that everything which occurs to us physically affects our emotions and minds, while each thought we think, each emotion we feel has its profound repercussions on our bodies. *Shema Yisroel—* Hear, O Israel! Man within himself is one, even as God is One.

When man too far forgets this or foolishly attempts to ignore it, he develops a so-called split personality; he becomes schizophrenic. At that point he needs something far more radical than religion to be cured. Religion cannot cure a sick mind any more than it can remove an infected appendix. But religion can help us prevent sick minds by encouraging us to strive for oneness within ourselves. Though few of us, thank God, will ever become schizo-

phrenic, most of us live lives that are impossibly splintered.
We chase off in a hundred different directions, with little
sense of coordinated or unified purpose. If we were pressed
to list in order the three foremost goals we pursue in our
mortal career, few of us could respond with anything more
than hesitant generalities. And even the few who could
answer properly would in most instances find themselves
spending only the smallest portion of their energy and time
on the objectives which, in theory, mean most to them.

Some weeks ago a very intelligent, sensitive college
student came to me for counseling. One of his key questions was: how do I establish priorities in my life? How do
I achieve order out of the chaos which threatens? Knowing
that in a single lifetime I cannot begin to accomplish even a
tenth of the objectives which now seem important to me,
how do I choose which to pursue and coordinate my best
efforts in that direction? I could not answer that boy's
questions. I did not even try. My only effort was to think
out loud with him, even as I think out loud now with you.
For each of us must make this kind of decision himself.

To be either happy or healthy or both, we must be one
within ourselves. We must know what we want most to
accomplish and which of our efforts will lead us in that
direction. We must try to integrate intellect with emotion,
reason with faith, what we know with what we believe.
Unless these aspects of our lives are consistent and coordinate, unless they mesh together purposefully toward the
same primary ends, we will forever be at war with ourselves. And a man at war with himself can be no happier or
healthier than a man at war with the universe.

There is a special aspect of this second application of the
Shema to which I would speak briefly before concluding,

an aspect particularly congenial to Judaism. In order for any one of us to be truly at one with himself, there can be no sharp schism in his life between the sacred and the profane. Every apparently vulgar or mundane experience must be seen as a temporarily unrealized opportunity for sanctity. Life must be divided not into the hallowed and the profane, but into the hallowed and the not-yet-hallowed. Judaism at its best has always recognized this. Only thus can we understand why our fathers recited a Hebrew blessing even when satisfying their most elementary and alimentary physical needs. For us, as for them, no moment or experience in life can be beyond use as a means of sanctifying ourselves, of unifying us with the divine.

This means that even the way we spend our leisure hours must help promote the best in ourselves. Even our social enterprises must be opportunities for growth toward further maturity. The way we behave toward our children and mates in the home, the methods we use in relating to our employees or competitors or customers in business, the manner in which we meet our political responsibilities as citizens—all must be permeated and pervaded with the ethics of Judaism, must lift us up from what we were in the past toward what we may yet become in the future. There is no corner, not even the tiniest, in any man's life which can be exempt from the challenge of the divine.

Chasidic literature illustrates this in many ways. There is, for example, the comment of the Baal Shem Tov himself on the Biblical verse, "All that your hand finds to do, do in your strength." This means, said the Besht, that a cobbler at his bench must sew together the upper leather and the sole in such manner that he will simultaneously be joining God and his *Shechina*, His holy spirit. For us that means that the meanest, seemingly most menial and insignificant task on earth must be performed so that it helps unite the performer to his universe and to the best in himself.

All this from the six short words of the *Shema!* This and much more. We have not even touched on the essential oneness of men with each other, which is also a necessary implication of these words. Yet we have said enough, I hope, to indicate that each week or each day as we recite the watchword of our faith, we rehearse thereby the unity of the universe and of man within the universe and within himself.

Near the beginning of this sermon I quoted Kaufman Kohler. I close now with an altogether different kind of quotation. This is from the pen of a scientist who, in the language of his own discipline and of this twentieth century, confirms what our ancestors have meant since Bible days whenever they recited the *Shema*. These are the words of Ralph W. Burhoe, Director of the Center for Advanced Study in Theology and the Sciences: ". . . the scientific faith is essentially akin to the ancient religious faith in holding that the infinity in which we live and move is in reality one, not many. The scientific faith that all things are variants in a single system, that one law rules the Cosmos from end to end, from the biggest to the littlest, is a faith that grows stronger with each succeeding new discovery. . . . Today this faith is so high that we have little doubt but that there is continuity from man to amoeba to molecule. There is no separation of man from his origin nor from his fellow man. We are indeed all brothers. . . ."

12
God's Voice—Or My Own?

One of the most persistent and compelling myths in the entire literature of mankind is the tale we read a few moments ago from the Torah. It is open to so many varying interpretations that every rabbi finds himself preaching on it repeatedly. The fact that Abraham's apparent willingness to sacrifice his beloved son Isaac is correctly characterized as a myth does not mean that its importance is to be minimized. For the role of the myth in the collective life of society is recognized now to resemble that of the dream in individual experience.

In a literal sense, neither the dream nor the myth is true. Indeed, more often than not, they both portray events which are factually impossible. Yet we know that dreams, however improbable or implausible their content, can accurately reflect conflicts or memories or urges which have been repressed beneath the surface of individual consciousness. In much the same way, we now begin to realize, myths can express anxieties or hopes no less significant in the experience of the group.

Perhaps this is why a myth like that of Abraham and Isaac holds an almost hypnotic fascination for so many of us. The extent of my own preoccupation with this story may be measured by the fact that of the ten Rosh Ha-shonah occasions on which I have thus far been privileged to preach from this pulpit, this is the third time my sermon has been based on the story of Abraham and Isaac. Yet each time my theme has been quite different from the others; because each time I discovered in this myth a profound and enduring message that I had never seen in it before.

This past summer as I read the story again—perhaps for the hundredth, perhaps for the thousandth time—I found myself confronted by a dilemma which must have been excruciating for Abraham. According to the Torah anecdote, Abraham hears what purports to be the voice of God twice. The first time it says to him: "*Kach na et bin'cha . . . v'ha-a-lay-hu . . . l'ola;* take now your son, your only son Isaac, whom you love . . . and offer him . . . for a burnt-offering." The second time Abraham thinks he hears God speak, at the very instant when he stands with knife poised ominously to sacrifice his own precious flesh and blood, the instruction is quite opposite: *Al tishlach yad-cha el ha-na-ar v'al ta-as lo m'uma;* lay not your hand upon the lad, neither do any harm to him!"

How did Abraham know which was the authentic voice of God? If on grounds of immediacy, he might well have chosen the first, for the voice which ordered him to kill Isaac is described directly as the voice of God Himself. The second, saving voice, is attributed in the Torah only to *malach Adonai,* an angel or emmisary of God. How did he know? How can any of us know when it is God who speaks to us and when we are just using God as a stamp of approval, so to speak, for what we want desperately ourselves?

Those of you who have visited mental hospitals know the frequency with which desperately ill psychotics claim to hear the voice of God or to speak for God. A few years ago in our newspapers we read of a woman who had kept her son locked in a dark, damp, dismal room from birth to adolescence because, she said, God had ordered it. Members of certain religious sects refuse to accept or permit blood transfusions even when the alternative is certain death because they believe such transfusions to be against the will of God. In the early 1960s three faithful Catholics in New Orleans accepted excommunication from their church because they were convinced that God wanted segregation. The problem, you see, was not just Abraham's. The dilemma confronts us too; it will for the rest of our lives. How do we know when it is really God speaking to us? How can we distinguish right from wrong? What criteria can we employ to know the difference between God's voice and our own?

I have no simple or easy answers, no spectroscope by which to take an exact reading on each moral issue and thus know precisely what to do. In fact, we should beware of those who do profess such certain knowledge. The best I can offer—for you or for myself—is a set of guide-lines by which, in each separate instance, we can evaluate and measure, then do the very best within our power to identify the genuine voice of God. These guide-lines I derive from my fundamental conviction that God is to be found within nature itself, including human nature; that God is the dynamic, creative, emergent Urge which permeates nature— directing and propelling it toward the fulfillment of a massive plan. If, then, I want to know the will of God, I search not for voices from on high nor for the mysterious promptings of oracles, but rather for the directions in which nature has already moved at the behest of the divine. Which means to say, I search with all my mind and heart for the tendencies and trends already exhibited by nature before man first appeared.

When I do that, what do I discover that helps me identify the voice of God? First, that nature has progressed to its present point through the cooperative integration of small units into larger wholes. You can supply examples as easily as I. In an earlier chapter we noted that electrons, protons and neutrons must combine and in a sense "cooperate" in order for atoms to exist. Atoms must prevail in the right relationship to each other in order for molecules to emerge. Then, progressively, molecules must do the same for the sake of cells . . . cells to form organs . . . organs to function within organisms . . . organisms within families and tribes . . . tribes within nations . . . nations within all of human society . . . and perhaps one day all earth's humanity within a cosmic society which will include the inhabitants of planets other than our own.

This is both elementary and obvious. Each small unit in nature exists for the sake of the next larger unit. Were this not so, evolution would have been blocked on the level of the electron, if indeed it would have developed that far. This is not speculation; it is fact. It is the way in which nature operates. It is therefore our first clue to the voice and will of God. When the molecule combines with other molecules to form and function within the cell and when I cooperate with you for the eventual welfare of all of us together, both the molecule and I are heeding the voice of God. The only difference is that the molecule lacks both consciousness and choice, while I possess both.

Does this mean that in nature the individual unit has no importance of its own? Quite the contrary. It requires no argument—does it?—to establish that the cell which cooperates to make human life possible is more valuable and important, even in and for itself, than the cell which goes berserk and, by becoming cancerous, abruptly ends its own life along with that of its larger host. Or that the man who cooperates to make society possible is more valuable and important even on his own account than one who rejects society and condemns it. This is one of the most precious paradoxes of nature, hence one of the most accurate ways to discover the voice of God: the small individual which, so to speak, sacrifices part of its own hegemony for the sake of the next larger unit of existence thereby becomes not less significant but more.

What I am really struggling to say here is that our best ethical insights and values are potentially present within nature from the beginning; that the Ten Commandments, far from being an intrusion of the unnatural into the natural, are as much a product of nature as is our complicated human brain. Because this thought is still new enough to sound radical, let me share with you the words in which one of our most eminent American scientists has said very much the same thing. Dr. Kirtley F. Mather has written: ". . . biologists and paleantologists have been increasingly impressed by the importance of the role played by mutual aid and cooperation in evolutionary development . . . especially with respect to man's lineage, evolution tends toward the development of ethical behavior in complete harmony with the high principles of the best religious traditions."

Now let's get back to Abraham. I haven't forgotten him. If Abraham had killed Isaac, he would have been destroying a unit of life equal to himself, rather than cooperating with it to make possible an even higher dimension of life. The only excuse for one human being deliberately to terminate the life of another is if that other has itself so far rejected the discipline of nature that in no other way can that discipline be maintained. This was clearly not the case with Isaac. Hence, in accordance with our first clue, there can be no doubt: the voice which called upon Abraham to save his son was truly the voice of God.

A second clue which has already been adumbrated now begs to be elaborated. It too finds the voice of God within nature itself, especially in nature's own hierarchy of values. It emerges from the fact that evolution has moved not merely from smaller units to larger units and from simpler to more complicated forms of existence, but also to higher and higher levels of value. First there were just things on this earth—plain, passive, unresponsive, insensate things like water and earth and rocks. Out of these things in the course of cosmic time there developed life. And more recently— only a moment ago as the planets and suns measure time—a very special kind of life: man. Man, who is more than a thing, more even than just another animal. Man, who is part beast and part God. Man, who can not only procreate but can love, who can not only move but can think, who can not only ingest and digest but can create and appreciate ineffable beauty, who can not only manipulate and adjust but can distinguish the difference between evil and good.

In short, nature has moved inexorably, through its own inherent direction and propulsion, from the mere existence of the amoeba to the intellect and aesthetic capacities and exquisite conscience of man. The Power within nature which has been responsible for such movement, we call God. Any action or thought on man's part which helps nature move still further in the evolutionary direction for which it has shown so strong a preference is in fulfillment of God's will and voice. Any step which reduces man to a thing or even to nothing more than another animal is in defiance of God. Every voice we hear which urges us to increase our margin of superiority over things and animals is God's voice. Every prompting within us more vigorously to pursue truth, beauty and ethical goodness is divine prompting. When Abraham sacrificed an animal, a ram, rather than his human son, he was without the slightest doubt heeding the voice of God. He was acting consistently with the nature of the universe and of himself. He was prefering and promoting the larger and nobler values of collective humanity rather than the smaller, meaner choices of the animal within himself.

The question with which we began this investigation is not as difficult as we may at first have feared. The voice commanding Abraham to spare his son was in truth the voice of God—not because it was the second to speak, not even just because it was consistent with Abraham's desperate desire as a father—but because it was appropriate to a higher level of evolution than the first.

What does all this mean, specifically and concretely, for us? This is the heart of the matter. Our inquiry into Abraham's dilemma is valid only if it helps us resolve our own. Abraham was fortunate in one respect: he heard only two voices. We today are exposed to many thousands of voices, all purporting to express God's will. What, then, does Abraham's experience mean for us? It means that for us also the voice of God is the voice which prompts us to act on behalf of the human totality at its noblest and best. It means that the man who is generous to his entire family is more responsive to God's voice than he who is concerned only with himself. But such a man isn't really quite fully human yet, because even certain species of animals have developed a rather touching degree of loyalty and affection for their own kin. The man whose generosity reaches out to encompass his congregation and all congregations and the Com-

bined Jewish Philanthropies is a stage higher in his consciousness of God's voice. Until finally, the man or woman
whose heart bleeds whenever a human being goes hungry
in Asia, wherever the yearning for freedom is thwarted
behind the iron curtain or in Mississippi—he whose heart
not only bleeds for all this but impels him to action on
behalf of its victims, he has indeed become part of nature's
tidal wave. He has heard the voice of God.

The voice of God says *yes* to blood transfusions because
they mean the preservation of some human lives with no
damage or harm to others. The voice of God says *no* to
segregation and discrimination because they set up conflict
instead of cooperation between equal units of humanity.
The voice of God repudiates exploiting the military need
of our nation to gain unconscionable profit or the accumulation of wealth by a drug industry which refuses ade-
quately to test its products first, not just because these
happen to be violations of Federal law but because they are
the way of the cancer cell, the way which obstructs nature.
The voice of God condemns continued, uncontrolled,
competitive testing of nuclear weapons because such tests
can destroy the whole purpose of evolution. For us, as for
Abraham, the voice of God is the voice which calls upon us
to act in concert for our common good, to give our highest
priority to that which makes us most human.

Does this mean that life will henceforth be easy for us,
that our moral dilemmas will yield to simple solutions? Not
at all. Abraham faced many moments of painful searching
even after he had successfully identified which voice be-
longed to God. We shall have many such moments also.
There will be times when our guide-lines, however clear
they seem this morning, will appear to be hopelessly knot-
ted and snarled, other times when they seem to point simul-

taneously toward opposite directions. But they are the best we can expect, the very best. If they cannot guarantee us any easy success, at least they can help us as we search.

There is an ancient oriental fable with which I would close. It tells how the evil spirits conspired to hide God from man. They thought of all sorts of places—mountains, caves, forests—but knowing man's insatiable curiosity, they were afraid that he would eventually find the hiding place. So at last the most cunning of the evil powers suggested that God be hidden in the heart of man himself, for man would never think of looking for Him there.

The voice of God will come to us not from the heavens and not through angels. It will come from within ourselves. It will bid us act together on behalf of our highest human values. May we, like Abraham, hear and heed.

13

I Believe in Miracles

Anyone familiar with my theology must be puzzled by tonight's title. Such persons know that the very heart of my religious faith is confidence in a universe of purposeful order. Hence I cannot believe in miracles according to the common definition of the word; I do not believe that the laws of nature are ever interrupted or suspended.

There is, to be sure, a great deal we do not know yet about the laws of nature. Some of the conclusions concerning nature's procedures about which we seemed most certain only a generation ago, are now seen to have been grossly mistaken. Some of the phenomena we find it impossible to understand or explain today will no doubt be comprehensible and clear to our children and grandchildren. But I believe, with firm conviction and positive faith, that nothing will ever be discovered to upset the picture we now have of a universe characterized by purpose and order.

In such a universe there is no room for miracles in the form of exceptions. If I thought for a moment that God could suspend the rules of nature, it would be impossible for me to believe in God at all. The evidence which, as much as anything else, impels me to the conviction that God exists is precisely the fact that this is so unexceptiona-

bly a universe where things happen sensibly and reasonably. A universe of inexorable law, of cause and inevitable
effect, is a universe which becomes intelligible only in
terms of a Force or Power or Mind which is responsible for
such order. A universe, on the other hand, of coincidence
and accident, one in which things occurred haphazardly
and undependably, would be a universe which not only
needed no God to explain it but indeed by its very acciden-
tal nature would preclude even the possibility of God.

Joshua Liebman expressed this thought with his customary clarity: "At first it seems daring, if not heretical, for us
to say that God is . . . limited. We ask in amazement,
'How can God be limited? If He is not all-powerful—able
to do anything that He wills—then surely He cannot be
God!' I deny this conclusion. If I did not believe that God
is *limited* by the very nature of the world He created, then
I would have to surrender my faith."* To which I would
add: if God is limited by the very nature of the world He
created, then obviously there is no room for miracles as our
ancestors understood them.

Perhaps it would be more accurate to say: as *some* of our
ancestors understood them. For it would be a serious mistake to assume that this matter of miracles didn't bother
many of our progenitors in Judaism, despite all their apparent naivete. The Talmud tells us, for example, that the
Torah preceded Creation and was used by God as a blueprint in the establishment of the universe. What is that but
a poetic recognition of the fact that God Himself is limited
by His own rules, hence not free to act by caprice or
whim?

The well-known miracle stories of the Bible were ex-

* J. L. Liebman: Peace of Mind, p. 160 f. Simon and Schuster, 1946.

plained by our ancient rabbis (who, after all, could not be expected to reject them out of hand) as having been included by God in His original Plan of Creation and therefore not exceptional to that Plan. They said God made a bargain with the sea, for example, at the very beginning to split apart at the appropriate time so that the children of Israel could pass through it in escaping from Egypt. A neat solution for them, you will admit, even if scarcely a tenable one for us. Elsewhere, in at least two unrelated passages, the Talmud states explicitly: "We do not rely on miracles."

The most telling rejection of miracles I can remember in Jewish tradition comes from Chasidic literature: "Rabbi Bunam told this story: 'Rabbi Eleazar of Amsterdam was at sea on a journey to the Holy Land, when, on the eve of New Year's Day, a storm almost sank the ship. Before dawn Rabbi Eleazar told all his people to go on deck and blow the ram's horn at the first ray of light. When they had done this, the storm died down.' 'But do not think,' Rabbi Bunam added, 'that Rabbi Eleazar intended to save the ship. On the contrary, he was quite certain it would go down, but before dying with his people he wanted to fulfil a holy commandment, that of blowing the ram's horn. Had he been out to save the ship through a miracle, he would not have succeeded.' " So I am neither heretical nor alone in saying tonight that I do not believe in miracles as they are ordinarily defined.

At this point your confusion must be even greater than at the beginning. My title is: *I Believe In Miracles*—yet thus far my argument has been completely to the contrary. Let me proceed, then, to the positive phase of our discussion. I believe in miracles, not as interruptions in the laws of nature, but rather as developments and phenomena which are ineffably beyond man's capacity to comprehend. I believe that a universe of constant law and order is a more magnificent miracle by far than would be one of occasionally spectacular disorder. I believe in the kind of miracle described by one of the greatest of modern Jewish theologians, Dr. Kaufman Kohler: "The whole cosmic order is one miracle. No room is left for single or exceptional miracles."

I believe in miracles as did Rabbi David Nieto, spiritual leader of the Sephardic community of London at the beginning of the 18th-century. He wrote this modern parable, very much in the spirit and style of an ancient midrash: "A skilled architect once built a great and beautiful city, with market-places and streets. He erected stately residences for the aristocracy and a royal palace which, for structure and beauty, had no equal. All who saw it said that there was not a skilled architect like unto him. One day the king said to the architect: 'I would like you to tear down a room in my palace, because, on a certain day, I want to give a banquet, and I do not want this room to be in the way of my guests. And, after the banquet, rebuild the room as it was at first.' The architect did as he was commanded. When the room was reconstructed, the young men marvelled at the skill of the architect. But the elders, who knew that the architect had built the whole city, and the houses, and the terraces, said to the young men: 'How can you marvel at the fact that he demolished and then reconstructed a single room? Surely, this is nothing for him, seeing that he had originally built the whole city!'" In short, I believe that for God to have created the universe at its inception, to have sustained and evolved it through all the millennia since, is a miracle of incomparably greater proportion than if he had in fact divided the Red Sea or sent manna from heaven in the wilderness.

The trouble with many of us is that we remain blind to the miracle of the ordinary. Some years ago Harry Emerson Fosdick put his finger on our difficulty when he recounted this story: "An Eastern king was seated in a garden, and one of his counselors was speaking of the wonderful works of God. 'Show me a sign,' said the king, 'and I will believe.' 'Here are four acorns,' said the counselor; 'will your Majesty plant them in the ground, and then stoop down and look into this clear pool of water?' The king did so. 'Now,' said the other, 'look up.' The king looked up and saw four oak trees where he had planted the acorns. 'Wonderful!' he exclaimed; 'this is indeed the work of God.' 'How long were you looking into the water?' asked the counselor. 'Only a second,' said the king. 'Eighty years have passed as a second,' said the other. The king looked at his garments; they were threadbare. He looked at his reflection in the water; he had become an old man. 'There is no miracle here, then,' he said angrily. 'Yes,' said the other; 'it is God's work whether he does it in one second or in eighty years.'"

How manifold indeed are the miracles—like that of oaks growing from acorns—which we so blithely take for granted. There is a miracle of spectacular beauty in the design of every snowflake and in the fact that no two of them have ever been identical. There is a miracle in the fact that although a worker bee lives only about six weeks and a queen bee at most three years, a man or animal which befriended a bee colony can go back to it ten years later on a day when anyone else would be attacked and will be received in safety by the descendants of bees long since dead.

The instinctual behavior of a newly-hatched chick is also a miracle. It will ignore a duck flying overhead but react with stark terror to a hawk. How does it know the difference? The outlines of the two in flight are nearly identical. Their outspread wings are alike and the long neck of the duck corresponds to the long tail of the hawk. The only basis of differentiation is whether the long end precedes the short one or follows. So acute is the perceptivity of chicks in the first hours of their life that if a black cardboard silhouette of a gliding bird is pulled over a wire above them with the long end first, they ignore it: it's a duck. If the short extension comes first, they are terrified: it's a hawk! Nature is so full of such miracles that long volumes could be written on them.

What else but a miracle is it that the entire present population of this earth, more than two billion of us, developed from egg cells that would fit into a one-gallon container and spermatozoa equal in volume to less than an aspirin tablet? Do you know any word more descriptive than "miracle" for the fact that within the tiny, sub-microscopic cell each of us was at the moment of conception were already contained the seeds of all the physical traits, all the mental characteristics, all the emotional proclivities, all the creative possibilities of the adults we are today? Tell me what that is, if not a miracle. Compared to that, a sea-splitting in two or a whale swallowing and then regurgitating a man is simple child's play. There are more miracles in this universe than the wisest of us could ever identify. The trouble is that most of the time we're looking for them in the wrong places.

There is one more kind of miracle in which I believe—the miracle of the human spirit, what my late beloved friend, Rabbi Milton Steinberg, called "the achievement by spirit of what by every law of logic and common sense seems impossible." And he added: ". . . when the immovable is moved, when the insuperable is conquered, when the impossible is achieved, what else is that but a miracle?"

Is it necessary to illustrate in detail? A decade ago the wife of my most precious friend died in New York, eight years after her first operation for cancer, three years after it became apparent that the end was inevitable. Ten days before her death she was making toy animals for the children in the hospital and practically forcing her roommate to eat and trying to get the Negro who cleaned the room each morning to laugh. Elsie Rudin was a miracle.

I remember on the morning of 19 February 1945—D-Day at Iwo Jima—standing with a young Jewish boy at the rail of our ship just before his turn to go over the side in the first wave of attack. He was so horribly frightened he couldn't keep his entire body from trembling violently. Later I learned that upon landing he helped save another man's life and earned a medal for bravery. That boy was a miracle.

Have you ever seen the ceiling of the Sistine Chapel in Rome? Michelangelo, who painted it, lost his mother when he was six years old. He grew up under the domination of a selfish, rasping father and with brothers who despised him. He did so poorly at school that he was repeatedly beaten. A passionate lover of beauty, early in life he suffered a major disfigurement which made him repulsive in his own eyes. Through the course of four long years he lay on his back under the ceiling of the Sistine Chapel—on a scaffold from which at least once he fell, nearly killing himself—often forgetting to eat or sleep, painting ten thousand square feet of fresco with the most eccentric angles and curves . . . finally producing what is perhaps the most magnificently inspiring piece of religious art in history. Michelangelo was a miracle.

I believe in miracles. I believe that the beauty and order of nature and the imperishable courage of the human spirit are radiant and majestic miracles. I believe in miracles as Walt Whitman did:

Why, who makes much of a miracle?
As to me I know of nothing else but miracles,
Whether I walk the streets of Manhattan,
Or dart my sight over the roofs of houses toward
        the sky . . .
Or sit at table at dinner with the rest,
Or look at strangers opposite me riding in the car . . .
Or birds, or the wonderfulness of insects in the air,
Or the wonderfulness of the sundown, or of stars
        shining so quiet and bright,
Or the exquisite delicate thin curve of the new
        moon in spring . . .
To me every hour of the light and dark is a miracle,
Every cubic inch of space is a miracle,
Every square yard of the surface of the earth is
        spread with the same,
Every foot of the interior swarms with the same.
To me the sea is a continual miracle,
The fishes that swim—the rocks—the motion of
        the waves—the ships with men in them.
What stranger miracles are there?

14

"I Can Pray at Home"

In order not to invite massive disappointment a few pages hence, let me commence by gearing your expectations to my intentions. I do not address myself here to the general subject of prayer. I shall deal only with one specific phase of that topic—with the person who excuses his absence from the synagogue by saying: "I can pray at home." Thus does he convey his conviction that prayer, as a very personal bridge between God and himself, can be voiced anywhere—independent of time, place or his fellowmen.

Some indeed would go so far as to claim that prayer expressed by a solitary human being, facing his God alone —in his home, at the seashore, on a mountain peak—is superior to that proclaimed in unison at public worship. This and only this is our concern now. What shall we say to such a person? How shall we react to the man who insists—more often than not defiantly—"I can pray at home"?

Well, the first thing to say is: of course you can. Not only can you pray at home . . . there is something woefully lacking in your religious life if you don't. There is a great deal lacking religiously also, however, if you fail to perceive that even as there are times when private prayer is preferable, so there are times when public worship is better. The fallacy to be avoided here is the either-or assumption that prayer should be private or public when in fact it should be both.

In this respect prayer isn't really as different as some people think from other kinds of experience. One can get his exercise alone too, either through calisthenics or by regular solitary walks in the woods. Yet sometimes the exercise obtained with others through a game of volley-ball or golf has advantages over calisthenics or walking. One can enjoy a great symphony at home with his record-player or drama on his television set. Yet who will deny the advantage of gathering with hundreds of others at Symphony Hall or theatre to share the appreciation and enjoyment?

Admittedly, there are times when the deeply religious person not only wants but needs to be by himself for prayer. There are occasions—whether of deep sorrow or exhilarating joy—when one wants to be alone with his God, without even the company of his best friend or wife. But for the mature religious man there are also moments when only in the presence of others who share his emotions and needs can he realize the fullness of prayer. Judaism has always been wise in providing for both kinds of prayer. The minute an observant Orthodox Jew awakens in the morning, he prays at home and alone. No witnesses or companions are required when he winds his *teffilin* and pronounces his morning devotions. But when he recites any of the three prescribed daily liturgies or *kaddish*, a minimum of nine others is needed.

Here, then, we have the first of our answers. I can not resist the temptation, before leaving it, of recalling the story of the little girl who wanted her father to go with her to Services on a Saturday morning. "Come," said the father, "let's go instead to the beach; we can say our prayers there." The little girl, more perceptive in this respect than her father, quickly replied: "But we won't, will we?" So, when a congregant or friend challenges me by asserting— "I can pray at home"—my irresistible impulse is to reply: "Of course you can; when was the last time you did?"

My second reply is to remind him that in prayer—no less than in any of life's activities and more than in most—we need discipline. Despite all the time we have saved through modern technology, our lives are far more hurried and harassed than were our fathers'. There isn't a single one of us who could not easily make a long list of important things he has always wanted to do but never even started because life is so frantically rushed. For many of us a visit to nearby museums or historic sites might be on that list. Or the reading of great books or a course of study or the pursuit of a hobby. For nearly all of us prayer has a place on that list. Unless we discipline ourselves, establishing a stipulated time and place for prayer, weeks will go by—sometimes months, perhaps even a year—without a single word of worship crossing our lips.

The distinguished British Jewish scholar, Israel Abrahams, was very wise when he said of prayer: "What can be done at any time and in any manner is apt to be done at no time and in no manner."

Again, a comparison with similar types of activity will be instructive. If my wife and I did not have a season's subscription to the symphony—much as we love music, we would attend less than one concert a year. Our intentions would be the best. Concerts would always be high on our list of things we honestly wanted and intended to enjoy.

Yet somehow we would seldom get to one. The more insistent and clamorous demands of life would crowd them out.

The late Rabbi Milton Steinberg understood this well and expressed it persuasively: "A musician must practice by prearranged schedule, regardless of his inclination at the moment. So with the devout soul. It may not rely on caprice or put its hope on chance. It must work. The man . . . who folds his hands, waiting for the spirit to move him to think of God—who postpones worship for the right mood and the perfect setting, a forest or a mountain peak, for example—will do little of meditating or praying. After all, how often does one find himself in a 'cathedral of nature', and when by infrequent chance he does, who shall say that he will be in a worshipful temper? The effective pious man then is very likely to be none other than one who toils over his religion according to a program of specified acts at stated hours."

One of the important values of public prayer in the synagogue is that it offer us "a program of specified acts at stated hours." It counteracts the temptation to let prayer wait until all the more peremptory demands of life have been met.

Public prayer can add to our religious lives qualitatively as well as quantitatively. Not only does it increase the frequency with which we pray; it also has a tendency to increase the maturity of our prayers. Did you see the recent *Dennis the Menace* cartoon which showed the young scamp kneeling at his bedside in the posture of prayer? His mother is seated on the bed. Dennis is looking at her apologetically and saying: "I'm sorry . . . I didn't mean to ask Him for ice skates . . . I get Him mixed up with Santa

Claus." The temptation to confuse God with a perennial giver of gifts is much greater for adults too in their solitary devotions.

Voltaire once said: "When God and I pass each other, we salute, but we do not speak." The prayers most of us proclaim at home are I fear, likely to be in the nature of either a perfunctory salute or a desperate cry for help. Here in the Temple everything conspires—the architecture, the music, the books we hold and the presence of others—toward relaxed conversation with God.

A 15th century Jewish authority named Simeon ben Zemach Duran was well aware of the difference. He said: "Praying together with the congregation is more praiseworthy than praying by oneself. For when a man prays by himself, he might include in his prayers some petition which could be detrimental either to another individual or to the public. Whereas, when the congregation is at prayer, it asks only for those things which are of benefit to everybody . . ." That was his way of suggesting that when men pray together in public they are less likely to treat prayer as a panic-button, to be employed only for their childish personal benefit, and more inclined to use it as an instrument for religious understanding and growth.

This brings us to the next advantage of prayer in the synagogue. It affords the lonely man an opportunity to share his anxieties and guilts, his worries and his fears, with other lonely men. Let no one underestimate the value of such sharing. Modern psychotherapy has in this respect only recently begun to approximate the wisdom of ancient Judaism. In emphasizing of late the value of group therapy, it has duplicated the insight of Judaism in establishing the Shivah week and requiring that a *minyan* be present to recite *kaddish* with the mourner. There is enormous relief and blessed healing just in knowing that one is in the presence of others whose hearts harbor the same pains and hopes as his. This is why we in Reform Judaism rise as a congregation to repeat the *kaddish*. Even those who are not in immediate mourning themselves rise to share the grief of those who are. Any one of you who has recently lost a loved one knows that the comfort which came to you here from the very physical presence of your fellow congregants exceeded greatly any you could have received by repeating the *kaddish* solitarily at home.

It isn't only the mourner, though, who can benefit in this way. In all areas of experience men gathered in one place for a common purpose reinforce each other. A hundred individuals, sitting in a room together concentrating on a single objective, can accomplish much more than one hundred times the potential of each as an individual. This is true whether their goal is encouraging their school team toward victory or resolving a civic problem or planning for peace. It is especially true in religion. Any man who probes for the quintessential meaning of life, who reaches out with his soul for the Soul of the Universe, is strengthened and encouraged by the presence of others, who are involved with him in the same search. We enrich each other in prayer no less than do the individual voices in a chorus. Could it be that the 13th century mystic was trying to say this very thing in *Sefer Chasidim?* He wrote: "Two men carrying a load would not be able to carry it as well separately as together. Two men raising their voices are more apt to be heard than if they cry separately."

There is another aspect of this sharing which carries it a step further. Martin Buber had it in mind when he said: "To begin with oneself, but not to end with oneself; to start from oneself, but not to aim at oneself; to comprehend oneself, but not to be preoccupied with oneself." The man who prays only alone runs the risk of beginning and ending with himself. The man who prays with the congregation may very well begin with himself—we all do—but the very nature of public prayer leads him to an awareness of the group and of his place in it. Thus can corporate worship expand our horizons to encompass others. In the very act of receiving from them, we find ourselves giving to them.

Allow me to indulge for a moment in personal confession. Never do I feel the bonds which unite me to my fellowmen so intensely as I do standing on this very spot. There are times when I look out from this pulpit into your faces and feel an almost mystic thread uniting my heart with every heart in this sanctuary. At such sacred moments we become one—all of us one. No man can experience that and still feel forsaken and alone.

This can be true of any group, worshipping through the rites of any faith. But I am a Jew. And you are Jews. And the prayers we speak are the prayers of Judaism. In a very special way, then, the hours we spend together here bind us to one another not only as individual persons but also as Jews. Religion is more than the quest of the individual for a relationship with God. It is also the quest of his people. When we pray together we unite with each other and with all Jews in historic time: with Moses, with Amos, with Isaiah, with Akiba, with Maimonides, with Achad Ha-am, with Leo Baeck—all of them! They stand here with us when we pray together and suddenly we become aware of the peoplehood of all Israel. In this very congregation on any Friday night there are apt to be Jews born in Germany, Austria, Israel, Hungary, Poland and Egypt. I have specific names in mind when I mention these countries. Nothing unites all of us quite so firmly into one people, the Jewish people, as when we gather in this place to worship the one God.

What priceless insight Judaism has exhibited in this regard! Our blessings, even when recited by an individual, are worded *asher kid-sha-nu*, who has sanctified *us*—not me, but us. *V'tzee-va-nu* . . . who has commanded *us*. On Yom Kippur we confess: . . . for the sin which *we* have sinned. So intimate and integral does Judaism evisage the relationship between the individual and his people in prayer that the Talmud enjoins even a blind man to recite the blessing thanking God for sight, because he belongs to a group in which he benefits from the sight of others!

Here, then, are my answers to the man who tells me he can pray at home. I gladly admit that he can and hope that he does. But I add that he who prays also in public is more apt to pray regularly at home. And that we need, all of us, the discipline provided by public worship if prayer is to become a meaningful part of our personal lives. And that public prayer can make our religious meditations more mature, can alleviate our personal sorrows and pains through sharing, can enlarge our perspectives to include others, can reinforce in action as well as word our participation in the peoplehood of Israel.

Abraham Joshua Heschel tells a parable with which I would close. There was a small town, he relates, far from the highways of civilization. In it were all the trades and crafts essential to the community except one: there was no watchmaker. Because of this, in the course of time all the clocks in town became annoyingly inaccurate. Many of their owners therefore gave up in disgust, ignoring their clocks and discarding them. Others, however, kept winding their clocks each day, even though they knew there was no sense in depending upon them.

One day a watchmaker did come to town. Everyone rushed to him with his clock. But the only clocks he could repair were those that had been kept running. The others had grown irreparably rusty and were useless.

Prayer which is reserved only for emergencies is like a clock which has been allowed to rust. When needed most, it can accomplish lest. Those of us who pray as a regular discipline in our lives—both at home and here—are the ones for whom prayer can avail. "Therefore," said Maimonides, "a man should join a congregation, and not pray (only) alone, if he can pray with a group."

15

The Conquest of Inner Space

Our generation is at once the most advanced and the most retarded in the whole of history. In the physical sciences, especially in space research, our achievements have surpassed anything our fathers dared dream. The wildest, weirdest extremes they imagined in science fiction have for us become commonplace accomplishments. We have probed the heavens, accommodated ourselves to weightlessness, explored space in a variety of vehicles, and confidently announced that we shall soon land more men on the moon. We have far outstripped the generation of Babel, which proposed to build a "tower with its top in the sky—*v'na-a-seh lanu shem*—to make a name for ourselves." We have indeed made a name for ourselves through our spectacular conquest of outer space.

If this be so, why did I begin by saying that ours is also the most retarded period of human experience? Because our record in inner space is anything but successful. An alarming proportion of our American population is victimized each year by mental and emotional illness. During a period when the population of our nation was increasing by a factor of three and the number of marriages by four, our divorce rate multiplied twenty times. From 1958 to 1965, the rate of serious crime in this country skyrocketed at six times the level of population growth. The number of young people today who indulge in hallucinatory drugs in the hope of finding in induced illusion the happiness which reality seems to deny them is scandalous.

Here, then, is our painfully perplexing paradox. Astonishing success in outer space, contrasted with dark, dismal doom within ourselves. Science has done so much for us, yet at the same time so little. Someone quipped a year or two ago that science has brought us to the point where a man can have breakfast in New York, lunch in Los Angeles, dinner in Honolulu and baggage in Dallas. What is ever so much more pertinent is that science has enabled us to contemplate reaching the moon but not yet to find happiness and peace on earth.

My thesis now is a simple one. I hold that exactly the same principles through which we have achieved such fantastic success in outer space are necessary and valid for the conquest of inner space. Nor is there anything mysterious or esoteric about those principles. We are able to send manned satellites into the atmosphere (a) because we have assiduously studied the physical laws of nature, and (b) because, having discovered many of those laws, we have scrupulously conformed to them. Both (a) and (b) are indispensable. Millions of research hours had to precede our very first effort to launch a satellite. We had to gather every scrap of accurate information we could about nature's patterns of behavior: about gravity, about atmospheric pressures, about temperatures, about friction, about weather conditions, about radiation, about everything!

But that is only half the story. Once having amassed all this essential information, we then had to use it. We couldn't say, for example, that we do not like the fact that water normally freezes at 32° Fahrenheit and boils at 212° so we'll proceed as if that were not true. We couldn't reject the universe as it is in favor of an imaginary universe more to our fancy. We had to conform to cosmic reality, not expect that cosmic reality would bend to our will. We succeeded in outer space because we accepted and followed the dictum of Francis Bacon: "Nature, to be commanded, must be obeyed." Or, to paraphrase Brooks Atkinson, we "joined the universe on its own terms," not on ours.

So far there is no room for misunderstanding or disagreement. The matter becomes more complicated and elusive, however, when we proceed to the next step. Nature is characterized no less by inherent spiritual laws than by physical laws. To be sure, by very virtue of the fact that they are spiritual, hence intangible, these are much more difficult to discover and assess than are such physical laws as those of gravity or energy or thermodynamics. But they exist nonetheless; make no foolish mistake about that. The conquest of inner space—which is, after all, just another way of saying, the achievement of happiness—depends as much on identifying and following these spiritual laws as the conquest of outer space hinged on realistic conformity to nature's physical laws.

It remains to inquire, then: what are the spiritual laws of nature, insofar as we are thus far able to distinguish them? That question, you will immediately recognize, poses potential for a lifetime of speculation, not just for these few pages. To the extent that time permits, however, we owe ourselves the obligation to catalogue at least the most important laws of nature—specifically and precisely of human nature—on which the conquest of inner space depends.

The first is the surrender of egocentricity. That is a

rather highfalutin way of saying that in order to be happy a man needs a purpose much larger than himself. The precedent here in physical science is instructive. The conquest of outer space also required a surrender of egocentricity, in that instance of astronomic egocentricity. If we had remained chained to the pre-Copernican notion that our earth is the center of the universe—that sun and moon and all the hosts of heavenly bodies revolve around us—we would have achieved nothing. The first requirement for success in the conquest of outer space was to recognize the true relationship between our earth and the rest of the cosmos, to accept the fact that the moon moves around us and we around the sun; that ours is only one planet in an enormous galaxy which, in turn, is but one among innumerable galaxies.

In much the same manner, the first prerequisite if inner space is to be conquered is that each of us perceive his own true relationship to the collectivity of other men on earth, that each of us surrender his exclusive egocentricity in favor of larger purposes. There is much convincing evidence that this is more than just grist for the sermonic mill, that it actually corresponds to reality. We know, for example, that the incidence of neuroses and psychoses declines in time of war but rapidly increases once a war has ended. Apparently—in some devious, perverse manner—war serves an important purpose in the economy of the human mind. Perhaps this helps explain some of the utterly irrational, explosively violent behavior of alleged patriots against professed pacifists during our misadventure in Vietnam. War, with all its heartache and horror, apparently gives men the purpose larger than themselves which they so often fail to find in time of peace. Thus is the acute anxiety which contaminates their inner space relieved.

I hope no one will interpret the foregoing to be a plea for waging war. What we need is not war, but creative, constructive, peacetime purposes larger than ourselves and our own egoism. Joseph Wood Krutch, one of the most sensitive observers of our time and its problems, has put the matter in a series of questions which, by implication, carry their own answers. Commenting on our frenetic obsession with owning more things and moving at faster speeds and on the utter failure of this twin-preoccupation to bring us happiness, he asks: "Is it possible that we really want something else also; that it is not in accord with our nature to assume that a high standard of living is the *summum bonum* . . . ? Is it possible that man is not by nature a creature whose happiness is directly proportioned to the wealth he commands and the speed at which he can travel? . . . wouldn't it be worth-while to ask whether or not there is something else he wants—either instead of or also—and to see if it can be provided?"

My answer to these trenchant queries is to assert, as the first of human nature's ineluctable spiritual laws, that the conquest of inner space depends upon subsuming the immediate needs of the creature, man, to purposes and causes outside of and more significant than himself. The second such law is that to achieve happiness, man must fulfill his potential. A cow, deprived of any opportunity to yield the milk she carries, suffers excruciating pain. A hen, blocked from laying the egg she bears, is in agony. A human being who possesses creative potential but is prevented by either internal or external restraint from expressing it reaps a harvest of turbulence and misery.

Dr. A. S. Maslow is among the many psychologists who have recognized how true this is. He writes: "Capacities clamor to be used, and cease their clamor only when they are well used. Not only is it fun to use our capacities, but it is also necessary. The unused capacity or organ can become a disease center or else atrophy, thus diminishing the person."

Franz Kafka expresses a similar thought more poetically and imaginatively. Do you remember his short parable called *Metamorphosis?* In it he describes a typical middle-class salesman who enjoys all the material comforts he needs. He eats well, lives well, is clothed well, follows the identical routine day by day, week by week, month by month; and awakens one morning to discover that he is no longer a human being but a cockroach. You and I know men and women, fashioned physically in human form, who have so defaulted on their human potentialities that they have in effect, like Kafka's hero, become cockroaches.

The creative potential will not be the same for all of us. For me, insofar as I have succeeded in truly knowing myself, it rests in study, in teaching, in creative writing. If circumstances deprive me of all opportunity to express these potentials for more than a few days, I find myself growing irritable and restive. If the door of creative self-expression were to be denied me for a long period of time, I have little doubt that I would become ill. For you, the potential is probably different. It may be to sing, to dance, to compose, to empathize with others, to bring even a humble light into lives that would otherwise be darkened. The point to be made here is that each of us possesses such potential, that he must strive to find out what it is, and that there can be no lasting happiness for him until he discovers ways in which it can be fulfilled. This is as much a law governing the conquest of inner space as is the law of gravity in the conquest of outer space.

Our third law is that, for men who would remain men rather than degenerate into cockroaches, the moral life is a prerequisite to the happy life. This is an issue on which Freud made a serious error. Before I identify his inadequacy, make no mistake about my intention: this is not to be construed as an attack on or rejection of Freudian psychology. Freud was one of the gigantic geniuses of our century. His contribution to the understanding and welfare of man is incalculable. But even Freud was human and therefore subject to error. His most devoted disciples, after surviving a period of uncritical adulation, are now able to perceive some of these errors and to correct them. Freud's mistake here was to see man basically as an animal—an aggregate of psychobiological instincts—and morality as an artifical straight-jacket, imposed upon him externally. He believed that many, if not most psychoneuroses were due to the raging conflict between man's instincts and needs on the one hand and the moral restraints of civilization on the other.

The trouble with all such views is that they reduce man to the level of being only an animal. True, we are animals in every physical sense. We have emerged and are still emerging from the animal kingdom. But we are not animals —*period*; we are animals—*plus*. It won't do to evaluate us purely in terms of what nature appeared to be before man himself evolved. We ourselves are aspects of nature. We are nature grown aware of itself and its almost limitless possibilities. Our moral values at their best—I repeat, at their best!—are as characteristic of nature at its current stage of development as are our kidneys or hands or brains. And we can no more live happy lives in contempt or disregard of those moral values than we can by walking on all fours, as do most of our animal predecessors. In short, to attain success as men, we must act as men—both physically and morally—not as beasts.

Some of Freud's more idolatrous disciples have compounded his initial error of theory in applying it to their therapeutic practice. They have given their patients—in many cases perhaps inadvertently—the idea that the way to relieve anxiety is to adjust their moral standards to their desires rather than the reverse. This is like telling a motorist that the cure for an overheated engine is to smash the temperature gauge. Each year in London the Queen's birthday is celebrated with an impressive parade in her honor. It commences at 11:00 A.M. The Queen is never late. She can't be. If she isn't there at 11:00, the clocks are stopped. There is perhaps something whimsical and quaint about thus protecting the Queen's honor. But no man can expect happiness through trying to force either the cosmic or the moral clock to follow his personal time schedule. The process must be reversed.

The moral values enunciated by Moses are valid, not because Moses pronounced them, but because, properly understood and implemented, they square with reality, that is, with the realities of human nature. Because, both individually and collectively, they chart the only course through which, consistent with human nature, men can conquer their own inner space. In the words of the distinguished Viennese psychoanalyst, Dr. Viktor Frankl, "Moral values are intrinsic to man's existence."

The Hitler nightmare provided us with a startling example of how true this is. There were more suicides among concentration camp guards than there were among inmates! The prisoners—however horrible and unspeakable their plight—were living more in accord with man's essential moral nature than were their guards. They came closer than their tormentors to the conquest of inner space.

Our time is all but expired. Not being the Queen of England, I must at least come close to obeying the dictates of the clock. Let this be said, then, in summary: There is no instant, magical way to conquer inner space, any more than there was to negotiate outer space. The basic rules are quite the same in both instances. We must use our intelligence to discover the immutable laws of nature—in the one case her easier physical laws, in the other her far more elusive but none the less compelling spiritual laws. We must accept the truth as we find it, whether we happen to like it or not. We must see ourselves as indigenous to nature and happiness as accessible only in conformance to nature, including human nature. We must bend ourselves to nature's will—I would much prefer to say God's will, but they mean the same—rather than petulantly expect nature to accommodate itself to ours.

This is the only road to happiness. More than that, it is the only road to peace, to the survival of human life on this earth. The spiritual laws by which alone inner space can be conquered are within our power to know. My listing of them tonight has been only suggestive, not complete. There are others already known to us, and still more awaiting discovery. Among them are at least the following: We can conquer inner space only if we serve purposes far more consequential than ourselves, if we strive to fulfill our creative potentials, if we implement our moral insights in our lives. Erich Fromm put it very well when he wrote: ". . . well-being is being in accord with the nature of man."

The ancient psalmist, without our technical vocabulary,

but with much more poetic sensitivity than we possess, in a sense both anticipated and summarized this sermon by saying:

> *"Happy is the man that has not walked in the counsel*
> *of the wicked,*
> *Nor stood in the way of sinners,*
> *Nor sat in the seat of the scornful.*
> Kee im b'torat Adonai chef-tzo
> Uv-torato ye-h'geh yomam va-lei-la.
> *But his delight is in the law of the Lord;*
> *And in His law does he meditate day and night."*

16

Twelve Months to Live

This night is the holiest and most awesome of the entire Jewish year. Its primary purpose is to provoke in each of us the most penetrating kind of ethical inventory. On other occasions we may inquire into the moral deficiencies of our society or our fellowmen. Tonight the proper ground for each man's search is himself. Any one of us who leaves this hour of worship without feeling honest remorse for his mistakes of the past and genuine determination to improve himself in the future will have failed to observe this night at its deepest dimension.

In the hope of stimulating such spiritual assessment, in myself no less than in you, I have chosen to cast this sermon in a form which some few of you may think is morbid. I do so as a consciously calculated risk; this is, if you please, a kind of spiritual shock therapy. My theme is really a very simple one. Suppose you knew tonight that you had exactly twelve more months to live! What would you do about it? What plans would you make? What changes would this knowledge cause in your present scheme of living? The question is not quite so fantastic as it may seem, you know. The fact is that all of us actually do have a limited number of months to live. Pretending that number to be twelve would simply serve the purpose of speeding our rate of spiritual metabolism, so to speak, of exposing the values by which we live as if to the magnified view of a microscope. There are, moreover, people who actually are called upon to answer this question, people who literally do know that they have a year or less to live.

I first thought of this subject a number of years back when the late A. H. Friedland, one of America's most eminent Jewish educators and Hebrew poets, was told by his physicians that he could anticipate at most one more year of earthly existence. I watched him turn that year into the most prolifically creative period of his life, writing Hebrew sonnets all day and most of the night, as if with one eye constantly on the clock, to make sure he would squeeze out the last drop of his creative urge before the ink of life could run dry on him.

I thought of this theme again on reading an article by Helen Keller called "Three Days to See." It was prompted by the careless remark of a friend that she hadn't seen anything particularly interesting on a walk from which she had just returned. This provoked Miss Keller to reflect on how little many people really use the sight with which they have been blessed, and to wonder what she would choose to see if the curtain of blindness could be lifted from her eyes for three days. She listed a number of objects most of us normally take for granted, among them the faces of her friends and of a baby, a walk in the woods at twilight and the colors of rugs, pictures and books. I wondered, after reading her essay, what each of us would choose if he had but seventy-two hours more of sight.

A similar curiosity came to me on a different level when I read some years ago of a tragic fire in a Maryland nursing home for the aged. One poor old woman had actually been rescued from the flames and was safely out of the building when she thought of her favorite chair, a plain wooden kitchen chair. She struggled loose from the doctor who had rescued her, ran frantically back into the fire to get her chair, and later was found sitting on it . . . burned to death. That woman, Helen Keller and A. H. Friedland all revealed what was most important to them in life. An unfinished book of Hebrew sonnets, a list of things to see, and a kitchen chair. What would you choose as the most important thing in your life if you knew you had but twelve months to live?

I can think of at least four ways in which one might react to such knowledge. The first, especially if you are a husband and father, would be to embark upon a feverish attempt to amass for your family all the wealth you could possibly collect. For want of a better term, suppose we call this the way of hoarding. No one who has a wife and children of his own would minimize for a moment the perfectly normal, understandable desire of a man to leave those whom he loves with a measure of economic security. Despite which, allow me to suggest that the way of hoarding is far from an adequate goal for one who has twelve months to live. Even though it be cleverly and unconsciously disguised as a desire to provide for one's family, what it actually boils down to is that money and the things money can buy become the most important objectives in life, that material things, which should be but the necessary means of life, become instead the all-absorbing ends of human striving.

I quite agree that a man whose days are numbered should indeed concentrate on what he wants to leave his family. The question gnawing at my mind isn't that, but whether, having provided a margin against actual destitution, he should not then begin to accumulate something more important than material possessions to leave them. Our ancestors seemed to understand this far better than many of us. One of the most distinctively eloquent forms of medieval Hebrew literature is the so-called Ethical Will. These wills provide brilliant insight into our grandparents' scale of values. It wasn't money which these men were so desperately anxious to leave their sons and daughters. They loved their children at least as much as we do ours, but when they sensed life's end approaching they wrote wonderfully inspiring wills in which they bequeathed to their offspring such things as character and ethical values and a proud, passionate love of the Jewish people and faith.

You wouldn't think them foolish or impractical at all if you could sit with me in my study and listen to the people who bring me their heartaches and anxieties. I can't remember more than three or four across the long span of years whose basic trouble was lack of economic security. Quite to the contrary, some of the most desperately unhappy among them were people whose parents gave them not only security but even wealth. It wasn't enough! It wasn't enough, because something else far more important than either security or luxury was missing. The wise parent with twelve months to live would try to discover what that something else is instead of concentrating exclusively on the way of hoarding.

I would not want to be misunderstood at this point. I am not advocating poverty as a way of life—neither for others nor for myself. Asceticism is foreign to the essential nature of Judaism. What I do propose, however, is (a) that he who makes wealth the foremost objective of his life will never reach a point of fulfillment and (b) that he who gives his dearest ones only wealth or even primarily wealth has given them nothing. If I had twelve months to live, I would want to remember the wisdom of the rabbis, who ask *ayzehu asheer*—who is a wealthy man?—and immediately answer *ha-sa-may-ach b'chelko*—he who is satisfied with his portion.

Well, if the way of hoarding won't do for one who has twelve months to live, how about the way of distraction? I am sure there must have been some few among you whose instinctive response when I posed my question at the beginning was that with your days so numbered you would want to pursue all the fun you could find, to drown your dismay in distraction. It should not take more than one minute—literally—to dispose of that. To say, in the first place, that fun as a camouflage for reality may be a valid juvenile goal —I'm not even sure of that—but certainly isn't an adequate aim for adults, however long or short their time to live. And to add, secondly, that the trouble with distraction is: it never works.

I think very nearly the greatest fallacy of all the forms of foolishness we hear so frequently is the suggestion to a person who is broken by grief or threatened with emotional upheaval that he should go away on a trip. Away from what—from himself? A trip to where—to a place where he doesn't have to take himself along? No, dear friends, the way to mental health, for the man with twelve months to live or for any human being, isn't the way of self-deception or distraction. We can't hide ourselves permanently from the facts, be they pleasant or unpleasant. The way to health is the way of facing facts and accepting them, not trying to pretend them out of existence.

The trouble with many of our currently popular forms of so-called religious revival is that they encourage people to put blinders on their eyes rather than strengthening them to face truth and triumph over it. If Jacob had run away from the angel, he would have forfeited his unique place in history. It was because he confronted the angel and wrestled with him that his name became Israel . . . *Yisra-ayl* . . . "for you have striven with God and with men and have prevailed." The man with twelve months to live would have to accept that unpleasant fact and adjust himself to it. He couldn't forget it by playing foolish games with himself.

Then how about the way of self-pity? There is always a strong temptation—is there not?—when the problems and disappointments of life seem overwhelming, to take refuge in feeling sorry for ourselves. There would be, I am sure, a very special temptation in that direction for the man who had just discovered that he had only a year to live. He could spend every minute of that time, so to speak, prematurely mourning his own death, steeped in morbid grief over the approaching end. Do you remember the bizarre newspaper account a few years back of the man who went through the complete ritual of his own funeral in advance because he wanted to see and hear it himself? All of us know people who live their lives in constant dread of death. A Bernard McFadden who parachutes at the age of eighty-three, a woman who won't allow her hair or skin to grow old gracefully and beautifully, a William Randolph Hearst who for years wouldn't permit anyone even to mention the word *death* in his house: all these are pathetic instances of human beings obsessed in one way or another with the ultimate and inevitable end of life.

There would be many things wrong with the man or woman who spent his last twelve months on earth in the gloom of self-pity. Above all else, whether he consciously meant it so or not, he would be revealing that to him the highest value in life, the thing that counts most in life, the criterion above all others by which to judge life, is its length. But see how foolish it is—how utterly, unforgivably foolish—to weigh life chiefly by its length. Do we do that in any other area of spiritual experience? Do we judge music by the number of notes it contains? Or poetry by the quantity of its verses? Or genius in painting by the area of its canvas? Then why should we thoughtlessly assume that the man with twelve months to live necessarily has less for which to be thankful than the man with twelve years to live?

Who among us has not experienced from time to time more of love, of beauty, of warmth in thirty minutes than at other times in half a year? If you had your choice between a year of torture or even monotony and a week of tingling, exultant joy—which would you take? Be careful how you answer, even to yourself. You may be disclosing more than you intend about the kind of human being you really are. But whatever your answer, understand with me that the measure of a man's life is not its length but what he does with his portion of days or years. Twelve months to live? That's just incidental. The real question is: what will you do with them? Will you make them, for yourself and for everyone whose life touches yours, months of unforgettable beauty and strength? Or will you waste them in miserable, corrosive self-pity?

So the way of self-pity won't do, any more than that of hoarding or of distraction. How, then, shall we face our twelve months to live? The answer is implied in everything that has already been said. We must live every hour of the next twelve months as consciously creative partners of God. Knowing that most of you are strange to this kind of theological language, let me try to explain what I mean more simply. Humanity at large is thus far the highest, most refined product of the whole process of evolution, which has gone on now for something like three billions of years. We are literally the heirs of every experiment in animal life which preceeded us on this planet. But there are vast, imponderable differences between us and every previous form of life. Chief among these differences are the facts that evolution with us is on a spiritual as well as a physical level and that we are no longer merely the passive instruments of evolution. That is to say, we, unlike our animal predecessors, can consciously affect the future course of evolution; we can deliberately hasten or retard the rate of evolutionary development by the measure of our cooperation with the great Creative Power behind evolution, with God.

To be even more specific: when the pivotal hinge on which the whole future of evolution depended was the development of arms in place of front legs, the species of life in which this change was slowly taking place themselves knew nothing about it and could in no way affect it. The process from their point of view was an unconscious one in which they were passive instruments rather than active agents. Today the pivotal hinge on which future forms of life depend is a spiritual hinge, namely, the development of such traits as character, creativity and conscience. Spiritually we stand, as it were, at the birth of a new species of life whose great promise we can at present but dimly glimpse. And the spiritual area of life is precisely the place where we ourselves can consciously affect the future, where we can be, if we wish, conscious partners of God! Which means to say that spiritually our future development will depend not just on the automatic action of the Great Power which has been and will continue to be the

Driving Force of evolution, but depends in part also upon our own conscious, active, deliberate cooperation with that Power.

What does all this have to do with our twelve months to live? I think everything. It means we have a totally new motive or purpose in life. If all this be true, then what really counts about a man's existence on earth is not how long it happens to last, but how much it has contributed to the on-flowing, up-reaching, ever-aspiring stream of life. Has he used his precious years on earth to leave this newer spiritual development exactly where it was before? Or to retard it to an even lower level? Or consciously to elevate it still higher?

In this light every single thing we do takes on new significance. Every time a human being composes lovely music or paints breath-taking beauty or thinks ennobling thoughts, he has, by the effort of his own life in coopera-tion with God, advanced the course of evolution. Each time that any one of us, when tempted by a lesser good for himself, chooses instead a greater good for others, he moves the whole level of life to a higher dimension. Whenever we help lift from the weary shoulders of a fellowman some burden of worry or of grief, whenever we bring into the lives of others some bit of hope or courage or love, we have added our strength to God's, we have become partners with God, we have justified the experiment of human life on this planet.

Twelve months to live? Here is the way to spend them. Not in greedy hoarding, nor in foolish distraction, nor yet in miserable self-pity. But in doing the work of God for which we were created. You can, if you really will it, do more of that in the next twelve months than you have in the last twelve years.

Now let me return at the end to the place where we began. Was this really too morbid for Kol Nidre night, this question of how to live with only twelve months left? It should not have been. Any more than our medieval rabbis were morbid in commenting on the sentence, "Repent one day before thy death." How can we do that, they asked, when none of us knows the day of his death? And they answered: because we know not the day of death, we must repent every day of our lives.

Perhaps it would be better for all of us to act *as if* we had but twelve months to live. For truly every one of us has just twelve months from this Day of Atonement to the next. Then will be time enough to plan our lives still further. Will Rogers, whose homely humor embraced so much of wisdom, was asked once by a friend: "If you had but forty-eight hours to live, how would you spend them?" He answered: "One at a time."

So let us live our years one at a time. In the words of the Kol Nidre itself: *Mi-yom kippurim zeh ad yom kippurim ha-ba alaynu l'tovah*—from this Day of Atonement to the next—may it bring us welfare and happiness—let us live as if we had but twelve months left; let us live as conscious partners of God; let us live as men.

BETWEEN THE JEW
AND THE
MODERN WORLD

17

Are We the Chosen People?

Of all the doctrines and concepts developed by Judaism, that of the Chosen People is perhaps the most widely known and the most grossly misunderstood. For centuries it has been the object of criticism and complaint by non-Jews. Our friends among them have asserted that it exposes us Jews to unnecessary suspicion and animosity. Our enemies have insisted that it shows us to be arrogant, presumptuous and chauvinistic; that indeed it places us in the same category as the Crusaders, who killed those they believed to be religiously inferior to themselves, and the Nazis, who based their brutality on the fiction of Nordic supremacy.

It would be manifestly unfair, however, to give the impression that only non-Jews have expressed discomfort with the idea that we are the Chosen People. Even so erudite and perceptive a scholar of Judaism as Dr. Mordecai Kaplan urges us to relinquish this doctrine. He argues that it is so subject to misinterpretation and distortion as to bring upon us a great deal of avoidable animosity, adding that its implications of exclusiveness are inconsistent with the universal values both of Judaism and of democracy.

In considering the retention or rejection of the Chosen People concept, I have three questions to propose. First:

what does the idea of Jews as the Chosen People really mean? Second: does it correspond to reality? Third: should we or should we not retain this teaching today?

In approaching the first of our questions, it would be disingenuous and naive to deny that at its earliest inception perhaps the idea of Jews that they constituted an *am s'gulah*, a Chosen People, did spring from feelings of superiority. Almost every ancient people went through the stage of believing that it stood in a special, monopolistic relationship to God which was denied to everyone else. But anyone who is more than superficially acquainted with Judaism knows that very early in its career it successfully emerged from whatever chauvinism there may have been in its beginnings. To decry this or any other religious doctrine because its origins were in primitive superstition or exclusiveness is as sensible as to disparage man because his origin was in primeval slime.

What we really need to know, then, is not at what point did the notion of a Chosen People begin in Judaism, but how was it interpreted by our fathers in the course of time? Not how did it at first resemble the exclusivist beliefs of other groups, but how in the course of the centuries did it grow to be different? When we search for evidence in answer to this question, we discover in Jewish tradition an embarrassment of riches.

For example: one of the earliest statements that Jews are to be a Chosen People is to be found in the biblical book of Exodus. It reads as follows: "*Im sha-mo-a, tish-m'u v'kolee u-sh'mar-tem et b'ree-tee, vi-h'yee-tem lee s'gu-lah mi-kol ha-ameem*—If ye will hearken unto My voice and keep My covenant, then ye shall be Mine own treasure from among all peoples." There was an important *if* involved in the Election of Israel, an *if* which was repeated time and time

again throughout the Bible. Jews were to consider themselves Chosen only if they accepted the special moral obligations of the Torah and fulfilled them. They were chosen
not for privilege but for responsibility, not for special favor
but for extraordinary obligation!

This is how our fathers understood their status almost
from the beginning. In the Midrash, for example, commenting on the verse I have just read, they played an
intriguing linguistic game to demonstrate their interpretation beyond doubt. Because originally the Hebrew of the
Bible was written without punctuation, frequently the
meaning of a passage can be radically altered or its emphasis
changed by choosing a different point at which to pause. In
this case the rabbis, to reinforce their interpretation, read
the sentence not *vi-h'yee-tem lee s'gu-lah*—ye shall be unto
Me a treasure, but *vi-h'yee-tem lee—s'gu-lah—if* ye shall
be on My side, *then* ye shall be a treasure. This is what it
means in Judaism to be chosen.

Similar passages and interpretations can be cited almost
endlessly. The purpose for which Israel was chosen is made
manifest by the prophet Isaiah. He pictures God as saying:

"Behold, My servant, whom I uphold
Mine elect, in whom My soul delighteth; . . .
He shall make the right to go forth to the nations. . . .
He shall make the right to go forth according
*   to the truth."*

To return for a moment to the Midrash, we find this
interesting and instructive passage: *"Lu-lay to-ra-tee she-
kee-bal-tem, lo ha-yee-tee ma-keer et-chem v'lo ha-yee-tee
may-teev ba-chem may-ashair ov-day ko-cha-veem* if it
had not been for the fact that you accepted My Torah, I

would not have recognized you, nor would I have treated you any differently from the worshipers of idols." Elsewhere rabbinic tradition plays an interesting variation on the same theme by saying: "Because God loved Israel He multiplied suffering for him."

It is important to recognize that the idea of being chosen did not mean to our ancestors that they stood in a monopolistic relationship to God which was not open or available to others. One of the most significantly characteristic expressions of this point is to be found in the formula we still recite whenever we read from the Torah. We say: "*Ashair ba-char ba-nu mi-kawl ha-ameem v'na-tan la-nu et to-ra-to* —who has chosen us from among all peoples and has given us His Torah." Note that the index of chosenness consists not of extra privilege but of the multitudinous extra burdens imposed by the Torah. And bear in mind also: the same tradition which thanks God for having given us the Torah also states that it was pronounced from Mt. Sinai simultaneously in seventy languages so that every people in the world which wanted to accept it could do so.

Finally, the prophet Amos gave voice to what for me has always been the most eloquent exposition of what chosenness means in Judaism. He attributed the following words to God, words obviously addressed to and meant for the people of Israel: "*Rak et-chem ya-da-tee mi-kawl mishp'chot ha-a-da-mah*—you only have I known of all the families of the earth—*al kayn ef-kod a-lay-chem et chawl a-vo-no-tay-chem*—therefore, I will visit upon you all your iniquities!" No one who understands such passages as these can possibly confuse what our fathers meant by the Chosen People with the notions of racial superiority and divine favoritism which have often been proclaimed by other groups. Our first question has been answered.

Let us turn now to the second. Does the doctrine that Jews have been a Chosen People square with reality? Is there in fact something unique or special about us? In our quest for an answer, suppose we examine a few facts. This people of ours envisioned one God when others were worshiping many gods. It insisted on an invisible, intangible, nearly incomprehensible God when every other group in the world was bowing down to concrete, visible images and idols. This was also the first people in the world to proclaim "Thou shalt not kill," at a time when all others gloried in killing. It was the only people in antiquity publicly to blame the historic catastrophes it suffered not on some weaker scapegoat but on its own moral deficiencies. It was the first and foremost people to demand on food for the hungry, clothing for the naked, freedom for the captive, justice for the oppressed. It had the audacity to proclaim, "You shall love your neighbor as yourself," at a time when vengeance and spite and hatred were the rules of human life.

The plain truth of the matter is that those who today would drop the doctrine of the Chosen People find themselves stumbling against the uncomfortable but stubborn facts of history. The truth is that historically we *have* been chosen in the sense that we were unique. We did differ from every other people in the world. No amount of clever manipulation or subtle reinterpretation can change that. A distinguished Christian biblical scholar, Dr. William A. Irwin, has written: "Whatever hypercriticism may say of the arrogance of the dogma of the divine choice and the peculiar people, it cannot be denied that at this point we touch solid reality. Israel's God was vastly different from the deities of all other nations, and Israel was, as a fact of history, the people of God."

Another articulate writer on Christianity, Dr. Kirby
Page, has written: "The Jews have made an incomparable
contribution to the life of humanity. It may be said without
exaggeration that in the whole history of human progress
no other nation has made such a mighty contribution to or
exercised such a lasting influence on the thought of the
world."

Let me hasten to add at this point that a recognition of
the fact that we Jews have been chosen by no means
excludes others from sharing that privilege. As a matter of
historic fact other peoples have been chosen too, for shorter
periods of time and in more limited spheres of concern.
The ancient Romans were chosen, which means to say,
uniquely qualified and gifted, in law. The Greeks were in
aesthetics. The modern American nation has shown in its
very short career thus far a potential for chosenness in the
field of political democracy. Only we Jews have exhibited
such capacities over an uninterrupted span of thirty centuries and in the most decisive area of all, man's relationship
to the universe. In this sense, the verdict of history is clear.
We have been, whether certain individuals like it or not, a
Chosen People.

This brings us to our third and final question. Shall we or
shall we not retain today the doctrine that we Jews are a
Chosen People? My answer is that we should. This is one
of the few substantive matters on which I disagree with
Mordecai Kaplan. I think it would be an irreparable loss for
Jews to stop thinking of themselves as chosen. Too many
of us have already lost all sense of deeper meaning in the
fact of our Jewishness. We look upon ourselves as Jews just
because we happen to have been born as such. We don't
feel excited or disturbed enough about it negatively to do

anything to change it; but neither are we particularly impressed by our Jewishness affirmatively.

I would want us to retain our sense of chosenness but
only if we live up to its responsibilities. This means a
number of things. It means that individually as Jews we
must set an example, a special example, a unique example, if
you please, of personal ethical conduct. Not for the reason,
I hasten to add, which prompts some of us when we talk
about a special Jewish obligation to live ethically. Not
because we would hopefully use ethical conduct as a
weapon in our war against anti-Semitism, not because we
think that by living exemplary lives we can show the world
what a wonderful people we are and thus change enemies
to friends.

This I reject as being ethically unworthy and historically
unrealistic. The conduct of Jews can have little bearing on
anti-Semitism because the conduct of Jews has little or no
relationship to the primary causes of anti-Semitism. But the
conduct of Jews can have a great deal to do with how well
we discharge our obligations to our fellowmen and to God.
I want my fellow Jews to set an ethical example for all
mankind not from fear but from faith. I want them to feel
themselves chosen—all of them: businessmen, manufacturers, teachers, doctors, lawyers, rabbis, all of them—to
feel themselves individually and collectively chosen to
show the world just how decent human life can be and thus
to encourage emulation toward ethical perfection on the
part of others.

I want my Jewish contemporaries to feel chosen also in
the sense that theirs is the distinctly Jewish responsibility to
speak out for justice. Every human being, to be sure,
should be concerned with the contrast between inexcusable

poverty and inordinate wealth. Every human being should strive for decent wages and economic security and equal civil rights and adequate medical care for all of his fellowmen. But Jews should care about these things in a very special way just because they are Jews! Because this is what it means to be a Jew! Because we Jews have always been the nagging conscience of the human race!

It is in this sense that I would urge retention of the idea that we are a Chosen People. Not simply for the vain and tedious purpose of flattering our collective ego or enlarging sense of security and importance, but as a blueprint for the kind of life we must live. The German Jewish poet, Richard Beer-Hofmann, understood the sense in which I believe we Jews should still consider ourselves chosen. In his unforgettably moving drama, JACOB'S DREAM, he puts these words into the mouth of Jacob:

> *"This is what 'chosen' means: Not to know*
> *dreamless sleep,*
> *Visions at night—and voices round by day!*
> *Am I then chosen? Chosen that all suffering*
> *Calls me, demands me, and complains to me?*
> *That even the dumb look of the dying beast*
> *Asks me: 'Why so?' "*

Are we today a Chosen People, as were our fathers? The answer is for us to determine by the quality and depth of the life we live. Each of us must provide his share of the answer for himself.

18

Mixed Marriage: Phobia or Threat?

Mixed marriage is far and away the most frequent practical problem with which the modern American rabbi must deal. Seldom does a week go by without one or more such instances being brought to my attention for guidance or help.

I want to deal here with three questions and to do so from the most intensely practical point of view within my power. One: why is Judaism officially and almost universally opposed to the practice of mixed marriage? Two: why do some Jewish young people seem to be so greatly tempted toward mixed marriage? Three: what should be the attitude of intelligent Jewish parents when the problem strikes them personally? Now that you have my prospectus before you, let us proceed at once.

Why the overwhelming Jewish opposition to the marriage of our sons and daughters outside the faith? It goes without saying that Orthodox and Conservative rabbis are unanimously opposed to such marriages. What may not be quite so well-known but should be emphasized at the start is that Reform rabbis are scarcely less opposed. In 1909 and again in 1947 the Central Conference of American Rabbis adopted a statement which read in part: "The CCAR declares that mixed marriages are contrary to the tradition of the Jewish religion and should therefore be discouraged by the American rabbinate."

No one knows how many members of the Central Conference will officiate at such ceremonies. My own guess—probably no better and no worse than anyone else's—is that a maximum of 25% will do so. Clearly, then, I have not exaggerated the extent of opposition to mixed marriage among Jewish leaders.

There are two reasons for this opposition. First, we who are concerned about Jewish survival cannot look with equanimity on the practice of mixed marriage because we know that ultimately it would lead to the complete disappearance of Judaism and the Jewish people from the stage of history. Recent studies give us reliable and persuasive data on the extent of mixed marriage in the United States, the trend of such marriages, and the resultant effect on the totality of Jewish life. A comprehensive survey of Washington, D.C., for example, shows that in 1956 the ratio of mixed marriages to the total number of families in which either or both spouses were Jewish was 13%.* But alarming as this figure may immediately sound, it conceals at least as much as it reveals. Unless we know what the trend appears to be across several generations, the statistic itself is deceptive.

On this count the Washington survey becomes even more frightening. It discloses that among the immigrant generation to this country the percentage of mixed marriages is a negligible 1%. In the second generation—the native-born children of immigrants—the percentage rises to 10%. In the third generation—native-born children of na-

---

* All statistics here are rounded off to the nearest whole number.

tive-born parents—it has reached 18%. From one to ten to eighteen percent in three generations! It is this figure, then, rather than the more palatable over-all average, which tells the true story. The trend is unmistakable. Almost one in five third generation households in the Washington area where at least one spouse is Jewish contains a mixed marriage.

Are the Washington figures reliable for other metropolitan centers in the United States? Pending the completion of similar studies in these other cities, we can only guess. From everything we know on other scores, however, I would without hesitation suggest that the differences, if any, can be only of minor proportion. Washington may be a generation or a half-generation ahead of New York or Boston in setting the trend, but not more. There are, as a matter of fact, areas of the country where the situation is already worse than in Washington. A reliable study of Iowa, for example, indicates that the ratio of mixed marriage there during the span of 1953 through 1959 averaged out at 42%. But again, the trend is more significant than the average. In 1959, the final year studied, mixed marriages totalled 54%.

How about the children of these marriages? If it were to be the case that the majority of them eventually become Jews, the threat to Jewish survival would indeed turn out to be a phobia. Once more, however, the available evidence is worse than disquieting. It reveals that in 73% of the mixed marriage households in Washington the children are not Jewish. In an additional 10% some of the children are Jewish while others are not. It is my personal judgment that we can pretty well forget about most of these too. In only 17½% of these families are the children without exception identified as Jews. I hasten to add, moreover, that even in these there has been no effort to measure the extent or depth of their religious identification; it was simply stated to be Jewish by their parents.

To what, then, does all this add up? To the fact that the rate of mixed marriage among Jews in the United States, already alarming, is precipitously on the increase. To the further fact that at best only about 200 children out of each thousand born to such marriages are even minimal Jews. Even these conclusions assume their true significance only within the context of an expert estimate that the proportion of Jews to the total population of the United States is destined to decline disastrously. In 1937 we were 3.7% of the population. Today we are 2.9%. By the year 2,000, if current trends continue, we shall be 1.6%. To pretend that mixed marriage is not a factor of prime importance in this decline would be unforgivably irresponsible. Far from being just a phobic figment of the imagination, the threat posed by mixed marriage is so real that it can be ignored only at the risk of extinction for the Jewish people. Here is the first reason for firm opposition to mixed marriage among Jewish leaders.

The second emerges from the probability of happiness in such marriages. If there is one thing on which psychologists, sociologists and others in the relatively new profession of marriage counselling are agreed, it is that the more two people share in common of life's fundamental values, the greater is their chance for happiness together. The more they differ in important cultural and psychological respects, the less likely are they to be happy as husband and wife. Thus Clarence Leuba, Professor Emeritus of Psychology at Antioch College, writes: "In every marriage there are bound to be some outstanding differences in interests, attitudes, and beliefs; but a marriage cannot stand too many of them . . . Cultural, religious, or racial differences are of this sort; they are likely to have far-reaching effects on marital adjustments . . . Where the marriage partners come from different religious, economic, political, or social backgrounds, there are endless possible sources of irritation."

A glance at the record will swiftly indicate that this is more than mere theory. Marriage statistics in Hungary, for example, in the 1920's showed the divorce rate to be three to four times higher in cases of mixed marriage than when husband and wife came from the same faith. Here in this country, of much more recent date, the so-called Maryland Study discloses alarmingly similar results. A sober scientific study was made of twelve thousand young people and their family backgrounds. It was discovered that where both parents were Protestant, 6.8% of those studied came from broken homes. Where both parents were Catholic, 6.4% reported broken homes. In cases of mixed marriage, the broken homes amounted to 15.2%. Which means, to put it bluntly: the rate of divorce or separation was two-and-a-quarter times greater in mixed marriages than the average for others.

Let me add that for the sake of fairness and objectivity, I have chosen here one of the more conservative of available studies; others from the states of Washington and Michigan show even greater disparity than this. And a prognostic study made some years ago by two of the very best men in the field, Burgess and Cottrell, concludes that, where all other factors are equal, the chance for marital happiness is eleven times greater where the couple agree on all matters of religion than where they differ.

It should also be remembered that these statistics refer only to marriages that were dissolved by separation or divorce. We know that these are by no means the only unsuccessful matches in each group; there is no way to judge how many others, while apparently remaining intact, represent "lives of quiet desperation."

I must confess here to a feeling of deep frustration. How many weary times have I cited these studies to young couples who have come to see me, knowing full well in advance that their reaction would be: so the statistics show a great risk of failure in cases of mixed marriage . . . this we cannot and do not deny . . . but we love each other sufficiently to overcome the obstacles . . . we'll be one of the exceptional couples who succeed. And what is infinitely more frustrating and depressing: how many of those very couples who refused to listen, who insisted—so understandably but oh, so tragically!—that they would be different, how many of them ended their marital careers in divorce courts or shackled to each other in loveless prisons they ironically called their homes. Sometimes I think if I could be granted just one professional wish, it would be for some method by which to impress upon each such new couple the experience of those who have made the same mistake before them.

This brings us to those who say: "We can understand and appreciate that religious difference may be a major stumbling-block if the religious heritage of bride or groom or both means anything substantial in their lives. But frankly, our religious difference is purely academic because religion as such means little or nothing to either of us."

What can we say to such couples? First, don't assume that religion will always mean as little to you as you think it does now. Don't box yourselves in to prevent the spiritual growth and maturation you have a right to expect and experience, especially when your children are born and you drink more deeply of life's richest wells. Many a person who had no room in his life for religion at the age of 20 or 25 has been amazed to find himself profoundly religious ten years later as a parent.

As long as I live I shall be unable to forget a man who cried profusely and bitterly across my desk a few years ago. Religion had meant so precious little to him when he married that he had glibly promised to rear his children in the Lutheran faith of their mother. He had come to see me just six months before his son's thirteenth birthday. Suddenly it had occurred to him that this boy would be the first male in his family literally for centuries not to observe a Bar Mitzvah ceremony. And this man, to whom religion —so he firmly believed at the time of his marriage—meant nothing, wept before me like a baby!

A second reaction to the couple who are convinced that their mixed marriage will work because neither of them is religious is to feel great pity for them. Nothing can add more of substance or depth to the life of two people who are truly in love than religious commitment fully shared. How my heart bleeds for a groom and bride who permanently shut the door to such happiness for themselves, who, in effect, declare an armed truce on religion from the start, thereby closing off an area of sublime joy which they may never taste together.

Bishop James A. Pike writes: "A person's religion is his frame of meaning, the source of his priority scale of values, the measure of his hopes, the wellspring of his most secure joy. When two people decide for a lifetime to pool their strengths and weaknesses, their hopes and fears, the religious dimension in the personality of each of necessity plays its part—consciously or unconsciously—in their most significant relationships, decisions and responses to each other. Lacks, conflicts or closed doors in the matter of religion cannot be brushed aside as a mere matter of the private taste of each party. . . . In the long run the best single thing a marriage can possess is a common religious grounding . . ."

Incidentally, the fact that I have referred only in connection with one brief personal experience to the children of mixed marriages should not be construed as minimizing in any way this aspect of the problem. Indeed, more often than not the children are not only a chief cause for the later unhappiness of their parents, but are themselves the principle emotional casualties of such matches. If time permitted, I could cite evidence and experiences almost without end to prove this. Instead, let me just tell you about the girl who came to me two years ago to undertake a course of study that would lead to conversion. When I questioned her as to her reasons for taking this step she said: "Rabbi, I was myself the child of a mixed marriage between a Protestant and a Catholic. I would do anything within my power to save any future child of mine from the excruciating emotional tensions I had to face as a consequence. For the sake of my child or children, before I marry a Jew I must myself become a Jew." So much, then, for the first of our three questions.

The second was why some of our Jewish young people tend so strongly toward mixed marriages. The simplest and most obvious answer is: they just happen to fall in love with individuals who just happen not to be Jewish. Psychiatrists tell us, however, that seldom, if ever, does any experience which is deeply emotional "just happen" to us. There are usually profound underlying reasons for such apparent coincidences. I do not rule entirely out of possibility the occasions when two young people of differing faiths fall in love with each other, innocent of any deeper psychological complications. But neither do I accept the premise that this is what happens in most cases.

Very often the desire of a Jew to marry a non-Jew is his unconscious way of rebelling either against his parents or against his Jewishness. Sometimes the choice of a marriage partner even where there is no question of crossing religious lines represents a rebellion against parental authority. This is even more apt to be so where mixed marriage is involved and especially where the dating pattern over a period of years has disclosed a consistent preference for Gentile partners. Such preference may be, without the individual's being consciously aware of it all, a rejection of parental discipline that has been too severe or of what the parent has represented to his child.

Or it may be, even more directly though still beneath the level of consciousness, a rejection of Judaism. What could be more natural than for a Jewish young person who has never really felt comfortable or at home as a Jew, who has always felt unhappy and inferior as a Jew, to escape the unpleasant and acquire that which has always seemed to him preferable and superior by marrying a Christian? Of course, he isn't himself aware of his motives; that's what makes it so baffling, at times so utterly frustrating an experience to deal with him.

The strong desire of a young Jew to marry a non-Jew is seldom a simple, uncomplicated phenomenon. More often than not, it masks an unconscious rebellion against parents or people or both. This insight, so modern and Freudian in tone, is as old as the Bible. In the Book of Genesis we read: "Esau realized that the Canaanite women displeased his father Isaac. So Esau went to Ishmael and took to wife . . . the daughter of Ishmael." From that day to this—sometimes consciously but more often beneath the level of consciousness—sons and daughters have married out of their own faith precisely and spitefully because they knew that such action would displease, perhaps even infuriate their parents.

II

With this understanding of Jewish opposition to mixed marriage and the reasons impelling many young Jews to defy that opposition, we proceed to our third and final question: how should intelligent Jewish parents act? How can they minimize the probability of mixed marriage for their children and what should they do if, despite their best effort, it appears to be inevitable?

The first effective ounce of prevention is to strive for healthy, wholesome, loving relationships with their children. This must be accomplished long before the age of marriage. Young people who love their parents maturely, who honor and respect them genuinely, are less likely to need mixed marriage as a weapon of retaliation or revenge than those who bitterly resent their parents or chafe under authority which they feel to be unfair.

This does not necessarily mean that every parent whose child intermarries has failed in his relationship with that child. Human behavior is far too involved and complex to permit any assumption as simple as that. A failure to meet parental responsibilities is one of several possible factors increasing the probability of mixed marriage. The attempt to succeed as parents is one of several steps calculated to reduce the danger.

A second step is for parents to remember the possibility of mixed marriage in choosing schools for their children. A number of years ago a mother in this congregation came to me in horrible distress. Her problem was similar enough to that of many others to be instructive and is far enough removed in time so that there is no danger of embarrassing her by recounting it. The reason for her distress was that her son wanted to marry a non-Jewish girl. I saw her and discussed the problem at length. Among the things I learned from her was that she and her husband had sent their son to one of New England's most exclusive private schools, where he was usually the only Jew in his class. After that he attended an excellent college, but again one with very limited numbers of Jewish students and in an isolated little community with almost no local Jewish population. I learned, moreover, that in this particular case the boy had shown a consistent pattern of dating Christian girls and that his parents had quite generally agreed with him that his dates were superior to the daughters of their Jewish friends. What surprised me was not that the boy had reached this critical juncture, but that his parents should be so distraught over it.

Admittedly, this was an extreme case. But the fact remains that a large proportion of our youth will fall in love some time during their college years. And it stands to reason—does it not?—that a young man or woman who must date non-Jews regularly because there are few or no Jews available, is far more likely to fall in love with one. It is too late to worry about the problem for the first time then. Here is a classic example of people who, in a sense, create their own problem by virtually asking for trouble, then complain bitterly when it comes. The intelligent procedure for parents is obvious. Among the factors to be considered in any choice of schools—even on the high school level, but ever so much more at college—is the availability of other Jews for social contact, both on the campus and in the community.

My third suggestion is the most important of all. Our best assurance against an increase in mixed marriage is a generation reared to know what Judaism is all about and to cherish it as a precious possession. That means Jewish education—more Jewish education and better Jewish education. It means also a generation of parents who will show by their action, by the quality and depth of their lives, that Judaism is important to them. I like especially the blunt emphasis with which Rabbi Eugene Lipman has expressed this truth. In a recent issue of his congregational Bulletin he wrote: "It is stupid for parents to prove for 18 or 20 years to their daughter that being Jewish is incidental, peripheral in their lives, with no conscious expressions at home or anywhere else, then suddenly to explode into life-or-death hysterics when the daughter announces her intention of marrying a decent Christian boy. . . . Our chances of all-Jewish marriages for our children are in almost direct proportion to the quality of the total Jewish commitment expressed by the total family. Our chances of retaining as Jews the participants in a mixed marriage are in almost direct proportion to the Jewish family life quality of the Jewish parental family."

Does this mean that parents who give their children a good Jewish education—who diligently, conscientiously practice the sancta of Judaism in both synagogue and home —that such parents can rest assured their children will not fall in love with non-Jews? No, of course not. There are no guarantees, only probabilities. But the probabilities are overwhelmingly in favor of the well-educated son or daughter whose parents have provided him with a good example of Jewish life and fearfully against those whose parents have been Jewishly negligent or indifferent.

If you will permit me to return for a moment to the

Washington study, I think I can quickly demonstrate how true this is. That study indicates that in the first or immigrant generation the quantity and quality of Jewish education apparently plays no role in the incidence of mixed marriage. In the second generation, strangely enough, those who experienced some Jewish education seem more likely to marry out of their group. Or perhaps, on more sober reflection, that isn't so strange. Two things should be remembered about that second generation. First, it was the generation most disastrously removed in many cases from its immigrant parents, hence in most violent rebellion against them. Secondly, the kind of Jewish education to which it was exposed was in all too many instances oriented toward Europe rather than America, in total disregard of the American environment and of modern pedagogy. The third generation, however, reflecting neither of these crucial deficiencies, is the important one. Here a little over 30% of the men in Washington who had no Jewish education married out of the faith, while among those who were educated Jewishly, the figure is cut almost in half to 16%! And while there is no statistical evidence available yet, we need have no doubt that Rabbi Lipman's second conclusion is no less valid: a solid Jewish schooling will also increase the likelihood—in those cases where mixed marriage does occur—of the Christian partner's converting to Judaism and establishing a Jewish home.

The best course of action for Jewish parents, then, is clear. It consists of no easy, magical solutions and offers no absolute guarantees. It involves the total effort of parents from the beginning, not a frantic, hysterical thrashing about after a crisis has appeared. It calls upon us to do at least three things: to aim at the kind of relaxed, wholesome, loving relationship with our children which will minimize

rather than maximize their need to rebel against us; to act
wisely in recommending a choice of college to them; and
above all, to demonstrate by our own action and by what
we teach them that Judaism is important and precious, that
Jewish survival is for us a *must*.

This brings us finally to the question of what parents can
or should do when all else has failed and mixed marriage
seems unavoidable. There are two things they should definitely not do. They should not discuss the matter on a basis
of "look what you're doing to me," or "how can you think
of ruining my life?" It isn't the parents' welfare which
should be primary at this point, it's the child's. All the
convincing facts there are should be brought into the open
in the most effective but least argumentative manner possible to establish the grave danger mixed marriage presents to
the welfare and happiness of the two people considering
marriage and eventually of their children, not of their parents.

The second thing parents in this situation should not do
is to threaten cutting all ties with their children if the
marriage occurs or in effect to sit *shivah* for them after it
has taken place. However deep their disapproval, however
painful their fears for the future, the love they bear their
children—and each other—must be unconditional. The acceptance which members of a loving family extend to one
another must not be predicated on following each other's
advice, even when it is good.

Even as sons and daughters often have their unconscious
motives in desiring mixed marriage, so parents sometimes
act out their unconscious needs and give expression to their
inner guilt in opposing it. How often have I noticed that
precisely the parent to whom Judaism seems to have meant
least through the years, the parent who couldn't be both-

ered with living an active Jewish life himself or providing the proper kind of Jewish education and home for his child, reacts most hysterically at the prospect of mixed marriage.

Parents are within their rights in asking a young couple so involved to wait even longer than they normally would before being wedded. If the risks are greater, the precautions also should be wise and the existence of genuine love be more positive. Parents also have a right to ask that the prospective son or daughter-in-law give serious consideration to conversion, not only for the couple's sake but even more for the security and emotional health of their children. But when all is said and done, when parents have advised and recommended and urged, they must in the last analysis be prepared to accept. Once this or any other marriage has actually taken place, be it foolish or wise, desirable or deplorable, be the prognosis favorable or precarious, it becomes the inescapable obligation of the couple, of their parents, of everyone concerned, to do their utmost toward making that marriage succeed.

My cherished friend, Alexander Magoun, has written many wise sentences about marriage. One of the wisest reads: "The only thing in the world as strong as love is truth, and there are reasons to believe as far as marriage is concerned they are different aspects of the same thing." It is because I believe that real love is impossible without truth and that couples who are contemplating mixed marriage run the risk of denying truth or at least of momentarily obscuring it, that I would warn them most earnestly to proceed with utmost caution or not at all.

Marriage is the most sacred relationship in human experience. It can bring men the most ecstatic happiness . . . or the deepest despair on earth. Before entering upon it, let the wise man or woman respect with reverence the wisdom of the ages.

19

Does Judaism Open Doors or Close Them?

Some weeks ago I spent an hour in my study with a young woman of far more than average intelligence and in many ways of exceptional sensitivity. The problem she had come to discuss with me was her identification with Judaism in general and with our congregation in particular.

She felt that her association with both was a constricting influence in her life, that whatever she did to label herself a Jew made her less a human being. She was convinced that Judaism closed doors in her life, confining her to one small corner of experience instead of inviting her to encompass the whole of it. She could see no reason to celebrate the festivals and holidays, the ceremonies and rituals of one particular people, when the whole human race was her province. She wanted her children, as they grew, to feel themselves brothers to all men and women everywhere, not just to one small group who happened to be called Jews.

I was well aware of the fact, as we quietly talked, that her concern was common to a considerable number of people. These words are intended not only as an expansion of my reply to her, but equally as an extension of that reply to others whose feelings are the same.

Included among those whom I address here are Jews who prate about the Judaeo-Christian heritage as if the teachings of Judaism and Christianity were identical. Also those who are obsessively preoccupied with interfaith ventures, though they have no viable faith of their own. Also those who repeatedly summon the rabbi to assist in every liberal cause in the community—as indeed he should and frequently does—but who are themselves never seen in the synagogue, if indeed they even belong to one. All these, like my recent visitor, see Judaism as too narrow to contain them. I speak to them now on two levels. The first is historical.

In point of actual fact, on the record of the past, has Judaism opened doors or closed them? If we begin with the Bible, the very charter of our faith, it contains so many expressions of opened doors one scarcely knows where to begin in citing them. At the very outset of the Torah, the whole human race is traced back to the same aboriginal ancestor. Adam is not described in Genesis as a Jew—nor is Eve, nor Noah, nor the sons of Noah. Not until Abraham is any person in the Bible identified as a Jew. The Midrash, expanding on this significant fact, tells us that God deliberately gave all men one and the same ancestor so that no individual or group would ever be able to say to another: I am inherently, innately superior to you. Does that sound like closing doors on men or on life?

Perhaps the loftiest biblical expressions of universalism —which is, after all, only a technical term for open doors —came from the pen of the Prophet Isaiah. He it was who pictured the day when all men and nations would flow to God's house, where they would freely accept His word, as a consequence of which they would beat their swords into ploughshares and their spears into pruning hooks and none would ever again wage war against the other. Does that sound constricting or restraining?

Another passage in Isaiah, though it is less well-known than the first, is perhaps even more important. Bear in mind that the two most powerful, fearful enemies the Jewish people had ever known up to the time of Isaiah were Egypt to the south and Assyria to the north. This is what makes most amazing the prophet's vision of God Himself proclaiming: "Baruch amee mitz-rayim v'ma-asay ya-dai Ashur v'na-cha-latee Yisra-ayl—Blessed be Egypt My People, and Assyria the work of My hands, and Israel Mine inheritance." Show me, in the literature of any other people or faith on earth, a statement of such wide and expansive universalism as this.

Or show me any other civilization which taught, as Judaism did in its post-biblical period, that the Torah was revealed simultaneously in seventy languages so that it might be available to every nation on earth. Or that a Gentile who obeys the law of God is equal to the High Priest himself. Or that the righteous of all peoples on earth have a portion in the world-to-come!

Let me return for a moment to Isaiah. There must have been some Jews in his time too who felt as did my visitor a few weeks back; who were so anxious to be men of the world that they burst the bonds of their Jewish identity. Who, then, ultimately contributed more to the cause of universalism—these imprudent, impatient ones?—or Isaiah, who remained proudly, assertively a Jew?

A few years ago a nationally prominent American Jew wrote to me in personal correspondence that he found the Jewish religion—and these are his very words—"lacking in spiritual spaciousness." He revealed by this phrase nothing about Judaism but more than he intended of his own abysmal, unforgivable ignorance. It is a point of incontrovertible fact that Judaism has opened more doors, wider doors —doors opening out upon more expansive vistas—than any other faith on earth.

But this is only half the historic part of our discussion. We have dealt thus far only with the past. The young woman whose views evoked this response would undoubtedly agree that Judaism has contributed greatly to the widening of man's horizons in the past but would say that all this has already been accomplished. Now let Judaism, like a seed which has produced its flower, disintegrate and vanish. One thing is glaringly wrong with the analogy. The seed, once it has emerged into a flower, has nothing more to give. Judaism, which has already contributed so substantially to the sum of human insight and knowledge, may have even more to give in the future than it has in the past.

A better analogy than the seed would be that of an individual human being. Mozart, for example, died at the age of 35. All that he contributed in his three-and-a-half decades to the musical heritage of mankind is permanent and indelible. But the sum of his contribution ceased on the day of his death. The minute he no longer existed physically as an identifiable entity he could no longer give of his uniqueness to the world of his fellowmen. Who will deny that if Mozart had lived to the age of 55, he would have composed and contributed much more?

So it is with our Jewish people. Let no one underestimate what we have already accomplished. But let no one foolishly suppose either that our capacity to contribute has evaporated. It will continue so long as we continue. It will disappear only if, God forbid, we disappear. It is not the man who wants to remain a Jew who closes doors; rather is it the one who is ready to call it quits. He closes the door to everything Judaism may yet give mankind in the future.

Christians are often able to recognize this truth with greater objectivity and insight than some Jews. Some years ago the Boston *Pilot* a Catholic weekly, editorialized as follows: "As we see it, the Jew in America has actually taken the melting pot notion much too seriously and has, as a result, put behind him many traditions which were really too precious to lose . . . Instead of making their traditions part of an ever-richer American tradition, they have often set aside their own and attempted to pick up the American one. Where this has happened, they are, as a result, poorer, and America is poorer."

Now let me speak to the same point on a second level— from the perspective of psychology. How does a man grow to become more than a man? By beginning with himself— with a wholesome, realistic, appreciative acceptance of himself as a unique personality, not exactly like any other personality. The man who for any reason is unable success- fully to negotiate this first step never gets beyond it to accept—successively and progressively—his family, his community, his state, his nation, the whole world. The man, moreover, whose development is arrested on any of the intervening levels never reaches his ultimate goal of universalism.

The Midrash says that if a man claims that he loves God but demonstrates by his conduct that he does not love his fellowmen, he is to be judged a liar. The same logic can be extended to the matter under consideration here. If a man proclaims that he loves all of humanity but demonstrates that he does not love himself or any of the intermediary groups to which he belongs between himself and "all of humanity," he may not be consciously or deliberately a liar, but neither is he in any wholesome, healthy sense a genuine universalist. In short, acceptance of myself and of the natural groups to which I properly belong is the key with which to unlock all the doors that will lead me out to mankind at large. If, wilfully or inadvertently, I lose that key, the doors remain forever closed.

There is a healthy and an unhealthy kind of universalism. The man who loves every human being because he loves himself and his own people is truly a universalist. The man who says he loves everyone but in fact detests himself and rejects his own group is only a rebel against reality. He is a quack-universalist, not a genuine one.

To say that in order to expand my human horizons broadly enough to encompass all men I must first surrender my identity as a Jew, makes no better psychological sense than to assert that in order to be a good American I must give up my individual uniqueness as a person. The contrary is closer to the truth. My uniqueness as a person makes me a better American. My distinction as an American and a Jew makes me a richer, more productive man.

May I illustrate, briefly and concretely? The love of one man and one woman for each other is a universal of human experience. But my wife and I—out of a whole complex of experience together across the years—have acquired certain intimate associations unique to ourselves, through which we express in our own lives that which is universal to all. There are certain phrases or words . . . places or songs . . . gestures, mannerisms, even silly little jokes, which evoke and increase our love for each other. Do these private rituals, uniquely our own, close doors in our lives? Or do they not rather open doors, enabling us to understand similar realities in the experiences of other couples, thus bringing us closer to them and through them to every man who

ever loved a woman and every woman who ever loved a
man?

The same thing is true of group life. Freedom is a universal value, a goal cherished and desired by all men. But
freedom means certain special things to me as a Jew. Here
again, out of a whole complex of historic experience together, we Jews have developed memories, associations,
rituals, sancta—by which we celebrate especially and inti-
mately for ourselves an ideal which is common to all. To
the Jew, freedom means the Maccabees and Chanukah candles, the Exodus from Egypt and the Seder ceremony. And
it is apt to be precisely the Jew who kindles his candles on
Chanukah and who conducts a meaningful Seder on Pesach
who is most concerned about freedom for others. All of
which means to say: I become more a man when I am more
a Jew. When I deny my Jewishness, I thereby and in the
same proportion diminish my humanity.

I diminish the sum total of civilization too. Judaism has
something especially its own to contribute to the world,
emphases and values which are not exactly like those of
other cultures. There is a uniquely Jewish attitude toward
peace, toward civil rights, toward marriage and sex, toward
the relationship between man and God. I do mankind no
favor when I so act as to reduce this Jewish uniqueness to a
pallid, least common denominator of uniformity.

The same man whose letter I quoted earlier once wrote
this to me: "I believe I am a human being before I am a Jew
or an American or anything else." Psychologically his
statement is absurd. Psychologically he must first be a son
to his parents and a Jew and an American before it can
mean anything for him to say that he is a human being.
Psychologically there is no such thing as universal man.
There are only Americans, Frenchmen, Germans and

Chinese—Christians, Mohammedans, Buddhists and Jews who are universal to the degree that they understand and accept themselves and each other. No spiritually sensitive person can live either in a no-man's-land or naked. He who divests himself of the garments of Judaism, yet is determined not to stand naked, puts on the garments of the dominant Christian culture, at least in one of its attenuated forms.

Here, then, is my answer for those who feel constricted by the fact that they are Jews. Judaism opens doors both historically and psychologically. Judaism is the best approach we possess for reaching out in love to all mankind. One world does not presuppose the surrender of all group identities. It certainly does presuppose—indeed demand—the surrender of all narrow parochialisms. The more intelligent and sensitive I remain an American and a Jew, the better candidate I become for citizenship in the one world for which we all so devoutly yearn.

Our rabbis understood this clearly. They observed that after the death of Joseph, his bones were carried back to Palestine for burial. But Moses was denied entrance into the Holy Land even after his death. They explained the discrepancy as follows. Joseph, they said, had never denied he was a Jew. From the moment of his arrival in Egypt as a slave, he identified himself at once. Moses, however, at least by implication did deny his Jewishness. When he first came to the land of Midian, the daughters of the land whom he immediately aided with their chores reported that "Iesh mitzree—an Egyptian man" had helped them. Moses did not correct their mistaken identification of himself. Therefore, the privilege of burial in the Promised Land was granted to Joseph, but withheld from Moses.

There is great truth in this Midrash. Those who consider

Judaism too small for them harm the Jewish people and do great injustice to the whole of mankind. They also cheat themselves. They exclude themselves from that Promised Land which can be the fulfillment of their happiness and the achievement of their highest hopes.

20

Sermon for Cambridge: to the Un-Jewish Intellectual

Soon after taking up residence in Boston I made a strange and disturbing discovery. I learned that across the river in Cambridge and extending in more recent years westward into such towns as Arlington, Lexington and Lincoln, there were communities of Jews who hold themselves apart from the Jewish community.

These are the so-called Jewish intellectuals. Or, more accurately, the intellectuals—pseudo or real—who happened to spring from Jewish origins. They are to be found, of course, in every center of American academic life. In this area they are identified chiefly with Harvard, M.I.T. and the several private laboratories engaged in scientific investigation and research.

With only the fewest of encouraging exceptions these men and women do not belong to a synagogue. They do not provide their children with any kind of Jewish education. Their names are not listed either as contributors, leaders, or even workers for the organized agencies of the Jewish community. They constitute a lost generation in contemporary Jewish life. What makes their deflection too tragic to be accepted in quiet acquiescence is the undeniable truth that included in their number are some of the finest, sharpest, brightest minds of our time.

I appeal to them here on three levels in my effort to persuade them that their estrangement from the Jewish community should be ended.

The first thing I would say to my un-Jewish intellectual friends is that the Jewish people needs them—the Jewish people past, present and future. Now how is it possible to speak of a people in the past needing those who are alive today? What I have in mind here is the unparalleled, immeasurable, almost unbelievable sacrifice and heroism exhibited by Jews through the centuries in their stubborn determination to remain Jews.

I would remind those to whom these words are addressed of what Judaism has meant to Jews through more than thirty centuries of time. Of the fact that at least until the Hitler period a relatively simple escape hatch was available for any Jew who wanted to avoid suffering. The door of conversion to Christianity was always open to him. All he had to do was give up the ghost, agree that Jewish survival wasn't worth the agony and pain it involved. At a cost only of surrendering his loyalty to the Jewish people and its faith, he could have purchased immunity and comfort for himself.

Yet very few Jews ever made the easy bargain. Nor was it just simple stubborness which motivated them. It was rather a deep, profound, abiding conviction that Judaism was worth preserving; that it possessed something unique and precious which warranted even the most unspeakable kind of sacrifice in order that it be maintained.

Shouldn't that count for something today? Shouldn't Akiba count for something—risking his life eighteen centuries ago by gathering his students secretly to teach them

Torah in stifling caves when Rome had forbidden such study at risk of life itself? Shouldn't the martyrs of nearly two millenia count for something—those who suffered and died on the stake, in torture chambers and crematoria, *al kiddush ha-shem*, for the sanctification of God's Name?

Shouldn't six million Jewish victims of Hitler count for something? Shouldn't those who willingly gave their lives that the State of Israel might be established and defended, shouldn't they count? Just what kind of person is it who can with easy conscience thumb his nose at sacrifice such as this? Who can tell so many millions of martyrs that what they proudly died for isn't worth our effort to preserve? That, in essence, is what I mean when I say that the Jewish people of the past needs our intellectuals today.

When I add that the Jewish people of the present and the future needs them no less, I have in mind something different, something even more important but different. I think I can understand what has estranged a certain number of Jewish intellectuals from their heritage. Judaism in some of its contemporary manifestations admittedly seems remote from modern life—remote, and perhaps even to a degree antagonistic. But observe: I said Judaism in *some* of its manifestations. On other fronts, Judaism is making a valiant attempt to absorb the most meaningful new insights of modern science and knowledge, to interfuse the new with the old out on the growing edge of man's spirit and mind.

This isn't a new experience for our heritage. Indeed, if there is one secret which explains the deep mystery of Jewish survival, it is the diligence of our brightest intellectuals in the past as they strove to coordinate Judaism and the secular world for the advantage and benefit of both. Time allows only two brief examples, though scores—perhaps hundreds—could easily be adduced.

As far as our records indicate, the most distinguished

Jewish intellectual in the first century of the Common Era
was a man named Philo Judaeus. The prevailing philosophic mood of his time was Platonic. With a mental acu-
men much more abundantly appreciated by succeeding
generations than by his own, Philo reconciled the philosophy of Plato with the religious ideals of Judaism. He did
not find it necessary to choose either Hellenism or Judaism
to the total exclusion of the other. He used the great gifts of
his mind to combine them, thus laying the groundwork for
Judaism's encounter with Christianity far into the future.

My second example is Maimonides. In his century, the
twelfth, the dominant intellectual atmosphere was Aristo-
telian. Modern science, moreover, was just beginning to
emerge. Maimonides embraced both of these disciplines: he
was a rabbi, a theologian, a philosopher and a scientist. He
was perhaps the most eminent physician in the world of his
time. He too found it altogether unnecessary to choose
either Judaism or philosophy or science at a price of rejecting the others.

Precisely because he was a truly great intellectual, Maimonides was able to help Judaism develop and adjust, to
adapt its values and principles without ceasing to be au-
thentically itself, to make room within itself for every
legitimate influence from Aristotle and from the scientific
method. Who can doubt that Maimonides himself and Judaism in particular and human culture at large all benefited
from the fact that this man remained a questing, practicing
Jew?

In our time, Judaism stands in dire need of precisely the
same process initiated so successfully by Maimonides and
Philo. The mood is no longer that of either Aristotle or
Plato. The mood now is a combination of Einstein and
Darwin and Freud. But the challenge in the twentieth

century is exactly what it was in the first and the twelfth. Every Jewish intellectual who abandons his ancestral faith, or who treats it as a matter of only minor consequence, decreases the probability of so re-shaping our tradition as to keep it viable and relevant. For this is a job which is especially dependent upon the intellectual. Here, then, is the first dimension of my approach to the un-Jewish intellectual: your people needs you!

Of no less importance, however, is the fact that the world needs you. The world needs you not merely as an individual, but specifically, precisely as a Jew. Basic to this assertion is the premise that Judaism—properly interpreted and applied—encompasses a syndrome of emphases and insights which no other group or culture expresses in quite the same measure or way. What are the unique emphases of Judaism which the world needs and which it will obtain from us only if we survive in identifiable form? For what does our tradition stand—especially, uniquely?

First, that the heart of all reality is spiritual, not physical. It follows from this that if man is to be truly man, and not just the most complex of all animals, his primary pursuit must be after truth, after beauty, after moral goodness— not just after pleasure and material wealth.

Second, there is a oneness about the universe and mankind. A physical oneness in the sense that everything emanated from the same creative beginning and that the same chemical components and natural laws are operative throughout all existence—from the remotest reaches of outer space to the minutest molecule within my body. There is also a spiritual oneness which inextricably binds each person on earth to every other person, each nation or religion or race to all others.

Third, our noblest ethical aspirations, which derive from

the very nature of reality itself, must be applied to every segment of life. There can be no asceticism, no withdrawal, no denial. All of man's experience is susceptible to sanctification. Life is to be divided, as Martin Buber put it, not into the sacred versus the profane, but into the sacred and the not-yet-sacred.

Fourth, every human being on this earth is my brother. The same ethic by which my family life should be governed must be extended to the stranger whose language I don't understand, whose mores may even be entirely beyond my comprehension. I who am descended from oppressed strangers must be forever compassionate to all who are either strangers or oppressed.

Fifth, religion is not a separate compartment of life but is rather a precious thread woven into the fabric of both the national and the ethnic. Which means to say: whatever I do as political man or civic man or biological man must be influenced by what I am as religious man.

Sixth, our greatest need today, if humanity is to survive, is for a synthesis of the particular and the universal. We must learn to live as citizens of our respective nations, yet simultaneously as citizens of the world. No one is in a better position to succeed at this excruciatingly difficult task than are we. For only we Jews on the world scene today exist in part as a separate nation, living on a soil of its own, yet also as a universal people, scattered over most of the planet. In mankind's ineluctable, urgent, desperate pursuit of peace, we Jews constitute—whether we deliberately will it so or not—as we have in other contexts so many times in the past—an experimental human laboratory, testing for the whole human race concepts and ideals calculated to achieve salvation.

So much, then, for our brief encapsulation of what Judaism offers to the world. I think I know the question some of my intellectual friends would pose at this point. Can't we cherish and foster precisely these emphases without identification as Jews? The answer is: to some extent, of course we can! But what kind of reasonable sense does it make to select from a variety of other sources—synthetically, as it were—that which has grown indigenously and organically in our own source, in Judaism? Isn't that almost like enjoying the physical appearance of my wife by reflection, through a series of photographs, each showing one perspective or angle, instead of living with her face-to-face, reveling in her beauty first-hand, alive?

Why go to the florist shop each day to purchase cut flowers while neglecting my own bounteous garden? Why live only on the accumulated capital of Judaism without making further investments, in order that it may offer the world additional and perhaps even greater blessings in the future?

If I told you, my Jewish yet un-Jewish intellectual friend, that a new organization was to be formed, dedicated to exactly the six ideals briefly summarized a moment ago, if I invited you to join such an organization in order that, together with others of similar intention and hope, you might encourage and promote these emphases, you would eagerly accept, would you not? Yet you deliberately scorn the great historic group already in existence for this purpose and into which you yourself were born. Thus you deny to the whole of humanity continued creative enrichment through ideals which you profess to cherish.

Yes, one or another of these values may by now be found elsewhere, in other cultures. But only Judaism originated all of them. Only Judaism holds them bound closely together in an integrated, organic whole. And Judaism can

best develop them as a pattern for the future. That's why
the world needs you as a Jew.

I said at the beginning that there were three dimensions
in which I wanted to address my Cambridge-type friends.
We come now finally, to the third.

In addition to the fact that your people needs you and
the world needs you to be identifiably Jewish, you, my
intellectual friend, need to be Jewish yourself. You need it
for the sake of your own fulfillment. You need it to attain
happiness and self-respect. If you are as balanced emotionally as you are gifted mentally, you know that self-denial is
not the road to happiness. Neither for the individual as such
nor for the renegade from an honorable historic people. I
am what I am—as an American, as a Jew, as a man. To the
degree that I acknowledge who I really am and struggle to
perfect myself as such, my life succeeds. In the measure
that I attempt to deny myself, I become ludicrous in the
eyes of others and more than slightly cheap in my own
sight.

You think I exaggerate? Last September I received a
telephone call from a Christian friend who happens to be
headmaster of a very fine New England private preparatory school. The purpose of his call was to ask my advice
on the kind of assembly program he could devise for pres-
entation on Yom Kippur. When I inquired into his reason
for proposing such a strange program in the first place, he
replied that about half of his Jewish students—and he has
many of them—attend school even on the Day of Atonement. "This bothers me," he added. "I hate to let them miss
so precious a spiritual opportunity. If their parents aren't
willing to impress upon them the values inherent within
Judaism, as their teacher, even though I am Christian, I
want at least to try!"

Don't think you fool the wise and perceptive among your Christian associates, my un-Jewish intellectual friend. Don't think you always succeed even in fooling yourself. The corrosive currents of guilt run deeper than you may suspect. May I offer a vivid illustration? It has to do with the death of Felix Frankfurter. In the earlier portion of his life, he performed valuable and valiant services for the Jewish people. Together with Brandeis, he was instrumental in effecting international recognition for the aims of the Zionist movement at the close of World War I. I bow to no man, moreover, in my esteem for Felix Frankfurter as an American jurist.

In the last forty years of his life, however, to my knowledge he had no positive Jewish identification at all. In his *Reminiscences*, he openly rationalizes his complete estrangement from the synagogue. In my entire adult life I don't ever recall seeing his name associated with a single Jewish activity or organization. Yet Felix Frankfurter directed in anticipation that the *kaddish* be recited at his funeral.

Garson Kanin recounts the following view, voiced to him by Frankfurter personally: "I came into the world as a Jew and although I did not live my life entirely as a Jew, I think it is fitting that I should leave as a Jew. I don't want to be one of those pretenders and turn my back on a great and noble heritage . . . So there's going to be Hebrew."

It has been a long time since I have heard or read words as sad as these. If Judaism is in fact what Frankfurter called it—"a great and noble heritage"—shouldn't it be more than just a pair of doors through which one enters and leaves this mortal life, with nothing of substance on the passage between? If children had been born to Frankfurter and his wife, would they have known they were

Jewish? And would *their* children in turn even have been
aware of their Jewish grandfather? And if they had not,
would they and their ancestors and the world have benefited from such ignorance?

Surely these questions answer themselves. Felix Frankfurter anticipated by more than a generation the Jewishly
alienated intellectuals to whom this message is beamed. In a
day when less was known than now about the uniqueness
of Judaism and the prerequisites for happiness, there was
more excuse for his behavior than for theirs. For their own
sake, for the sake of Judaism and the world, let those who
were born Jews proudly and affirmatively live as Jews!

21

Reform Judaism: Pro and Con

Since its earliest inception Reform Judaism has faced the need to defend itself. Like all great revolutionary movements, it has been vulnerable to vociferous attack from without and massive misunderstanding from within. Both opponents and adherents—from different perspectives and with different purposes, of course—have at times distorted the nature and meaning of Reform quite beyond the point of recognition.

The most common error made by those who have long been adherents of Reform Judaism is to charge that the movement has betrayed its original nature and purpose, that Reform is in fact becoming Orthodox Judaism. Included as evidence in support of this assertion are the facts that so many Reform Congregations have restored the practice of Bar Mitzvah, reinstated both *Kiddush* and *Kol Nidre* in their liturgies, increased the use of Hebrew in worship as well as in their school curricula, and either permit or encourage the wearing of the *Kippah* or skullcap in the Synagogue.

As long ago as 1953 a survey conducted by the National Federation of Temple Brotherhoods disclosed how dramatic the changes have been within our movement. Two hundred Reform rabbis and twelve hundred laymen answered a significant series of questions on their preferences in matters of ritual. 74% of the laymen wanted Hebrew taught to their children. Perhaps even more important is the fact that of this number only 51% said they would be satisfied with one day of Hebrew instruction per week; 49% wanted two, three, or even four days per week. 77% of the laymen wanted Bar Mitzvah observed in their Reform Congregations. 88% of them approved the wearing of a pulpit robe by their rabbis, 61% preferred the use of a talleet or talleet-stole on the rabbi's robe, and 90% endorsed the lighting of Shabbat candles in the Friday night service. On the over-all question of ritual and ceremony, 29% of our laymen nationally felt there should be more in our worship, while only 11% preferred to have less. The remaining 60% are presumably satisfied with the proportion of ritual now prevalent.

At least as important as these facts in themselves is the conclusion reached by Rabbi Morton Berman, director of the survey, as a result of comparing the attitudes of Reform Jewish laymen to those of their rabbis: ". . . . there is no wide gap separating laymen and rabbis in their eagerness for the acceptance of the new trends. . . . This is a movement in which laymen and rabbis share with genuine enthusiasm, which is extensive in both groups. . . ."

One need not be an historian or a scholar to recognize that what Rabbi Berman refers to here as "the new trends" is a far cry from the Reform Judaism of a generation or two ago. This is what prompts more than a few within the movement itself to accuse it of reverting to Orthodoxy.

I am convinced they are wrong. Reform is not becoming Orthodox; it is proving that it has never lost the capacity to change and thereby to correct its own most serious mis-

takes. Our movement is called Reform Judaism, not Re-
formed Judaism. There is no "ed" at the end of the word
Reform. If there were, it would indicate that all the re-
forming had been accomplished once and for all in the past.
That would make of us just a revised brand of Orthodoxy.
We call ourselves Reform Judaism to indicate that the very
essence of our approach to religion is a continuing, unending spirit of adaptability and change. If our interpretation
of Judaism ever stops changing, if it ever reaches the point
even for one generation where it loses the capacity to grow,
to recognize and then to rectify its mistakes, it will at that
very moment have ceased to be *Reform* Judaism.

What were some of the early mistakes of Reform Judaism and how have we been correcting them? In spelling
these out I want to make it perfectly clear that I am not
negatively criticizing the generation of Reform Rabbis who
made most of these mistakes. You and I in their historic
context would most probably have done the same. But
times have changed, circumstances have changed, and our
responses must change too.

The first mistake of early Reform was natural, perhaps
inevitable. Like a pendulum swinging on its natural arc
away from one extreme, it went temporarily to the opposite extreme. This is bound to be true in all movements of
protest, whether in politics, in culture, or in religion. It had
to be true, therefore, at least for a time, in Reform Judaism.
Our predecessors, in their zeal to clean house spiritually, in
their enthusiasm to strip from Judiasm some of the outer
trappings and trimmings it had long since outgrown, unfortunately also dispensed with some things that should not
have been surrendered. They almost threw out the baby
with the bath water. In permitting the pendulum now to
avoid both extremes, we are not returning to Orthodoxy;

we are preserving the essence of Reform while seeking to correct some of its most glaring errors.

A second mistake made by the immediate followers of Isaac Mayer Wise was to suppose that religion could be lived purely as a phenomenon of reason. This, incidentally, was an error committed also by the Quakers, the Ethical Culturists, and a number of Protestant churches and sects which tried to reduce religion to a purely rational experience, naked of all emotion. To be sure, it has always been a tenet of Judaism that religion must be both rational and reasonable. Our faith has never asked us to believe that which our intellect suggests is absurd. But to profess that religion must always be rational is not the same as to insist that it must dispense with emotion and color and warmth. To do that would be to divorce religion from life. For life generally is governed at least as much by emotion as by the rigid dictates of reason. So religion, if it is to express the highest aspirations of life and meet the deepest needs of life, must also clothe itself in symbolism and ceremony, the warm garments of emotion.

A third serious mistake of early Reform was that it acted as if religion were purely the private relationship of an individual to his God and, as such, could exist in a social vacuum. Earlier generations of Reform Jews overlooked the fact that, whatever its personal and private aspects, Judaism is essentially the product of a people's civilization and will thrive only so long as that people endures. The ceremonies of our faith are the dramatic devices whereby our people seeks to express its group solidarity and to symbolize the values in life which our own peculiar collective experience has led us to cherish most. Today, by our acceptance of Zionism, which means the peoplehood of the Jew, and of the Hebrew language, and of more ritual, we have once more rectified a grievous error. The Guiding Principles of Reform Judaism, officially adopted by the Central Conference of American Rabbis in 1937, express the matter with admirably brief eloquence: "Judaism is the soul of which Israel is the body."

Fourth and finally, Reform Judaism made the mistake of permitting itself to become too largely a spectator religion in which the rabbi and cantor and choir performed, while the congregation sat back to be entertained, not to participate. The trend of Reform Judaism toward more ritual is not a return to Orthodoxy, but a desire to correct an earlier mistake by encouraging the participation of the average Jew in his Judaism.

Those who see a reversion to Orthodoxy in the fact that Reform Judaism has embraced both ritual and the Hebrew language fail to understand either the intent or spirit of Isaac Mayer Wise. On the subject of traditional ceremony he wrote:

"We need only those ceremonies which in the consciousness of our age have the meaning and signification of worship and elevate the soul to God, or which unite us to a religious community all over the world. We must have ceremonies, to be sure. We must have outward signs and tokens to unite us into one religious community. Therefore, we choose the best and most useful."

The father of American Reform Judaism spoke with equal clarity and force on the role of the Hebrew language: "All Hebrew schools in which the pupils are not taught to read and understand the Hebrew Bible are perfectly useless . . . They deceive parents and children alike . . . they rob Israel of the rising generation, and Judaism of its sons and daughters. Hebrew schools for religious instruction must enable the pupils to read the Hebrew Bible, or else they are worse than useless." So, when Reform Judaism emphasizes more Hebrew and a richer ceremonial life, it is returning not to Orthodoxy but to Isaac Mayer Wise himself.

With all the changes of our generation, the crucial distinction of Reform from other interpretations of Judaism remains inviolate. The premise of Orthodox Judaism and, to a greater extent than most people suppose, of Conservative Judaism too, is that change in the practice of religion should be accepted reluctantly. The cornerstone of Reform Judaism is that change, far from being accepted warily, must be deliberately welcomed and encouraged. Indeed, that only if interpretation and form are flexible, can the essential core-truths survive! To confuse this with Orthodoxy is to be willfully obtuse and blind.

II

The most common misconception of Reform Judaism harbored by those who stand outside the movement is the notion that Reform is an easy, undemanding, diluted kind of Judaism—like instant coffee, a product which can be prepared with a minimum of effort or fuss but which comes only reasonably close to resembling the original. Far too many American Jews today think of the varieties of our religious life as positions on a quantitative spectrum. Orthodox Jews, according to this strange calculus, are the most religious; Conservative Jews occupy a kind of middle position; Reform Jews are the least religious of all. How often have I heard members of our own congregation, who surely should know better, refer to themselves as "very Reform" when what they meant was that they observe next to nothing.

It is important to dispel this illusion too, to establish the fact that Reform is not instant Judaism. I propose to accomplish this by taking a hard, accurate look first at the historical record, then at the position of Reform, respectively, on Jewish law, on the observance of ritual and on education.

The record of history is pertinent because it is frequently asserted that Reform Judaism was initiated by those who wanted either to make the practice of our faith easier or to escape its obligations entirely. Such claims can be made only by willfully perverting the facts. Those who—like Heinrich Heine—wanted to escape from Judaism during the nineteenth century period when our movement originated did so through the direct route of baptism or conversion; they needed no devious pretense on the way. Those who laid the foundations for Reform in fact made life more difficult and perilous for themselves, not easier. The easy, expedient thing to do was to go along with the past.

David Einhorn, who later became one of the most illustrious leaders of the movement in this country, was forced to wait ten years from the time of his ordination to his very first pulpit in Bavaria, because of the bitter, almost insane animosity of the entrenched official rabbinate. He was victimized by the meanest, most malicious kind of character assassination on the part of fellow-Jews who would have accepted and recommended him with alacrity had he only persisted in their kind of orthodoxy. Abraham Kohn of Lemberg was poisoned by fanatic opponents—Jewish opponents!—of his relatively mild religious reforms. Isaac Mayer Wise had to leave his pulpit in Albany—after being physically assaulted in the synagogue by an officer of his congregation on Rosh Hashanah!—because the changes he proposed in Jewish teaching and practice were unacceptable to many of his congregants. Any one of these men, or many scores like them, could have purchased immunity from harassment and scorn simply by yielding to the pressure of the past. To accuse such men of seeking expediency or escape, comes unforgivably close to libel.

Rabbi Gunther Plaut, in *The Rise of Reform Judaism*, lays this ghost once and for all. He summarizes an extensive anthology of source materials on the early history of our movement by saying: ". . . let us make no mistake about it: Reform was thoroughly Jewish. Its leaders were conversant with Talmud and Shulhan Arukh; they quoted freely from all Jewish sources and did so in Hebrew. They loved the holy tongue and, even though they were realists and introduced translations into the prayer book, they insisted that every Jew learn Hebrew to the limits of his ability."

Even so severe—and often unfair—a critic of Reform as Mordecai Kaplan has been forced to admit: "The Reform Movement, despite its apparent tendency to abrogate many traditional beliefs and practices, was impelled primarily by a desire to stem the flight from Judaism rather than by any light-hearted yielding to the pressure of the environment."

It would be improper to leave the historic record without observing that, of course, there were individual Jews —in the beginning as there are now—who misused Reform Judaism in their personal effort to depart from any meaningful dimension of Jewish life without assuming an intolerable burden of inner guilt. But the fault for that rests on them, not on the movement. It is no more reasonable to deprecate Reform because of their malfeasance than to castigate Americanism because of the shenanigans of Robert Welch. The testament of history is clear: Reform Judaism emerged out of a desire neither for expediency nor escape. Its initial objective was to make the practice of our faith more meaningful, not less demanding.

At this point we turn from an historic to a topical approach. There are three functional areas in which the accusation is frequently made that Reform is an attenuated kind of Judaism. The first is that of Jewish law, of *halachah*, the enormous body of post-biblical talmudic legislation by which every minute movement of daily life is governed for the observant traditional Jew. It is true, of course, that we Reform Jews reject the binding quality of *halachah*, which is accepted whole-heartedly by Orthodox and somewhat tortuously by Conservative Jews. Because of this, we have sometimes been compared to the Karaites, those Jews who, commencing in the eighth century, rejected the whole regimen of talmudic law and insisted that only the laws promulgated in the Bible are obligatory.

The gross inaccuracy of the comparison should at once be obvious to anyone with substantial knowledge of either movement. The fact is that Reform Judaism neither rejects all talmudic law nor accepts all biblical law. Our attitude, properly understood, is selective toward both. There are two kinds of *halachah* which we do accept and should observe; the first consists of those laws which are ethical in nature. The laws prohibiting businessmen from cheating the consumer or underpaying the worker or falsely advertising their products are as binding on Reform Jews today as on any other variety of Jew—whether they emanate from the Bible or the Talmud. The second kind of *halachah* for which we Reform Jews are still responsible is that which legislates the performance of rituals and ceremonies which are still viable and valid for our century.

There is a kind of *halachah*, however, which Reform Judaism unquestionably does reject. Some of you may recall that a few years ago the Orthodox rabbinate in Israel faced a serious problem. A *shemitah* year was about to commence—that seventh year prescribed in the Torah, during which the land must be allowed to rest. But refraining from cultivating the land at so crucial a juncture in the life of the infant state would seriously jeopardize the nation's food supply; even the Chief Rabbis recognized that. So, what to do in such a serious and threatening dilemma?

The answer given by Rabbis Nissim and Herzog was typical of how traditional *halachah* operates. They proposed a fictional "sale" of all agricultural land belonging to Orthodox Jews to non-Jews for a period of a year. During that year the regular ploughing and seeding would be done by the real owners, but always with an awning over them, to create the additional fiction that the work was being done not in the field, where it was clearly prohibited by the Bible, but in a private dwelling, of which the Bible says nothing in terms of the *shemitah*. One can admire the legal dexterity of such ingenious solutions, yet at the same time question their ethical impact on a sensitive younger generation or the respect they engender for law in general. *Halachic* Judaism says: when the law is archaic and outworn, manipulate and twist it to suit your contemporary purpose. Reform Judaism says: when the law has become anachronistic, abrogate or amend it honestly so that you mean what you say and say what you mean.

No one has understood the proper attitude of Reform Judaism toward Jewish law with greater accuracy than Rabbi Solomon Freehof: ". . . the law is authoritative enough to influence us, but not so completely so as to control us. The rabbinic law is our guidance but not our governance." Enough, then, to establish that in terms of its attitude toward *halachah* Reform is not instant Judaism.

Now how about ritual? A question I often propound to the Confirmation Class asks them to mark as true or false the following statement: "Ritual is less important in Re-

form Judaism than in Orthodox and Conservative Judaism." If I were to experiment with that question here, I
daresay that almost the same proportion of the adult congregation as of our prospective confirmands would mistak-
enly mark it *true*. The fact is, however, that ritual is every
bit as important to us as to the other branches of our faith.
The difference is not one of importance but rather (a) of
selectivity and (b) of motivation. Let me explain. As Reform Jews we believe in observing only those traditional
ceremonies which still have valid meaning, rejecting those
which, having served their purpose in another environment, are irredeemably meaningless in our time. And as
Reform Jews we observe our rituals not because we expect
thereby to change God's intentions toward us or to ward
off misfortune but because of the human effect such rituals
can have on us.

Those in our midst—and there are some; it would be
dishonest to deny it—who assume that Reform Jews have
no obligation to practice any of the rituals of Judaism don't
even begin to understand the meaning of our movement.
What they propose and often perform is no more than a
caricature of Judaism. The knowledgeable Reform Jew
recognizes that ritual is man's poetic, dramatic way of
symbolizing those values, sentiments, emotions, ideals, aspirations which mean most to him in human and cosmic
terms and which, for that very reason, are beyond the
power of words alone to articulate. To strip life of ritual—
Jewish, American, Christian, any kind of ritual—would be
immeasurably to impoverish the human experience.

So Reform Judaism is not anti-ritual, it is anti-rote. It
rejects the kind of ritual represented in the peculiar, triangular sway of the Yemenite Jew engaged in prayer. This is
quite a different kind of movement from that of any other

Jew as he *davens*. The Yemenite would be scandalized at
the suggestion that he should pray without his clumsy
motion. He thinks it is an authentic aspect of worshipping
as a Jew. He isn't even aware of the fact that he sways that
way because his ancestors frequently worshipped while
riding their camels and so acquired the habit of moving in
the triangular pattern of the camel rider as they intoned
their prayers. It has nothing whatever to do with Judaism
and can mean less than nothing to any Jew in the twentieth
century.

Obviously, however, there is an altogether different kind
of ritual which means much. The kindling of Shabbat candles and chanting of *kiddush* can add a dimension of aesthetic warmth to our Friday dinner table even as they
induce in us the *n'shama y'tayra*—the surplus soul—of
which our tradition speaks so eloquently. The performance
of the whole syndrome of rituals embraced in the Seder
ceremony can identify us with Jewish history and associate
us with Jewish communities throughout the world in our
time and motivate us toward the pursuit of freedom for
every minority group in the world which is still enslaved.
The illumination of Chanukah lights can symbolize our
loftiest ideals of religious liberty and reinvigorate those ideals in our own lives. Ritual is the acting-out of our faith—
the poetry, the emotion, the rich drama of our faith. Reform Judaism doesn't reject all this. It insists rather that it
be observed selectively and intelligently, not as the mecha-
nized routine of automatons, nor in the expectation of
magically affecting the universe. To call that instant Judaism is to distort the meaning of both adjective and noun.

Our third functional testing ground is education. If we
are to be intelligently selective—not compulsive or obses-
sive but intelligently selective—about the laws we practice

and the rituals we observe, it follows that we must be effectively educated. How otherwise can we hope to make the right choices? The fact is: we need to know not just as much as, but more than other Jews do about Judaism.

Reform Judaism at its best has always understood this. It was Leopold Zunz, one of the earliest of our leaders, who established the so-called Science of Judaism—*Die Wissenschaft des Judentums*—the very first attempt to study and understand the development of Judaism with the insights and techniques of modern science. It was our movement which first created in this country a Commission on Jewish Education, which became the prototype for similar commissions later established by the other branches. It was our movement—believe it or not—which set up the first school in the United States for the education of cantors! In education—as with reference to *halachah* and ritual—Reform is instant Judaism only for those who, innocently or willfully, fail to understand it.

Reform has never been instant Judaism. We must see that it does not degenerate into instant Judaism. Easy to be a Reform Jew? Not for the man or woman who truly understands. There are two positions which are easy in religion and only two. One is blindly to follow the paths of the past, to ask no questions and raise no doubts, to discard nothing old and experiment with nothing new. The other is undiscriminatingly to reject the past, to throw out our whole heritage of Jewish life. To be an intelligent Reform Jew—or, for that matter, an intelligent Conservative Jew—is the supremely difficult choice. It means that a man must know more in order to choose wisely.

No one has understood this more perceptively or expressed it more eloquently than the late Rabbi Abba Hillel Silver. His words should be pondered at depth by every one of us: "No religion is worth its salt which does not make great demands upon its adherents. . . .

"Too many of our people want an easy-going religion, one which does not interfere with their leisure, their sleep, or their television, which calls for no study and no observance, which does not challenge or disturb them—a religion without any spiritual travail, without any stab of thought or conscience, without any sacrifice, the religion of a self-pampering people. No religion has ever survived that kind of emotional and intellectual vacuum, Judaism least of all."

III

In refuting the two most common criticisms of Reform, we have performed an important task. But our responsibility in this respect is far from fulfilled. As Reform Jews we must also examine with scrupulous honesty the strengths and weaknesses of our movement. If I devote more space to the latter than the former, this is because my intention is not to induce a mood of self-congratulation, but rather to encourage the kind of correction and improvement we have embraced in the past.

Any cataloguing of our strengths must begin with the undeniable fact that Reform Judaism has given us freedom to select and reject from our heritage of the past. It recognizes the dynamic, evolutionary nature of our religious tradition, which has survived the vicissitudes of time precisely because it has been flexible and resilient. Therefore Reform encourages us to discard the outworn in our faith, to retain the eternal, and to create new tenets and rituals in response to new needs.

A second strength of Reform is the opening of ancient truths to interpretation by the light of new knowledge. Reform Jews are forced neither to close their minds to the discoveries of science, nor to compartmentalize their lives, as if knowledge and faith were unrelated to each other.

A third great strength—a consequence of the first two —is that our prayerbook has been exposed to adaptation and revision. Like the Orthodox *siddur* in its period of development—though most Orthodox Jews have forgotten it—from time to time outworn passages are dropped, while fresh, creative prayers are added. Only in a Reform congregation, or a Conservative group under the influence of Reform, is this possible.

Our fourth strength has been to embellish the aesthetics of religious worship. Decorum has replaced disorder; the organ, the choir, the unison and responsive readings, the encouragement of new, creative synagogue music—all these have made our Service a joy to the eye and ear as well as a solace to the soul.

Fifth, more than any other current interpreters of our faith, we Reform Jews have applied the social ethic of the Hebrew prophets to the political, economic and international problems of the time. It is no accident that of the three major Jewish religious denominations, only we have a Religious Action Center in our nation's capital.

Sixth and finally, we have brought religious equality in the synagogue to our women, seating them by our side in family units, inviting them to participate in pulpit prayers, at times even listening as they preach the sermons.

These are considerable accomplishments, neither to be taken for granted by us nor disparaged by our detractors. Why, then, am I worried about Reform? Because each of the strengths just described carries within itself a concomitant weakness. Our freedom to select or reject has too often been exercised only to reject. Our openness to the new insights of science has tempted us to contemn the old truths of faith. Our antiseptically revised prayerbook, with all its creative accretions, has become for too many of us a volume to be touched only once or twice a year. The decorum and aesthetics of our Worship Service threaten to turn us back into spectators rather than participants, into an audience instead of a congregation. And the equality we have so generously extended to our women comes perilously close to an equality of indifference, not of active concern.

Am I unduly exercised? Do I speak only out of a pessimism characteristic of the clergy, out of expectations too inflated ever to be met by reality? Well, I suppose the best way to determine that is to take a sober, honest look at our own congregation. I do so, not because I think Temple Israel of Boston is an extreme example of what ails Reform Judaism, but precisely because I am satisfied that in most respects we are a considerable cut above the average. So let's try to discover how accurate my fears are by measuring them against our own performance. To what degree does Judaism actually function in our lives?

Well, to begin with, we pride ourselves—and very properly so—on the fact that no other congregation in the Greater Boston area has so consistently high an attendance at Friday night Services of Worship. But if our commendable average of about 500 be realistically reduced by the number of nonmembers present and of students who are fulfilling a requirement for confirmation, it comes remarkably close to the findings of our 1962 congregational survey, which showed that only 14% of our adult membership worships with the congregation as frequently as two Friday nights a month. The percentage on Saturday morning, I must add with deep dismay, is miniscule.

No less significant than worship as a measuring-rod for participation in Judaism is study. That means life-long study, ending only at the grave, not just elementary education for children. In this congregation we have a variety of listings under the heading of adult education, but only two courses each year for those who take this privilege seriously enough to attend a dozen consecutive weekly classes, with preparatory study for each. To my knowledge, no neighboring Reform or Conservative congregation has a more valid or meaningful schedule of adult classes. But our average enrollment for each of the past three years has been slightly in excess of 100. That comes roughly to 5% or 6% of our adult membership, a figure which unfortunately speaks for itself.

Let me inject a hasty but essential word here about education for our children. Quantitatively we do much better here than on the adult level; over 90% of the children in this congregation through the sophomore high school year are students in our school. Still, the status of Reform Jewish education disturbs me immensely. I am convinced that our educational efforts are moving in the right direction. But to pretend that it is possible properly to educate Jewish children in Judaism within the pathetic confines of two or two-and-a-half hours a week is to indulge in the most destructive kind of illusion. In our congregation a substantial majority of the students in grades 4 through 7 attend classes a total of 5½ hours a week. But there are many congregations in which this is not true, and we ourselves leave much room for improvement above the seventh grade.

How about the practice of Judaism in our homes? I would estimate that half or less than half of us light candles and chant kiddush at home on Friday night; that a far lower proportion recite a Jewish blessing or prayer before and after eating, on retiring for the night, on awakening

again in the morning, on experiencing an occasion either of
sadness or of bliss. As I have come into your homes through
the years, I have seen almost no Jewish books, an abysmal
absence of Jewish art, a miserable paucity of Jewish music.
There are, to be sure, some notable exceptions in the homes
of our congregants, but not many. The effect, on balance,
is devastating.

One more congregational gauge should be read at this
point. A few years ago I invited those of you who were so
inclined to join me in assuming a set of Reform Jewish
commitments which are certainly a reasonable minimum.
Those who associate themselves with our *Breet K'tanah*,
organized at that time, voluntarily undertake such responsibilities as participating in at least two synagogue services a
month, enrolling in an adult education class, celebrating the
holidays in their homes, reading not less than six books and
two periodicals of Jewish content during the year. A total
of some 75 individuals accepted my invitation; about 60
have continued to meet with me one Shabbat afternoon a
month. I have no doubt that for this limited group the *Breet
K'tanah* has been an enrichment of major magnitude in
their religious lives. But the numbers involved—60 out of
approximately 4,000—testify dismally to the quality of our
Judaism.

What all this adds up to is that neither the appearance of
our homes nor the daily conduct of our lives nor the
quality of our attachment to the synagogue nor our readiness to assume even a minimum of Jewish religious commitment distinguishes us in any substantial way from our
Christian neighbors. The plain, simple, excruciatingly painful fact is that Judaism no longer functions for most of us.
In appalling measure we exemplify the pitiful, incredible
candor of a boy in our 1961 Confirmation Class, who

defined religion on his final examination as follows: "Religion is when you believe in one God and you go to Temple at least twice a year."

Why does this bother me so much? Because I know how very much Judaism can give to each of us in his search for a happy, fulfilled life. Because I have seen many times with my own eyes the prodigal strength which Judaism can bring in moments of bereavement and crisis to those who have faithfully practiced it. Because I am convinced that our religious civilization can contribute even more to the sum total of human culture in the future than it has in the past. And because I am positive that all will be lost—that our personal lives will be impoverished, our strength diminished, our civilization depleted and that Judaism will vanish —if we persist in our casual attitude toward its most precious traditions.

Jewish theology is important, immensely so. But man does not live by concepts and ideas alone, any more than by bread alone. Man isn't capable of sustaining himself only in the spiritual weightlessness of pure principle. He must have daily disciplines through which his principles are practiced and rehearsed. The person who professes the unique ideals and values of Judaism, but does nothing day by day to be reminded of them, to implement them in his life, is like one who prattles about love but never kisses or embraces his wife.

To experience the joys of love, one must practice the daily rituals and tokens of love. To benefit from the dividends of exercise, one must regularly flex his muscles. To profit from the accrued wisdom of Judaism, one must practice Judaism in visible, indentifiable form. I know: some of you became Reform Jews in the first place because you thought it would make no demands on you. Well, this is as appropriate a time as any to disillusion you. Reform Judaism is selective in its demands, but imperious none the less. If you aren't prepared to recognize and fulfill the responsibilities of your faith, don't expect to benefit from it. Joshua Liebman knew that. He wrote: ". . . when little is demanded of our people, little will be received, and little will be experienced in the way of happiness and spiritual integration. The greater our expectations of performances by Reform Jews, the greater will be the spiritual returns for all of us."

Let me back up a bit here to pick up my previous point on the relationship between noble ideals and daily discipline. A few specific examples are in order. One of the most precious insights of Judaism is that a great, creative Spiritual Reality permeates the whole of nature, relating us to every cloud, every bird, every tree. What a priceless opportunity to demonstrate and reinforce this truth is lost to the Jew who fails to build or at least visit a *sukkah* on the festival of *sukkot,* thus to participate personally in his relationship to nature and nature's God. We have taught mankind also that God is to be found in history, in man's ceaseless struggle for freedom and justice and peace. What a lamentable pity when a Jew fails to dramatize this truth with his own eyes and mind and gut, by participating in a real *seder* and in Passover synagogue worship.

Unlike most other faiths, ours has insisted that every experience in life is susceptible to holiness, that man possesses a capacity to infuse the sacred into the profane. What an unforgivable waste it is for a Jewish family to mouth such words, but not to symbolize them each week in their lives by framing the Sabbath between *kiddush* and *havdalah.* On a trip some years ago my wife and I were privi-

leged to observe successive Sabbaths in the homes of Rabbi
Soetendorp in Amsterdam, of Mons. Greilsammer—President of the Reform congregation in Paris—of Carl Alpert
and Rabbis Alvin Rubin and Jack J. Cohen in Israel. On all
these occasions we kindled the candles, chanted the melo-
dies, intoned the prayers which long centuries have rendered precious to our people. I wish it were possible to tell
you in words what these experiences meant to us. Not only
did they impress upon us again the unity of Jews throughout history and the world; they warmed and exalted and
inspired us, by the sancta of our faith, to live nobler,
stronger, more Jewish lives in the days that ensued.

Would we have felt the same had we celebrated *Shabbat*
in your home? If the answer is yes, you stand among the
minority in our congregation who don't need this sermon.
God bless you! If the answer is no, you typify the weakness of Reform Judaism; you are in danger of permitting a
priceless treasure to slip through your fingers, without even
suspecting its worth.

One Friday afternoon we took the famous synagogue
tour in Jerusalem. After an introductory lecture, the tour
proceeds to visit three or four of the most exotic Orthodox
synagogues in the city—if I recall correctly, one of Yemenite origin, one in which Persian Jews worship, one for Jews
from Iraq. In each we saw a small handful of elderly,
eccentric men, either studying or idly awaiting the arrival
of *Shabbat*. These shabby little synagogues are antiquities,
curiosities; tiny groups of Jews worship in them, while
many thousands visit them as mementoes of the past. Is that
what we're doing with our religious life here? Allowing it
to degenerate into a museum piece, a place to be pointed
out by sight-seeing guides, a building to be displayed on

postcards? That's not an easy question for a rabbi to ask. It happens to be, however, a question which neither he nor his congregants have a moral right to evade.

Here, then, are the strengths and the weaknesses of Reform Judaism. Here are my hopes and my fears, poised in precarious balance. Here is the disturbing challenge I beg you to take with you. Ponder it carefully. Examine it with reference to your life and your home. My concern is with the survival of our faith, of course it is. I would be a poor excuse for a rabbi if it were not. But I am no less worried about you—each one of you; about the quality of your life and your children's lives if Reform encourages you to profess Judaism but not to practice it.

Let me conclude with a story concerning the Baal Shem Tov, the founder of Chasidism in the eighteenth century.

When the Besht had a difficult task before him, he would go to a certain place in the woods, light a fire and meditate in prayer. When a generation later a Jew was faced with the same task, he would go to that place in the woods and say: "I can no longer light a fire, but I can still speak the prayer."

But a generation after that, facing a similar task, a Jew went into the woods and said: "I can no longer light a fire nor do I know the meaning of prayer, but I know the place in the woods to which it belongs and that must be sufficient." And when still another generation had passed, and a Jew was confronted with a similar task he remained where he was and said: "I cannot light the fire, I cannot speak the prayer, I do not know the place, but I can tell the tale of how it was done."

Reform Judaism will be weak if it is reduced just to the telling of a tale. It will be strong only if we know how to light the fire and speak the words ourselves.

22
The Two Faces of Israel

My second visit to Israel—like the first—was an experience I shall never be able to forget. For one thing, the changes that had taken place there in the short span of six years were difficult to believe even after one had seen them. But it is not of those dramatic changes that I would speak here.

For the diaspora Jew—no matter what his place of residence—there is an incalculable difference between visiting Israel and any other country. Elsewhere he is a tourist: he comes, he sees, he conquers pictorially, and he departs. In Israel he leaves something of himself and takes back with him a new ingredient which becomes a permanent part of his life. No longer merely a tourist, he becomes a participant in Jewish history.

This is, of course, entirely in accord with Zionist theory. The Jewish Homeland was always envisaged as more than just a physical refuge for homeless Jews. It was always anticipated that a dynamic relationship would exist between Zion restored and all Jews, wherever they continued to live. My most recent visit demonstrated vividly, how true this has already become in fact. Let me explain in some detail what Israel has already come to mean—first to Jews living in countries other than our own here; second, to us as American Jews.

The simplest, most effective way of describing the significance of Israel to Jews living in lands other than the United States is to assert that it represents—plainly, bluntly, literally—the difference between life and death. I know—you have heard these words or others like them so often from platform and pulpit that they begin to sound like cliches. But they would not impress you that way if you could have been with us the night my wife and I boarded an immigrant ship in the port of Haifa. It was a Turkish ship which had just docked with a human cargo of immigrants from North Africa and Eastern Europe.

How can I possibly reduce to words what we saw or how we felt? Through an interpreter we spoke with several men and women from both groups. We learned that those who came from Eastern Europe had applied for exit visas anywhere from two to fourteen years before! The instant they requested such permission they were deprived of citizenship in their native land and became, for the whole agonizing period of their waiting, outcasts. This, despite the fact that the cost of the visa, which they were forced to pay at once, was so exorbitant that most of them had to rely on the United Jewish Appeal to help cover it. If they had occupied positions of status in the national economy, they were at once deprived of these and had to live on whatever miserable crumbs of employment they could find. If they had occupied apartments, they had to sell them for a pittance, in many cases first being forced to redecorate them at their own expense for the new Gentile occupants. They were not permitted to take with them any gold, not even gold rings or watches. During all the anxious years of waiting they didn't dare have any more children, for if the number of individuals listed on their application changed, by virtue either of birth or death, the whole process had to be initiated again.

We saw a man whose left leg had been amputated. He had to inch his way down the gangplank seated, bumping himself awkwardly from step to step. Then he hobbled off painfully on two crutches. Like all the others, he had already received his blue document of Israel citizenship even before leaving the ship. He would immediately be given a light lunch right on the dock, plus a food package to carry with him as, that very night, a waiting car would take him to his permanent place of settlement. Soon he would be taken to a hospital where he would receive an artificial limb and whatever tender therapy he needed—as if the State of Israel had no more urgent task than restoring him to full humanity.

We spoke to one old man whose age I would guess to be about 70, though it is hard to say after what he had endured. He had once owned extensive timberland in his native country. When the lumber industry was nationalized, his property was expropriated with no compensation. For a short time the government employed him as a manager on what had been his own land, but soon that too was terminated. His two children had both been incinerated at Auschwitz. His eyes bore an unutterable pain. Our interpreter touched the old man's shoulder gently, pointed toward the glistening lights ascending the hill from the port to the top of Carmel, and asked: "What do you see?" He answered, so softly through his tears that we could scarcely hear: "It's beautiful . . . beautiful. Now I'm home."

That man came home only in the evening of his life. Others were more fortunate. There were young parents with children ranging in age from ten months to the adolescent years. The children—especially those from North Africa—huddled together fearfully; more than just a language barrier kept them from responding to our occasional questions. They were filthy, tattered, no doubt many of them diseased. Though we tried not to show any feeling of revulsion, there was an irresistible urge to pull away from them in passing in order to avoid direct contact. I confess that at first I was dismayed by what I saw of the children. Something in me wanted to cry out: "Is this the future of Israel . . . this refuse, this human trash?"

Then I remembered. I remembered that exactly one week earlier at Ashdod we stopped to chat with a group of boys and girls who had just been dismissed from school. They had been North African refugees too. They were 15 to 17 years old, had come from such places as Algeria and Morocco; none of them had been in Israel more than two years. No doubt the day or night they had landed they must have looked very much like these poor youngsters toward whom the snob in me had felt an initial revulsion. But how differently they looked and acted now! They were clean, neat, attractively clothed in their blue school uniforms. They were delightfully bright, eager to know about us and America, fluent in their use of Hebrew, which had been an unknown language to most of them when they first arrived. When I remembered them, suddenly I saw these poor, unfortunate children on board ship in a different light. I saw them as they too would be when an American visitor would stop to talk to them a year or two hence, and I knew—as I had never known before—what Israel means to such as these. It means life instead of death.

There are others for whom the significance of Israel is different. They came not because, subtly or otherwise, they were forced to, but because they freely chose to. There were, for example, the cantor of the new Liberal congregation in Haifa and his wife. They came from Holland. They are both alumni of Auschwitz. They could have remained in Holland; there is no discrimination against Jews there today. They came instead to Israel because, as they put it in answer to my question, they wanted their young son to "live in a Jewish environment."

There was the retired director of personnel training for a large British department store chain, who lives now in Haifa. She could have continued living a comfortable life in London, obviously so. She had never been a Zionist, never ideologically identified with the establishment of a Jewish State. When I asked why she had chosen to settle in Israel after her retirement, she looked half-puzzled for a moment —as if the question had never consciously occurred to her before—then quickly and simply replied: "Because I wanted to live among Jews, that's all."

I understood her motivation better for having visited the city of Florence en route to Israel. There we stopped at the church of Santa Croce, the Westminster Abbey of Italy. It is, as many of you know, a medieval structure but the facade was redone in the nineteenth century by a Jewish architect. This accounts for the fact that a large inlaid Star of David appears incongruously at the very top of the facade and another is beneath a side entrance. More than anything else, the architect responsible for the outer beauty of the building wanted to be buried there. But he was refused that privilege because he was a Jew; so they buried him under the threshold of the main door—just outside the church itself. He couldn't quite make the grade; they were willing to benefit from his genius as a craftsman, but he was still—in death as he had been in life—a second-class citizen.

That's what the story of the Jew has been for most of his

existence outside his own country, when he has had one. Even when his lot as an individual has been one of relative safety and comfort, he has always suspected himself to be accepted on tolerance. The cantor and the retired executive and other thousands like them—a few even from the United States and Canada—have come to Israel because there as Jews they have no doubt about the degree of their acceptance. So, this is what Israel means to Jews elsewhere in the world: to most, a blessed escape from persecution and death; to others, an opportunity to achieve full human dignity.

What does Israel mean, or what should it mean, to us as American Jews? A Jewish State should have significant meaning for us too; if not, Zionism is a delusion. For Zionism is more than philanthropy, more than an heroic effort to save Jews from the jaws of death. Therefore we must ask about the meaning of Israel for us too.

To begin with, it increases the favorable odds for Jewish survival. The time has come to stop entertaining any wishful thinking on this score. Barring anything unforeseen, and at the moment unforeseeable, the prospects for the survival of Judaism in Europe are anything but hopeful. I suspected it from my studies; I confirmed it on this trip by direct observation. In Florence there is a total Jewish population of 1500 souls. The magnificent synagogue there is a memorial to the past and a fascinating enticement for tourists, not a realistic harbinger of hope for the future. In Lisbon, once a great center of Jewish concentration, there are 800 Jews left; on a Sunday morning at 9:50 I was the tenth man for whom they had been waiting since 8:30 in order to have a *minyan* for morning prayer. In Athens there are 200 children in the Jewish school and the resources of the Jewish community are so impoverished that, except for one couple borrowed from Israel, the faculty consists of Christian teachers who are supposed to instruct the children not only in their general studies but also in Judaism.

While we were abroad, Albert Vorspan, Director of our Commission on Social Action, was in Yugoslavia. When we met in Rome he told us that in the city of Dubrovic he had met a Jew whose ancestors 400 years ago had helped build the synagogue there. During the second World War he personally had hid the Torah Scrolls, returning them to the sanctuary when the war ended. Now a man of 60, he maintains the synagogue for the twelve remaining Jews of the city. When he dies, he will carry the congregation and the Jewish life of Dubrovic with him to the grave.

Make no mistake: I am not suggesting that these valiant Jews give up the struggle or that we should, for a single moment, relax our efforts to help them in their determination to persist. But to count on them for Jewish survival just doesn't make sense. If we want Judaism to survive our generation anywhere in the world outside the United States, Israel is indispensable. I must add, in all brutal honesty, that the prognosis for meaningful survival even here is less than excellent without Israel. This is Israel's first meaning to us.

The second is that it reinforces in our minds and hearts the peoplehood of Jews throughout the world. Some of the Yemenites who came to Israel a generation or more ago had lived in such total isolation before that they were unaware of Jews living in any countries other than Yemen! There is real danger that the Jews of America may become almost that parochial. Perhaps this is truer of us Reform Jews than of any others. Our children are for the most part unable to worship meaningfully even with American Conservative or

Orthodox Jews. At a synagogue Service in any European country other than England they would be abysmally lost. A visit in depth to Israel discloses dramatically the full scope of Jewish peoplehood. There one sees—and if he is fortunate and perceptive comes to know—Chasidic Jews with *streimel* and *payot*, North African Jews who never saw a toilet or water running from a faucet, fanatically Orthodox Jews who throw rocks at busses on *Shabbat*, and Jews who insist that they have no use for religion.

The differences among and between such types of Jews are at first almost shocking. But there are similarities too. There is a kinship of fate, even if not always of faith, which binds us into a single people whether we are aware of it or not. And Israel is the one place where that kinship becomes most evident. Even if the differences seem unconquerable to the immigrant generation, their children become members all of one people. During our visit to the Technion we knocked at random on a dormitory door, asking if we might come in for a moment. There we found three students doing their work together—one from Argentina, one from Rumania, one from Bulgaria. When they first arrived in Israel last year or the year before, they may well have wondered what they had in common. Now they know. And we knew too, as we visited and spoke to them, that despite the very real divergences and discrepancies in our midst, we Jews everywhere are a people, one people. We who live in America need that understanding as much as anyone.

We need no less a third contribution of Israel to our lives, the Jewish cultural enrichment it affords. Another very real danger we confront as American Jews is that our Judaism will shrink to the proportions only of theology, that it will become no more than a system of beliefs. Now no one is more aware than I of how important theology should be for us; I have written at least my share precisely in this area. But to reduce Judaism only to theology would be to distort its essential nature grotesquely beyond recognition. Judaism has always been a way of life far more than a way of thought or faith. Indeed, the primary purpose of theology and philosophy with us has been to serve as a structure for Jewish living.

Judaism as a way of life means a moral code; it means a system of ritual observance; it means a rich cultural tradition. No one of these can be neglected without grave jeopardy to the others. And unless we have the example and encouragement of Israel, we are in deep danger of ignoring the cultural imperatives of living a Jewish life. Let me be specific. Without Hebrew as the spoken language of Israel, little or no Hebrew would be studied or spoken here. In anticipation of this journey, we spent many hours last summer reviewing our conversational Hebrew. What incentive would we have had for such study had there been no Jewish State to visit? Without Hebrew drama and music and dance there, how much of these could we realistically expect to enjoy? My wife and I brought back with us several very beautiful paintings which are distinctively Hebraic in content and flavor. For many years to come, our home and our lives will be Jewishly enriched by them. Where could we have found such paintings but in Israel? These are the fewest and simplest of examples but they should suffice to illustrate how great a difference Israel can make in the cultural life of American Jews.

Thank God, we do not need Israel in the exact sense that Jews elsewhere in the world do. Our lives are not threatened and our dignity as Jews depends more on ourselves than on outer circumstance. But it would be utmost folly to conclude therefore that our relationship to Israel is tenuous. We need it to increase the prospect of Jewish survival, to reinforce our understanding of Jewish peoplehood, to deepen the dimensions of our participation in Jewish culture.

Let me close now by telling you of a symbol for both faces of Israel. During our second week in Haifa we were invited for *Shabbat* dinner to the home of Carl Alpert, the Executive Vice-Chairman of Technion. His home, high up on Carmel, contains an exquisite outdoor terrace, from which the whole port and bay of Haifa are visible. The only artificial light on that terrace emanates from a huge ship's lamp. Carl told us, with much emotion, how he and his family came to Israel in 1952 on a ship called the *Artza*. About two years ago, when he read in the newspapers that the *Artza* was to be scrapped, he asked if he might have the lamp which he remembered having admired while they were in transit. When his request was granted, he mounted the lamp on their terrace. On a clear night, he told us, their lamp can be seen, shining brightly on the hill, from any spot in the port. And he added: "I like to think that our lamp shines its welcome to every immigrant who comes to Israel, even as it shed light on us when we were immigrants ourselves."

These are the two faces of Israel. For other Jews literally —for American Jews in an equally significant, if poetic sense—Carl Alpert's lamp transmits its message of welcome, of warmth and of strength.

23

The Future of Religion in Israel

To the average American Jew visiting Israel, few matters are more mystifying than the status of religion, that is to say, of Jewish religion. The more carefully and closely one observes the situation first hand, the less inclined will he be to give neat or dogmatic answers.

The first impression one obtains is that most Israelis are not religious. If you asked them to rate themselves, my guess is that from seventy to eighty percent would give a negative self-appraisal. On a warm, sunny Shabbat morning there must be hundreds of men and women cavorting on the promenades and beaches of Tel-Aviv for each worshipper in a synagogue. If you will permit me an impertinent parenthesis at this point, the ratio would probably be quite like the number of our members—among those who do not work on Saturday—who are on the golf course compared to those in the synagogue.

One twelfth-grade boy at the Leo Baeck School, with the refreshing frankness characteristic of youth at its best, expressed an attitude typical of many Israelis. I had spoken to his class that morning about the difference between a static and a dynamic approach to understanding God. When he met me after class, he said: "I found your lecture today interesting, but it didn't really touch me. I can't get excited," he continued, "about an ancient versus a modern interpretation of God because I don't believe in God. You'll have to convince me first that God exists, before I can really be impressed by your distinction."

Having already rushed in where any angel would fear to tread, let me return to the comparison between Jews in Israel and ourselves. One taxi driver, who came from a fundamentalist Orthodox background, told me that he now goes to Services only on the High Holy Days. When I inquired whether he never went on Shabbat, he answered: "O yes, once in a while if the son of a friend is celebrating his Bar Mitzvah, I may go, but that's all." I find it curious, if not in a sense perverse, to hear American Jews who attend Worship Services only on the occasion of the Holy Days or a Bar Mitzvah bewail the irreligiosity of their counterparts in Israel. Are they thus exposing their own unconscious guilt, making of the Israelis a handy scapegoat?

The evidence that most Israelis are not religious is infested with confusion. Sometimes the confusion is compounded with amusement. In 1958 my wife and I were in Israel with Rabbi and Mrs. Jacob Rudin. On the sixth night of Chanukah we were eating in one of Tel-Aviv's very few non-kosher restaurants. The minute we were ushered to our table we observed a *chanukiyah* in the center of the room. It held the proper number of candles, yet despite the fact that it was already 8:30, they had not been kindled. When we asked the waiter why, he answered that they were waiting for someone who knew how to light them. Ignoring the implausibility of his reply, we retorted that we knew how and would gladly oblige if he would bring the *chanukiyah* to our table. We then proceeded, all four of us, to chant the appropriate blessings. The minute we began, the owner, to whom it somehow had never occurred that Chanukah candles should be not only displayed but kindled, rushed over to our table, pointing frantically to his head, because we were chanting the *brachot* without benefit of *kipot*.*

At other times there is no amusement whatever interfused with the confusion. We spent an entire evening discussing religion with an exceedingly bright attorney in Tel-Aviv, a sixth or seventh generation sabra. He insisted, in a quiet but vigorous manner, that there is no room in Israel for Reform and no need, as a matter of fact, for any Jewish religion. He confessed to a certain nostalgia which prompts him—each year on the occasion of his father's *yahrzeit*—to visit the grave in Tiberias and join a *minyan* there to recite *kaddish*. It was, I presume, a similar mysterious nostalgia which moved him to celebrate his only son's Bar Mitzvah in an Orthodox synagogue for which he admitted he had little use and into which, he volunteered, neither he nor his son was likely ever to enter again. This is the strange, irrational, muddled kind of pattern one finds in Israel.

When I asked this attorney whether he thought his son would retain even his own rather tenuous nostalgia for Judaism, he said, "Probably not." I then inquired whether he thought—assuming that his attitude became general—the synagogue as an institution would endure in Israel for more than another generation or two. Again he replied, "Probably not." When I asked, finally, if the prospect of the synagogue's disappearing from Jewish life in a Jewish State bothered him, he said flatly, "Not in the least." For

* Skull caps worn by Orthodox and Conservative Jews when praying or studying.

him, the highest goal and ultimate loyalty in life is the
survival of the Jewish people. The State of Israel is an
indispensable means to that end. Religion is altogether superfluous. I cannot pretend to know for how many Israelis
this man speaks. I know only that it would be an unforgivable mistake to ignore his opinion and an equally eggregious
error to assume that his word on religion in Israel is the
final one. So, up to this point we have a baffling, bewilder-
ing pattern of attitudes, ranging from vigorous antagonism
to total indifference, with overtones and undertows of nostalgic devotion.

What of the future? If it is difficult to assess the present,
how much more hazardous to predict the future! Yet there
are symptoms and signs—mostly little ones, to be sure—
which do give us at least some basis for educated speculation. Press reports indicate that the attendance of young
people in particular at High Holy Day Services in the synagogues of Israel is on the increase. Every guide I met on
both of my visits to Israel knew and quoted the Bible with
accuracy and ease. Most of them are scarcely less familiar
with Talmudic literature. On one fascinating half-hour taxi
ride from Tel-Aviv to the Weismann Institute in Rechovot
our driver, as soon as he learned of my profession, kept
firing Biblical quotations at me, asking whether I knew
how the rabbis had explained each passage in the Midrash.
And the important point is that he did know, in every
instance!

A young teacher of physics at the Leo Baeck School
sought me out after my lecture to the faculty, asking if we
could arrange to spend an additional evening together. We
did, at the home of Carl Alpert. He picked my brain there
for two hours on a modern theology which would be
consistent with the findings of science. His alleged justifica-

tion was that since he teaches in a school avowedly oriented toward religion, he owes his students a pedagogic obligation to learn more about religion, even though he himself is not disposed in that direction. One did not have to be a Freudian detective to recognize that this was probably a face-saving disguise, beneath which to smuggle in, as it were, a deeply-felt personal religious need.

I recall an interesting and fruitful conversation with Joseph Zimmerman, an erudite, ebullient editor. Before I left his apartment he said to me: "Haged-na li'y'huday Amerika—I urge you to tell the Jews of America—she-yaysh yehudim ma-a-minim gam po ba-aretz—that there are also Jews who have faith here in Israel." He was obviously not referring to the Orthodox element. It would be wishful thinking to exaggerate the number of those thus described by Zimmerman; it would be no less a violation of truth to deny that there are some.

Several years ago a traumatic incident occurred at *K'far Ha-no-ar Nitzonim*, one of numerous youth villages in Israel. Prior to that event, the prevailing flavor of the village had been anything but religious. It happened, however, that a youngster there was so shattered by the sudden death of his father that he attempted suicide and almost succeeded. This caused the leaders and teachers of the village to take stock of themselves. Is it possible, they began to wonder, that with all our careful concern we are failing these young people? Is it possible that they need, after all, a kind of spiritual anchorage that we haven't even attempted to give them? Out of these questions there emerged, first, a series of discussions, then a few experimental Religious Services at which attendance was purely voluntary. Today a Service is held every Shabbat at *K'far Ha-no-ar Nitzonim* —not an Orthodox or traditional Service, to be sure, but religious devotion nonetheless—and almost everyone at the village participates.

The literary journals published by two of the national groupings of *kibbutzim* reflect a similar questing. What they have published thus far—and I saw several of them—would not be labelled *religious* by any Orthodox rabbi, perhaps not even by most of my Reform colleagues in the Central Conference of American Rabbis. But it discloses—beyond the slightest possibility of doubt—a restiveness, a dissatisfaction, a seething, troubled search for something spiritual which has thus far evaded their grasp. I doubt very much whether that search will ever lead all the way back to what we would call traditional Judaism. I have a strong suspicion, however, that it will produce new formulae and forms of faith which will be legitimate issues of our Jewish past. My friend in Tel-Aviv is far from the only one in Israel for whom, so far at least, the State and Jewish survival have been enough for their ultimate loyalty. I insisted, whenever I had an opportunity to converse with such individuals, that no State—however noble in spirit or design—and the survival of no national group—however gifted or chosen—is deserving of man's ultimate loyalty. A small but significant number of Israelis have already begun to feel this way. I believe a larger number is destined to agree.

One more significant factor must be mentioned. Most of us have come to recognize that two components are essential to religion. To qualify as a religious person, one must have faith in a Creative Reality within the universe and one must translate that faith into ethical action. Perhaps part of the tension between the Jews of Israel and ourselves can be traced to the fact that each community has seized upon only one of these components, neglecting the other. True, our theology is more advanced and mature than theirs. But their collective conscience is superior to ours. One must be extremely cautious about applying the label *irreligious* to any group which demonstrates the tender concern for each individual, the willingness to sacrifice in order that more and more and more Jews be brought home, the passion in so many quarters for social righteousness and justice, which are so adundantly evident in Israel. What disturbs me about ourselves in America is that the Judaism we profess is so much nobler than the Judaism we live. What distresses me about the Jews of Israel is that, without an underpinning of deep and abiding faith, their admirable ethic may in the end prove to be evanescent.

If you insist on categorizing my estimate on the future of religion in Israel, call it cautious optimism. That optimism is based not only on the foregoing factors, but also on a strange mystique about which one can read all his life in volumes of Jewish thought, but which one can truly understand and feel only when visiting Israel. This is the mystique which, since the time of Abraham, has bound the Jewish people to one tiny corner of earth on the Mediterranean. No historian has ever been able to explain it purely on rational or empirical grounds. But the stubborn fact persists that the people of Israel and the land of Israel have a nearly magical effect on each other which is one of the root realities of human history. We do something for that land that no other folk on earth has ever even approximated. And that land evokes talents and capacities from us which no other place can educe.

One becomes acutely sensitive to this mystique when standing beneath the waterfall at *mayan David*, the mountain oasis in the *Negev* where the young shepherd destined to be king hid from the paranoic fury of Saul. Perhaps it was on this very spot that David sang some of his incomparable songs of faith. One partakes of the mystique when walking in the hills of Judea near Jerusalem. This is the very ground on which the prophets stood—this, the very air they breathed, the very heavens they scrutinized, when they achieved the closest, most intimate relationship to God that man has ever known. Something in me refuses to believe that the descendants of those prophets today, returned to the same place, studying nature in the same setting, will not eventually rediscover the same Reality. If the insight of our ancestors was valid, that there is Spiritual Reality at the heart of existence, then I have faith that this insight will be reconfirmed by the same people in the same place.

Rabbi Robert Samuels, who has done superb work as a teacher at the Baeck School and as founder of the new Progressive congregation in Haifa, told me of an incident which may symbolize the future of religion in Israel. During the first High Holy Day Services held by his congregation, a man of limited learning was called to the Torah for an *aliyah*. He stood before the Scroll awkwardly, not knowing what to do or say. It was obvious that he didn't know the words of the traditional *b'racha*. But before anyone could even come to his rescue, he looked upward, and with almost childish simplicity said: "Ani mo-deh l'cha, elohim, al ha-hiz-dam-nut ha-zu—I thank you, O God, for this opportunity!"

These were not the words of tradition, were they? Yet they expressed the elemental joy of the Jew over the Torah far more eloquently than many a mumbled recitation by rote of the words which are accepted as correct. Many among the Jews of Israel today are as awkward religiously as that man. Either they have forgotten the exact words of tradition or they are unable to repeat them. But their minds and hearts are at least beginning to search for an abiding relationship with the universe. No one can predict exactly what words they will eventually speak. Yet I have confidence that, because they are Jews, and because theirs is the land of holiness, they too will find God.

II

Let us turn now from Jewish religion in general to its Reform variant. Is there a realistic prospect that Reform Judaism will take root and grow in Israel? This depends very much on what the questioner has in mind. If he means a carbon copy of American Reform Judaism, no. The Reform synagogue in the United States emerged from the effort to adapt Judaism to the unique circumstances and conditions here. Any attempt to transplant this particular adaptation to a totally different environment would be foredoomed to fail.

As a matter of fact, it would be wise to refrain from using the label Reform in Israel. The image of Reform in that country is anything but positive. Lamentably—but truthfully—the only thing the average Israeli knows about American Reform is that in the nineteenth and early twentieth centuries our movement was violently opposed to Zionism. For every Israeli who knows that Abba Hillel Silver was a Reform rabbi, there are five hundred who have not forgotten that Morris Lazaron and Elmer Berger are also. To insist on the use of our particular term would be pejorative in the extreme; it would necessitate the diversion of far too much energy from our constructive tasks to apologetics and defense.

In any event, the distinction between Reform and Conservative Judaism—whatever its validity here—is entirely without meaning in Israel. Both branches there would worship only in Hebrew, wearing *kipot,* with men and women seated together. Both would most probably use musical instruments of one kind or another as liturgical accompaniment and would be selective in their acceptance of *halachah.* The only religious division that makes sense in Israel is that between Orthodox and non-Orthodox Judaism. It would be better, therefore, to speak there of Liberal or Progressive rather than Conservative or Reform Judaism.

How much interest do Israelis have in non-Orthodoxy? A considerable amount of interest, based on abysmal quantities of ignorance. When in Israel, I make it my business to engage in lengthy conversation with just about every taxi driver I encounter. I find this an excellent means to take the pulse of the average citizen. So, shortly after announcing my destination, I always inform my driver that I am an American Reform rabbi, then sit back to await his reaction.

It is almost invariably uniform. A surreptitious glance in the mirror to see whether I am joking, then an immediate flood of questions, then a pronouncement of tremendous need in Israel for something like what I apparently represent. The questions are repeated by driver after driver, almost as if they had all met in advance to coordinate their curiosity. Do Reform Jews ride and/or write and/or smoke on Shabbat? Do we wear *kipot* when we pray? Do we accept converts to Judaism? Where do we derive the authority to reject substantial parts of traditional talmudic law? And so on and on, the number of questions depending only on the distance of my destination.

Again and again these drivers have told me that most young Israelis are fleeing from their faith, that only an implementation of principles similar to ours could possibly save them. One cabbie said that he had seen the Hebrew

Union College building in Jerusalem from the outside, that he was anxious to attend Services there the next time he happened to be in Jerusalem on Shabbat, that he was prepared to accept them provided they did not too closely resemble Christian Church Services. A driver who had come from Egypt some seven or eight years before once severely berated Rabbi Rudin and myself because our movement, in his judgment, has not been anywhere near vigorous or aggressive enough in establishing Israel congregations.

A young leader in the new desert industrial town of Arad had just been boasting of the fact that so far they had succeeded in having only one synagogue in the community, when he learned of our professional identification. At once he reversed himself, saying that the only circumstance under which he would gladly welcome a second synagogue would be if a Liberal group were to be established. I think I know what must be coursing through some of your minds at this point, so let me assure you: if you suspect that these reactions were prompted only by courtesy to tourists, you don't know Israelis; for good or for bad, they just aren't that polite!

On two evenings a few years ago I delivered English lectures on non-Orthodox Judaism under the auspices of the new Progressive congregation in Haifa. Every one of the approximately one-hundred-fifty chairs in the hall was filled, the second night against odds which included miserable weather, a dance recital by Inbal, and a concert of the Israel Philharmonic. I was told later that my audience had included a professor of languages at Technion, two nuclear physicists, a government inspector of schools, a number of physicians and several psychiatrists.

It would be a mistake, however, to assume that all the

interest of Israelis in non-Orthodox Judaism is favorable. Two young men who had spent a semester in the United States as exchange students, living in Reform homes, illustrated the divergence of opinion. One told me that from his observations American Reform Judaism is shallow, superficial, not genuinely religious, and has little hope for survival. The other was so impressed here that he wants to study at the Hebrew Union College and become a Liberal rabbi himself. I was told that when he first returned from the United States, he said to his classmates: "You think the Reform Jews of America will become assimilated? You'll be lost to assimilation before they will!"

So, there are two sides to the interest one finds in Israel. Beneath both is a substratum of genuine concern, most of it inchoate, amorphous, unchannelled. How about organized effort and accomplishment?

There are seven Liberal congregations in existence today under Reform auspices, several others affiliated with Conservative Judaism. Both American and Israel natives are among the graduates of the Hebrew Union College—Jewish Institute of Religion functioning in Israel as Liberal rabbis.

The story of the Haifa congregation is most illuminating. In the fall of 1964, some three or four weeks before Rosh Hashanah, Rabbi Robert Samuels inserted a modest ad in several newspapers. In it he invited anyone who would be interested in Liberal Services for the High Holy Days to contact him at a given number. Enough people responded, without benefit of pressure or even reminder, so that a hall seating about two hundred was rented. On Rosh Hashanah there were three hundred worshippers in attendance; for Kol Nidre night the congregation exceeded six hundred!

A similar response occurred in the fall of 1968. For three

years the Liberal Congregation in Ramat Gan had been holding its Services in a basement room whose capacity was under 100. With considerable trepidation the congregational leaders rented the largest theatre in the community for the High Holy Days. On the one hand, they felt strongly that with adequate facilities a large number of people could be attracted to worship with them. On the other hand, what would be the psychological damage—to themselves and their cause—if most of the seats remained empty? The best way to report the result is in the following terse excerpts from Rabbi Toviah Ben Chorin's summary:

"The success was beyond any optimistic expectations. Participation increased from day to day. First Rosh Hashanah eve, 500 participants. Second day, morning Service reached the peak of 800. Kol Nidre—over 1000. Help of police needed to turn people away at the door for lack of seats. Neilah—over 1200. Hundreds of young persons during the Service, with and without parents. Initial response, overwhelming. We are definitely the talk of Ramat Gan. . . ."

It would be naive to suppose that all those who were willing to benefit from these opportunities are ready to assume the responsibilities attendant upon organizing and maintaining a permanent congregation. But enough were so that congregations have been established in both communities, Services are held each Friday evening, and plans are already being discussed for permanent homes.

Where are we, then, in our survey of Liberal Judaism in Israel? We have taken note of much interest, ranging from bold antagonism through mild curiosity to enthusiastic experimentation. And we have outlined—all too briefly—the present progress of our organized effort toward the establishment of Liberal Judaism there. This brings us to the most important aspect of our concern. What are the prospects for the future?

The war for Liberal Judaism in Israel will have to be fought on two fronts. One will be against a rigid, intransigent Orthodoxy which, at least for the present, shares the reins of political power. The other will be against those who, for a variety of reasons, have no use for any kind of religion. The excruciating part of the battles ahead is that they will have to be waged simultaneously on both fronts, but with altogether different kinds of ammunition and tactics.

There will be two fronts on which to fight, and two formidable obstacles to victory on both. The first is the Orthodox fanaticism just mentioned. For more than a month after its first High Holy Days, the Haifa congregation was forced to hold its Shabbat Service in a different place each week because, no sooner did they find a room or hall to rent, than pressure was brought on the owner to withdraw it. Finally a permanent place was located. A revolutionary decision of the Israeli Supreme Court was necessary before the city of *K'far Sh'maryahu* was forced to extend the use of its public facilities to its Liberal congregation. In *Ramat Gan*, after an apartment had been purchased for use of the congregation, fanatical neighbors obtained a court injunction to prevent the remodelling necessary to accommodate those who wished to worship there.

When the *Ramat Gan* group persisted in convening its Services while awaiting final disposition of the injunction, opponents cut off the electricity, played their radios in surrounding apartments at top volume as a rude distraction, and placed hoses across the walk so that those who had come to pray would get wet as they attempted to enter! All this, believe it or not, undertaken by Jews against other Jews for the unforgivable offense of wishing to worship God! These are not pleasant or comfortable things to acknowledge, but they are facts, and our only hope of succeeding in Israel or anywhere else is by acknowledging the facts.

The temper of Orthodox opposition can be best judged by relating a devastating incident which took place during the summer of 1964 in Haifa's Dan Carmel Hotel. A delegation from the National Federation of Temple Sisterhoods was visiting. Rabbi and Mrs. Maurice Eisendrath were with them. Rabbi Samuels had arranged a Shabbat Religious Service in the hotel, to be followed by a beautiful, inspiring Oneg Shabbat program, performed by students of the Leo Baeck High School.

When the youngsters involved walked into the lobby, carrying their accordion, they were accosted by two Orthodox rabbis, who forbade them from proceeding to the assigned room. The point at issue was the accordion. It could not be played on Shabbat! Without it, the program was impossible. The manager of the hotel was sympathetic to Rabbi Samuels, but he explained that if he persisted, the hotel would lose its *hechshar*. So the Oneg Shabbat was cancelled. It was better to ignore the Sabbath entirely than to celebrate it with religious song and dance. There, in an ugly nutshell, is the first obstacle.

The second is money. It goes without saying that the location of premises for worship and prosecution of lengthy legal proceedings to secure full and uninterrupted use of those premises will be expensive. But the needs are even greater than I have thus far suggested. You see, when any group of Orthodox Jews wants to build a synagogue in Israel, they apply for government aid. The matter is referred to the Ministry of Religions and, if it is ascertained that in fact the community in question can make use of an additional synagogue, funds for its construction and for the salary of its rabbi are then supplied by the government.

Need I spell out the probability of a Liberal congregation's receiving such favorable consideration from a Ministry which is dominated by precisely the Orthodox fanaticism already described? Our congregations will have to be established with private moneys. And the people of Israel today, with the rarest of exceptions, don't begin to have that kind of money. Their incomes are modest, their taxes are colossal, and they receive no tax deductions for contributions of this kind! The World Union for Progressive Judaism, aside from some small sums supplied to the Leo Baeck School, last year gave $50,000 for the support of Liberal congregations in Israel. Compared to what had been given in previous years, that sum represented appreciable improvement. Compared to the real need, it isn't even peanuts!

If we had money enough and properly qualified rabbis enough, we could have a dozen or more thriving Liberal congregations in Israel. Until we have several dozens, we cannot hope to undertake the effort which will eventually be needed to break the Orthodox monopoly on performance of wedding and burial ceremonies.

On my last visit I had lunch one day with a member of the *K'nesset*, Israel's Parliament. He is himself a Liberal Jew, most anxious to aid on the legal front. I asked him if there was any possibility of our winning that aspect of the struggle. He replied: "Yes, it can and will be won, when there are enough adherents of Liberal Judaism in the country to arrest the attention of politicians. No politician," he added with refreshing realism, "will be favorably disposed until he has enough of a constituency who really care, to make his efforts in this direction politically profitable."

Time now to sum up. The possibilities for Liberal Judaism in Israel are hopeful. The obstacles to be overcome are frightening. The final resolution in this delicate, precarious balance depends on us. We who call ourselves Reform or Conservative Jews in America must find a way—without presuming to dictate to Israel's Liberal Jews what they should do—of supplying them with the sinew and muscle without which their cause is hopeless.

What this really means is that we are the ones being tested. The most crucial question, on which all else will depend, is how much Liberal Judaism means to us. Is it just something about which to brag and boast—just a device to channel our hostility and aggression against other Jews for their stubbornness? Or is it an interpretation of the Jewish way of life in which we believe so firmly that we live it ourselves and for which we are willing to make substantial sacrifice to the end that it may take root and flourish in Israel too? If we do not honestly mean business, if we do not take Liberal Judaism seriously enough ourselves, we have no moral right either to criticize the Orthodox Jews of Israel or to encourage and goad the brave little band which is willing, at considerable risk, to challenge the religious establishment.

My wife and I were privileged to attend the very first Bar Mitzvah ceremony ever held at the Haifa congregation. If I live to a hundred, I shall never forget the face of that boy. It was a round, eager, friendly, loving face—punctuated with unJewish freckles and topped by blond allegedly Aryan hair. As Rabbi Samuels stood with him before the congregation, speaking to him personally in Hebrew about the significance of the day and the nature of the responsibilities he was taking upon himself, the boy smiled back eagerly, nodding his head in vigorous agreement point by point. There were tears in my eyes and rich, deep pride in my heart by the time the moment of blessing was reached. That boy's face symbolizes for me the expectations and needs of Israel's Liberal Jews. I have asked myself numerous times, and feel constrained to ask you now, whether we mean to uphold his hands or let him down.

BETWEEN CHRISTIANS
AND JEWS

24

What Every Christian Should Know About Judaism

You will forgive me, I hope, for saying that much of the activity conducted throughout the nation during Brotherhood Week is both superficial and shallow. Merely to sit down once each year for the purpose of breaking bread together, to mouth pious platitudes which camouflage hypocrisy more often than they stimulate genuine understanding, is not the way to commemorate or to promote real brotherhood. There are, in my judgment, only two types of meeting which fully serve the purpose of this week. One is a gathering of Christians and Jews, of white men and black, who are intent upon working together for some common cause which transcends without obliterating or denying their differences. The second is a meeting to which one group comes for the express purpose of learning more about another.

I hope here to accomplish the second of these functions by addressing myself to a few of the questions Christians ask most frequently about Judaism. If, in the course of so doing, I can teach some Jews also things they had not known or had forgotten about their own faith, so much the better; this will be an extra dividend, so to speak, on my sermonic investment. What, then, are some of the things every Christian should know about Judaism?

First, that it is a religion of never-ending evolution and growth. This comes close to what is perhaps the most common of all Christian misconceptions about Judaism, namely, that our faith reached a dead-end in its development some two thousand years ago, from which it has never extricated itself. The corollary of this notion in Christian thinking is that Christianity took up where Judaism left off, that Christianity represents in a sense the logical fulfillment of truncated Judaism. Among Catholics and other orthodox Christians, this idea actually takes the form of referring to Abraham often as Father Abraham and of considering themselves to be the only true exponents today of what Judaism was meant to be in its beginnings. In short, many non-Jews believe that Judaism became stagnant and congealed; that its purpose on the stage of history was only to prepare the way for Christianity and, once having accomplished that purpose, it became a petrified remnant of the past. Arnold Toynbee has given this notion a certain academic elegance by referring to Judaism as a fossil.

Nothing could be farther from the truth. Judaism is not a lifeless, leafless stump; it is the trunk which has yielded many fruitful branches, the several forms of Christianity among them, but which has never stopped growing itself. Judaism is a contemporary of present-day Christianity, not just its antecedent. Judaism never terminated its evolutionary development either before or since the time of Jesus. It has always been and still remains a religion of growth.

Let me illustrate on the literary level. The Bible itself— our Jewish Bible—is a good example. The Bible, properly understood, represents not one static point in the development of ancient Jewish religious thought, but a whole series of points charting a steady course of development and maturation. We sometimes forget that the documents comprising our Bible were some ten to fifteen centuries in the making. They reflect a wide variety of religious opinion extending over a period of a thousand to fifteen hundred years. There were of necessity many changes during that time, changes which reflect themselves now in disagreements and inconsistencies within the written record. To select any one passage from that record as an illustration of ancient Jewish thought is therefore without meaning unless we can establish from which part of the biblical period it comes and whether it represents an early, tentative conclusion or a more definitive and mature doctrine. The Judaism of Abraham and that of second Isaiah differ from each other profoundly. To assume they are the same is nonsense.

It must be added here that even after the Bible itself became finalized at about the end of the first century, so that nothing could be added to it or subtracted from it, the way was always kept open for further change within Judaism. The rabbis then developed what has become known as the Oral Law, through which biblical provisions were explained and, where necessary, amended. When this Oral Law had been reduced to writing at about the year 200 in the form of the Mishnah, Judaism was still kept flexible and pliant through the Gemara, a fantastically wide-ranging series of further discussions and decisions. The Mishnah and Gemara together constituted the Talmud, which was completed roughly in the year 500. And from that time to this the precepts and laws of Judaism have been extended and revised in every century by talmudic commentaries and by the speculations of philosophers and theologians like Maimonides and Achad-Ha-am and Mordecai Kaplan.

This is the first important truth, then, for every intelligent Christian to remember about Judaism: that it is a faith as old as Abraham and as young as tomorrow; that it has never failed to keep up with the times; that it has abdicated neither its original purpose nor its final destiny to any other faith. Once this has been firmly grasped and clearly understood, it should be relatively easy to comprehend the additional items every Christian should know about our faith.

The second is that the ethic of Christianity is in no way superior to that of Judaism. If this sounds either apologetic or chauvinistic, let me remind you that the assumption of many Christians is to the contrary. Again and again we Jews hear the highest moral values of civilization referred to as Christian ideals, when what is really meant are Jewish ideals which were subsequently adopted by Christianity. Make no mistake about the nature of our complaint. We are happy and honored that our people's loftiest teachings have become so universal a possession of mankind. But we are also just human enough ourselves to appreciate and desire the credit which should follow upon accurate identification of those teachings. We are weary of hearing references to a lower level of ethics in our Bible having been superseded by presumably nobler ethics in the New Testament.

To some extent this misunderstanding about the relative merit of Jewish and Christian ideals has already been clarified by my comment on the evolutionary development of moral sensitivity within the biblical tradition of Judaism. This matter is so very crucial, however, that it deserves more specific attention on its own. Let me use as my illustration the common misconception that our Jewish ethic is accurately reflected by "a life for a life, a tooth for a tooth, an eye for an eye." This, we are told, is a doctrine of vindictiveness, compared to which Christianity teaches a philosophy of forgiveness.

Now what are the facts? First, that when the idea of an eye for an eye was first promulgated it represented a considerable ethical improvement over the prevailing practices of the time. It was common procedure then for a man whose eye had been injured even accidentally to revenge himself by blinding both eyes of his suspected assailant. It was quite the usual thing for the relatives of a man who had been killed to seek the life not only of the suspected murderer but indeed of his entire family. The ethic of the Jewish Bible was, therefore, from the beginning one of restraint. It taught that the punishment was to fit the crime; that, even when guilty, a man must be made to suffer for no more than the crime which he had in fact committed.

Just how substantial an ethical improvement this was more than three thousand years ago can clearly be seen if we bear in mind that in England as recently as the year 1700, men and women were put to death for stealing property worth slightly more than a shilling! So the first thing to understand about the doctrine of "an eye for an eye" is that at the time it was first proclaimed it represented ethical growth far beyond the level of common acceptance among other peoples.

The second thing to keep clearly in mind is that even before the close of the biblical period, Judaism had grown far beyond a literal interpretation of this equation. For the Talmud makes it quite explicit that only financial compensation is here intended. The real meaning of the passage is that an individual who has lost an eye or a tooth or a life is to be compensated financially for the precise damage suffered. This obviously is the basis of our whole modern law of damages. And this places the ethical attainment of Judaism in proper perspective.

We ought never to forget, moreover, that the same Hebrew Bible which speaks of an eye for an eye also commands: "If thine enemy be hungry, give him bread to eat, and if he be thirsty, give him water to drink." We ought remember that the God of Love taught by Jesus had been anticipated by Hosea eight centuries earlier. We ought keep in mind that the most exalted of all the teachings of Jesus—thou shalt love thy neighbor as thyself—was not originated by him but rather quoted by him from the Hebrew book of Leviticus, written perhaps a millennium before his generation.

How refreshing it is when, on occasions all too rare, Christians do remember this. Those of you who have visited the Cathedral of the Pines in Rindge, New Hampshire will remember that the two commandments given highest priority by Jesus are chiseled into the stones which mark both sides of the entrance. I recall the day when Douglas Sloane, the Cathedral's founder, first approached me with the request that I obtain for him stencils which would enable him to have the Hebrew original of these words cut on the stones together with the English, because, he said: "I want every Christian who enters this Cathedral to know where these teachings of our Christian faith come from." I have had the experience, standing near these stones, of hearing one Christian explain to another that Dr. Sloane had these commandments translated from English into Hebrew, if you please, so that Jews would know what they said too! Well, perhaps now you understand better than at the beginning why the second thing worth emphasizing for Christians about Judaism is the fact that our ethics require no apology or defense.

Since time allows for only one more truth about Judaism, let me choose the fact that Judaism is a religion of deed more than of creed. This is a matter which has been inadequately appreciated even by a good many Jews. Judaism is an intensely practical religion, perhaps in some respects almost a pragmatic religion. There is less pure theological speculation in Judaism and more concentration on ethical directives than in any other religion with which I am familiar. There are fewer pages than in any other faith devoted to philosophic argument or inquiry on the nature of God. A theological disputation on the number of angels that could be accommodated on the point of a pin, by no means an imaginary topic of concern for non-Jews in the Middle Ages, would have been utterly unthinkable for Jews. This does not mean that Judaism for a single moment minimizes the immeasurable importance of God or of belief in God. It means rather that we assume the existence of God; that we assume, moreover, our human incapacity to understand at best more than the tiniest fragment of what God is really like; and that we hasten from these assumptions to that which we can understand, namely, what does God want of us—what does our faith in God imply by way of human behavior?

This basic preoccupation of Judaism with conduct, this practical emphasis on deed rather than creed, this pre-eminent concentration on what God wants of us rather than what God is, can be illustrated in countless ways. Moses Maimonides, perhaps the greatest of all Jewish theologians, said in the twelfth century that it is possible to ascribe only negative attributes to God, not positive ones. He meant that man can comprehend and assert what God is not; exactly what God is, we cannot wholly comprehend. When the prophet undertook to summarize Judaism in a sentence, he began with the declaration: "It hath been told thee, O man, what is good and what the Lord doth require of thee." And he continued, not by saying, "to speculate endlessly on the nature of God," but by declaring: "to do justly, to love mercy, and to walk humbly with thy God." It would be by no means inaccurate to say that for Judaism only the man who has already learned to do justly and to love mercy and to walk humbly with his fellowman has the remotest chance of understanding God and walking with Him.

Rabbi Jochanan ben Zakkai may have been the most authentic Jew of the first century. He once came very close to expressing the essential heart of Judaism when he said: "If you are about to plant a tree, and someone tells you that the Messiah has come, finish your work and then go forth to meet the Messiah." Finish your work first; then go forth to meet the Messiah! The Talmud attributes to God Himself a pious wish that would be foreign, I suspect, to any religion except Judaism. It pictures God, saying of the Jewish people: "Would they might forget Me and keep My commandments!" It should be altogether unnecessary for me to assure you at this point that the rabbis who wrote the Talmud were not atheists. They simply understood, as Judaism always has, that the person who truly strives to live by God's ethical commandments will never be in danger of forgetting Him.

Here, then, are the three things I would select above all others for my Christian friends to know and to remember about Judaism. First, that ours is a changing, evolving religion, no less able to meet the spiritual needs of men and women today than it was two or three thousand years ago. Second, that the ethical values of this dynamic Judaism are equal to our noblest human insights. And third, that in

Judaism more important even than what we believe is how we act because of our beliefs.

If, even in some small way these paragraphs have helped us understand important truths about Judaism, I may dare to believe that a valid purpose of this Brotherhood Week has thereby been served.

25

Can Jews Accept Jesus?

This sermon is in answer to an article published three months ago by Norman Cousins, Editor of the *Saturday Review*. Entitled *The Jewishness of Jesus*, it appeared in the Rosh Hashanah issue of *American Judaism*. I knew the moment I had finished reading this piece that somewhere along the line I would have to comment on it from the pulpit. The delay from September to this night has been caused not by any reluctance on my part to speak, but rather by the fact that this Christmas week is the timeliest season for Christian and Jews to reflect on the similarities which unite them and the divergences which divide them.

Even before turning to a brief resumé of the article, one more introductory statement must be made to put my own attitude in proper perspective and to set my conscience at ease. Norman Cousins is one of the most spiritually sensitive, ethically dedicated human beings I have ever been privileged to know. However vigorously I may disagree with some of his approaches to Judaism or his views on Jesus, I feel nothing but deep affection for him as a friend and profound respect as a creative religious spirit. I would not want any of the following to be construed by him or by you as denigration of himself.

Having said that—and already I feel better for saying it

—let me remind you of Mr. Cousins' argument in the article under consideration. He begins by asserting what should be the obvious fact that Jesus was a Jew, as were the Apostles and his earliest followers. From this he proceeds to elaborate on the core-inconsistency in the customary Christian understanding of the Crucifixion. He calls it "perhaps the greatest single paradox in the history of Western religion." On the one hand is the theological doctrine that the time and manner of the Crucifixion were fore-ordained by God, that Jesus was meant to die exactly as he did in order to serve as a vicarious atonement for the sins of all who would believe in him. This is without any question a key premise of Christianity. Were it not for the Crucifixion and the events which allegedly surrounded and followed it, Christianity would not, indeed *could* not have come into being.

On the other hand is the oft-repeated Christian motif that his fellow-Jews were responsible for the death of Jesus, a guilt from which they can eventually absolve themselves only by accepting his divinity. These two views, Mr. Cousins correctly insists, are utterly irreconcilable. He writes: ". . . these two cries—'They killed our Lord!' and 'He died for our sins!' are basically at war with each other. The first assumes an active human free will. The second assumes an active divine determination. If Jesus died on the cross in order to purge man, then every act that leads up to it is essential, explicable, predetermined. In the same sense, if Christianity could not have come about without the Crucifixion, and if it was the will of God that Christianity should have been born in this way, then all the circumstances of the Crucifixion are part of a design, and the people who figured in the event, whatever their role, were carrying out the parts divinely assigned to them."

It follows that what Christians must do, if the "sense of spiritual community" for which Mr. Cousins pleads is to be attained, is to make up their minds that if indeed Jesus was crucified according to a divinely predestined plan, then at worst Jews must not be blamed for their alleged complicity in that plan; at best they should be congratulated for having served to that point at least as instruments of the divine will. In either event it becomes incumbent upon Christians to acknowledge that Jesus was born, lived and died as a Jew; and that the most precious ethical and spiritual insights of Christianity are inextricably rooted in Judaism. To quote Mr. Cousins directly: "It is by setting aside the reluctance to see Jesus as a Jew that a creative and compassionate basis can be found for Christianity's new approach to Judaism."

At once, then, he continues with the second aspect of his argument: "The same is equally true of Judaism in its approach to Christianity. . . . The modern synagogue can live openly and fully with Jesus. It can do more than take pride in the fact of his being and in his existence and his ideas and his claim on history. . . . If it will help the Christians to come to terms with the fact of Jesus as a Jew, so it may help Judaism to give way to the same fact of Jesus' Jewishness—openly, fully, freely, proudly." Thus does Mr. Cousins, having spoken his message to Christians, urge upon his fellow-Jews also an acceptance of Jesus. It is, obviously, to this second emphasis that I would now address myself.

When Jews are asked to open their hearts and minds to Jesus, the first question to be faced is: to which Jesus? Norman Cousins writes as if there were only one Jesus. The ineluctable historic fact is: there were three. The first, as we have already seen, was Jesus the Jew, or perhaps more accurately, Jesus the Reform Jew of nearly two millennia ago. The ethical imperatives of this Jesus were, of course, Jewish in origin. The God of Love concerning whom he preached so eloquently was recognized and acknowledged eight hundred years earlier by the prophet Hosea. The Golden Rule which he pronounced in affirmative form was issued negatively a generation before him by Hillel. When this Jesus was asked, "What is the first of all the commandments?" —he answered: "Here, O Israel, the Lord our God, the Lord is One: and thou shalt love the Lord Thy God with all thy heart and with all thy soul . . . this is the first commandment, and the second is like unto it: Thou shalt love thy neighbor as thyself. There is no commandment greater than these." Surely, there isn't a person here who needs to be reminded that Jesus was consciously quoting these words from the Hebrew Torah, a tradition which antedated his own career by many centuries.

More evidence could easily be given if it were needed. All of it would confirm the conclusion expressed even by so otherwise anti-Semitic a biblical scholar as Julius Wellhausen: "Jesus was not a Christian: he was a Jew, and, as a Jew, his life-story is that of one of the prominent men of the Jews of his time, while his teaching is Jewish teaching. . . ."

Now then, if this is the Jesus Mr. Cousins has in mind, his plea for Jews to accept him is, to say the least, superfluous. It amounts to urging that Jews should accept a carbon copy of Judaism when the original is already in their possession. Granted that Jesus was a particularly attractive personality and a most imaginative and effective teacher of these Jewish doctrines. The fact remains, however, that he originated none of them, that all of them were evolved and enunciated by the authentic teachers of Judaism long before he had ever been born. What have we to gain, then, by accepting them in the particular form enunciated by Jesus? How does the injunction to love our neighbors, as voiced by Jesus in the gospels, add anything to the original of that lofty challenge, as expressed earlier in Leviticus?

Let me reinforce my point additionally by way of analogy. Frederick Chopin, in his *Butterfly Etude*, composed a melody line of exceptional beauty. A hundred years later a composer whose name isn't even worth remembering took the exact notes of Chopin and made of them a popular song called "I'm Always Chasing Rainbows." Who deserves credit for this melody—Chopin or his imitator? To whom does it really belong? What kind of sense would it make to urge that a man who knows and appreciates Chopin should buy a recording of the popular song in order to hear his favorite melody?

I don't mean to suggest for a moment that Jesus was a cheap imitator like the man who musically chased rainbows. What I do mean is that he taught values and ideals which he learned from Judaism. Why, then, should Judaism go back to him to recapture that which it already possesses?

So much for the first Jesus, the one on whom Mr. Cousins concentrates. The second Jesus spoke in accents irreconcilably foreign to Judaism. He recommended celibacy, for example, as the noblest goal of human sexual conduct, specifically praising those who "make themselves eunuchs for the kingdom of heaven's sake." Judaism urges not sexual frustration but legitimate sexual fulfillment in marriage as God's purpose for human life. The second Jesus, in effect, taught that morality has nothing to do with politics, that the two are in altogether separate categories of experience. He said: "Give unto Caesar that which is Caesar's and unto God that which is God's." Judaism insists that morality enters into every area of life, including that of politics; that nothing belongs to Caesar unless first it has been consecrated by the values we associate with God.

The second Jesus castigated the rich purely because they were rich. In the parable of the rich man and Lazarus, the former inherits hell not because he has committed any evil but plainly and simply because he posseses wealth. This Jesus said: "Woe unto you that are rich, for ye have received your consolation; and woe unto you that are filled, for ye shall hunger." He also said: "It is easier for a camel to go through the eye of a needle than for a rich man to enter the kingdom of heaven." Judaism teaches that we must show prejudice against or favortism for neither the poor nor the rich but treat all men justly. Judaism implies that what counts is not whether a man has wealth, but (a) how did he obtain his wealth and (b) for what purposes does he use it?

Perhaps the most frequently quoted precept of the second Jesus is this: "Whosoever smiteth thee on thy right cheek, turn to him the other also. And if any . . . would take away thy coat, let him have thy cloak also." Thus did Jesus articulate his doctrine of non-resistance to evil, another emphasis completely contradictory to Judaism, which teaches that evil must always be resisted and justice always pursued. In the words of the late Dr. Joseph Klausner, perhaps the greatest Jewish interpreter of Jesus, "what room is there in the world for justice if we must extend both cheeks to our assailants and give the thief both cloak and coat?"

The second Jesus urged his followers to love their enemies. Judaism is far too realistic and sober a faith to endorse so psychologically impossible a precept as that. Judaism orders its adherents to help their enemies when they are in trouble, to rescue the animal of an enemy when it lies helplessly under a heavy burden. Judaism proclaims: "If thine enemy be hungry, give him bread to eat, and if he be thirsty, give him water to drink." But never would Judaism torture its adherents with guilt by expecting them to *love* their enemies!

The temptation is to go on and on. It would be easy to do so; the evidence in the form of direct quotation from Jesus is plentiful. But isn't this enough to identify the second Jesus? And to establish the utter inconsonance between his teachings and those of Judaism? Or, for that matter, the inconsistency between these precepts and his own when he speaks as the first Jesus? Which Jesus is it, then, which Mr. Cousins would want Jews to accept? If, as I strongly suspect, it is only the first, would he then, for the sake of the spiritual bridge he so yearningly seeks, ask Christians to relinquish the second? And if he did, is there any realistic probability they would do so? These are questions which come close to the essential heart of the matter.

The usual explanation for the antipathy of most Jews to the very name of Jesus is that they and their ancestors have been subjected to such inhuman suffering in his name. Perhaps there is another reason in addition to this. Perhaps the generations of Jews were perceptive enough, even if only by intuition, to recognize that so much of the teaching attributed to Jesus is the very antithesis of Judaism, the direct negation of what Judaism pronounced as valid. Obviously the problem is considerably more complicated than Mr. Cousins makes it out to be.

It becomes still more complicated when we remember that there is yet a third Jesus—the Christ. Though I devote only a passing paragraph to this Jesus, let it not be forgotten that for the overwhelming preponderance of Christians this Jesus outweighs by far the first and the second. This is the Jesus alleged to be God incarnate, born of a virgin, the fulfillment of Hebrew prophecy, the Messiah ordained by God, the second partner to the Trinity. This is the Jesus without whom, for all practical purposes, Christianity disintegrates for without him, Christianity becomes simply a branch of Judaism. I hesitate to be flippant on a matter so sacred to millions of my fellowmen, but I feel almost compelled to quote here the comment of Heine: "Christianity without Christ is like turtle soup without turtle." It's all very well to say that this third Jesus is not the historic one, that this one is a product of what later enthusiasts did to Jesus the Jew. But saying so doesn't alter the fact that for all but a very small fringe of Christians this is the Jesus who counts, the central figure of their faith.

I think I know Norman Cousins well enough to feel sure that he isn't asking us to accept the third Jesus. I'm not absolutely sure whether or not he would have us accept the second, though I suspect not. If, then, we agree to accept the first, would this lead to "the nourishment of reconciliation" for which Mr. Cousins pleads? I think not. In a paradoxical, almost a perverse way, it might in fact have the opposite effect. For this in reality would mean to ask that Christians "water down" Jesus to what many of them would consider a least-common-denominator. This would come perilously close to making the whole development of Christianity a superfluity based on distortion. I suspect that this—far from bringing Jews and Christians closer together in amity—might well exacerbate the existing enmity, fanning it into aggravated warfare.

Mr. Cousins' motives are beyond reproach. His spirit is

that of unbounded love for humanity, all humanity. He wants brotherhood and peace so passionately that I'm afraid he has used the materials of history and of fact too selectively to be valid. The real road to inter-religious harmony—a long, hard, often discouraging road, but one nonetheless worthy of our most intense effort—is for Jews to be the most devoted kind of Jews they can be and for Christians to strive toward understanding who Jesus really was and what he truly taught.

Can Jews accept Jesus? Only the first Jesus. Only the one who learned Judaism from his parents and rabbis and who preached it as he understood it, when he understood it. We can and do accept Jesus as a Jewish teacher, one among many teachers—as a magnetic personality, as an expert in the use of parables—one among many such experts whose words are recorded both in Bible and Talmud.

As for the amity Mr. Cousins so properly seeks, the late Rabbi Milton Steinberg pointed the only realistically hopeful way to achieve it. He asked: "Will the gap be filled? Will the two religions, mother and daughter, ever be reconciled?" And he answered: "Many . . . in both camps see no reason why the two faiths need coalesce. Let each be as pure and strong in its own character as it can. For the rest, there is need not for filling in gaps but for bridging them with mutual candor and understanding."

26

The Jewish Schema

One week ago today Vatican Council II at long last issued its substantive pronouncement on the Jews. Since the matter was first proposed there has been so much backing and filling, so many false starts and trial balloons, that the statement itself comes almost as an anti-climax. It represents nonetheless a move of major historic consequence and as such deserves the careful consideration of every thoughtful Christian and Jew. For three years I have resisted the temptation to speak publicly about a document which was still being formulated. Now that it stands completed, awaiting only *proforma* promulgation by Pope Paul VI, the time has come for pulpit comment.

Perhaps the place to begin is with the multiple convolutions and gyrations suffered by the schema since the Council began. When John XXIII first announced his intention to open the window, that fresh air might ventilate the ancient truths of his church, it was generally assumed that some attention would be given to the Catholic attitude toward our Jewish people and its faith. Notwithstanding this assumption, nothing of this nature was introduced at the first session in 1962. At the second session—the following fall—a strong resolution was proposed, absolving Jews, both past and present, of collective guilt in connection with the crucifixion of Jesus. No action was taken on that resolution.

Between the second and third sessions of the Council—which means to say, between the meetings of 1963 and those of 1964—a concerted effort by conservative forces within the hierarchy resulted in a watering down of the original wording and the addition of an offensive paragraph expressing the hope that all Jews would speedily convert to Catholicism. Before the third session reached its end, three important events transpired. The strong original wording about deicide was substantially restored; the offensive plea for conversion was excised, and the statement as a whole was adopted in principle by an impressively overwhelming vote. These improvements came about largely through the efforts of liberal American church leaders, among them Richard Cardinal Cushing.

But behind-the-scenes intrique and maneuver had not ended. Between the third and final sessions, all kinds of rumors and replies, of reports and counter-reports, filled the air. Pope Paul himself, despite the pronouncement already adopted in principle, acquitting Jews of complicity in connection with the death of Jesus, preached a sermon on Passion Sunday last April in which old indictment was revived. Speaking of the Jewish people at the time of Jesus and their attitude toward him, the Pope said they "not only did not recognize him, but fought him, slandered and injured him; and, in the end, killed him." Efforts to explain this astounding accusation as an unfortunate slip of the tongue or an attempt to address simple people in simple words proved less than convincing. Many religious liberals —Catholic and non-Catholic alike—feared that the pontiff was deliberately trying to move his Council toward a more ambiguous and less effective position than it had seemed ready to embrace.

Probably no one will ever know the full story of the pressures exerted by the Pope and on the Pope in the last few weeks. The final outcome was revealed in the statement overwhelmingly adopted last Friday. It was a disappointing document in two respects. First, where earlier versions had both deplored and condemned anti-Semitism, this one merely deplores it. I want to be both honest and fair in commenting on that change. I strongly suspect that if the word *condemn* had not appeared in public print previously, if the 1964 draft had also just *deplored* anti-Semitism, no one would be bothered now about the use of one word rather than both. In any event, though I too would have been happier with the original stronger verbiage, I am not disposed to argue it.

The second cause for disappointment, however, is far more serious. The draft circulated to the Council on 8 November 1963 by Cardinal Bea's Commission clearly and unmistakably removed from us Jews every taint of guilt for the crucifixion. An official Vatican communique summarized its content as follows: "The responsibility for Christ's death falls upon sinful mankind and not upon the Jews. 'Therefore, it is unjust to accuse this people of deicide or to consider it cursed of God.'"

The amended phrasing now adopted is far more hedging and equivocal. It eliminates the word *deicide* altogether and reads: "Although the Jewish authorities and those who followed their lead pressed for the death of Christ, nevertheless what happened to Christ in his Passion cannot be attributed to all Jews, without distinction, then alive, nor to the Jews of today." It then continues: "Although the Church is the new people of God, the Jews should not be presented as rejected by God or accursed, as if this follows from Holy Scriptures."

Here we have far more than just an insignificant choice of vocabulary; nor is our strong Jewish objection to this change an instance of quibbling. Authorities on anti-Semitism are agreed that the seminal cause of this extremely complex form of prejudice—the root cause from which most other causes flow and for which they are often only clever rationalizations—is the alleged complicity of the Jews in the tragedy which befell the Christian saviour. The first time the average impressionable Christian child even hears the word *Jew* is in connection with the death of Jesus. His first emotional impression of Jews, therefore, is of a people that brutally killed God's son, if not God Himself. Until this cause of anti-Semitism is effectively extirpated, all other moves will be nothing more than a superficial nibbling away at the edges.

Several Protestant church bodies have done a far more thorough job on this crucial matter than did the current Vatican Council. Back in December of 1961 the World Council of Churches referred to the blame for the crucifixion in terms of "responsibilities which belong to our corporate humanity and not to one race or community." The 61st General Convention of the Protestant Episcopal Church adopted a pronouncement which included these words: "The charge of deicide against the Jews is a tragic misunderstanding of the inner significance of the crucifixion . . . . . all men are guilty of the death of Christ, for all have in some manner denied Him; and since the sins that crucified Christ were common human sins, the Christian knows that he himself is guilty."

Compared to such acknowledgments as these, that of the Vatican Council is a timid half-step forward where history demands a gigantic leap. It accepts and confirms the historically doubtful complicity of *the Jews* in the murder of Jesus by attributing his death to "the Jewish authorities and those who followed their lead," making no mention at all of Romans. The clear implication here is that only the exceptional Jewish contemporary of Jesus can be absolved of guilt. There is, I submit, a collosal difference between saying that Jews should be exonerated of this crime because they did not commit it, and saying instead that they should be exonerated even though they did it. The Pope and his Council, by choosing the second of these alternatives, have missed a rare historic opportunity to achieve greatness.

Let me interrupt the main line of my argument at this point with an important parenthesis. It would be unfair to criticize the changes incorporated in this final version without acknowledging that in one respect it is an improvement. Speaking of the Jews, the draft under Council scrutiny a year ago contained these words ". . . the Church expects in unshakeable faith and with ardent desire the entrance of that people into the fullness of the people of God established by Christ.

"Everyone should be careful, therefore, not to expose the Jewish people as a rejected nation, etc., etc., etc." This was as rash and naked an appeal for conversion of all Jews to Catholicism as modern religious literature can yield. It insinuated, moreover, that the chief reason Jews are to be treated decently is in order to make them more amenable to the missionary enterprise. Last week's statement has been changed in this respect to read: "In company with the Prophets and Paul, the Apostle, the Church awaits that day, known to God alone, on which all peoples will address the Lord in a single voice . . ." The oblique reference to Paul makes it clear that the bishops haven't really changed their minds in substance on the ultimate conversion of all Jews, but at least they have phrased their hope in more acceptable and less offensive language. End of parenthesis; resumption of my main argument.

Where do we go from here? Next Thursday Paul VI will promulgate the Council statement, thus making it official Catholic doctrine. How much good will it accomplish? What can we Jews reasonably expect by way of favorable results?

Let me commence my answers to these questions by urging that our understandable disappointment with some aspects of the current declaration should not blind us to the fact that potentially it marks considerable improvement. It is no small matter when the Roman Catholic Church publicly declares that other religions too reflect a ray of truth; and that whatever of sanctity or value inheres in other faiths is to be cherished. It is no minor or ephemoral accomplishment when the highest authorities of Catholicism, speaking of those who adhere to other religious denominations, call upon their own people to "recognize, preserve and promote those spiritual and moral goods as well as those socio-cultural values found among these men." We must not minimize the immense importance of more than two thousand bishops' declaring that their church "deplores hatred, persecution, displays of anti-Semitism directed against Jews at any time and by anyone." These confessions and declamations can lead to tremendous steps forward. They can . . . but will they? That depends on several crucial conditions.

First, the Pope must make up his own mind, then help his subordinates to make up theirs, whether we Jews are or are not guilty of the Crucifixion. The truth can not be shared by both sides of the argument. It will not do to announce in

December that our ancestors collectively did not kill Jesus, then to preach in April that they did. It makes no sense to assert that there is no corporate guilt for the crucifixion, then to repeat the canard of the Gospels that "the Jewish authorities and those who followed their lead" were in fact guilty. If the highest Vatican authorities have so much difficulty making up their minds, what can we reasonably expect from the relatively unsophisticated parish priest in South Boston?

Nor will it suffice to rely only on soothing and sweet-sounding generalities, such as urging Catholics not to "teach anything that is inconsistent with the truth of the Gospel." It was precisely the Gospel—especially that according to John—which originated the gross anti-Jewish libel from which the church is now painfully and valiantly struggling to extricate itself. The Gospel itself is impossibly ambivalent about Jews—on the one hand exhorting its readers to love them, on the other hand branding the Jews as crass murderers. So, the first condition, if the potential good within the new ecumenical spirit is to be realized, is that Christendom must once and for all decide whether we Jews are innocent or guilty of the Crucifixion.

The second is that Christians must stand ready to accept us for what we are and intend to continue being, not for what they would like us to become. Fortunately the final pronouncement of the Council couches the hope that all Jews will ultimately convert to Catholicism more subtly and less offensively than did an earlier draft. But the hope is there nonetheless. And even though it is conceded that God has not rejected us Jews, the reason given for His continued love is anything but comforting. After reminding their communicants that their own faith originated in Judaism, and that Jews as a whole did not accept either the

Gospel or the Christ, the bishops then continue: "Nevertheless, God holds the Jews most dear for the sake of the
Fathers . . ." Compared to church doctrine in the past, this
is an improvement. But as a modern Jew I do not want to
be told that God cherishes me only because of the biological accident that I happen to be descended from the patri-
archs. I am a Jew today—not four thousand years ago. And
he who truly wants me as his brother must accept me as a
practicing Jew today and my grandchildren as practicing
Jews tomorrow. In short, I insist on being accepted or
rejected as a Jew, not a potential Christian.

If I appear to be somewhat sensitive on this point, there is
alarming historic justification. The participants in Vatican
Council II are not the first to predicate their professed love
of me on the hope that I would eventually convert to their
interpretation of truth. Both Mohammed and Martin Luther began their careers of spiritual rebellion by saying
favorable things about Jews. Both obviously were motivated by the hope that their honeyed words would induce
our ancestors to convert. And both, when they realized that
hope was vain, became vicious anti-Semites. There is ample
precedent, then, for my refusal to be accepted only as grist
for the Christian conversionary mill.

The third condition for genuine ecumenism is a logical
and practical extension of the first two. Once the highest
levels of Catholic authority have made up their minds
where we stand, they must then work out a host of mechanisms and devices to communicate their intentions to every
local parish priest and through them, to every Catholic
man, woman and especially child. This means, specifically,
either the elimination or the drastic revision of the Passion
Plays presented annually throughout the world. It does no
good to urge brotherhood toward Jews and then each year

to incite against them—through emotionally loaded drama —the ugliest, most inflamed kind of hatred. There must also be a thorough reappraisal of every textbook and catechism used in church instruction, a task which happily the churches, both Protestant and Catholic, have already begun. The church must also publish a variety of manuals and teachers' aids, indicating precisely how the Gospel stories are to be taught so that their message of love will come through, not their encouragement to hate.

It is not presumption which prompts me to make these specific and detailed suggestions, but rather an honest recognition of the fact that words themselves—even the most eloquently pious and poetic of words—are meaningless hypocrisy unless they be implemented by deed. There is rich promise in the Jewish Schema, despite our deep disappointment in certain last-minute changes. That promise can be fulfilled only if conditions such as the three I have detailed are realized.

Am I implying that the entire responsibility rests on Christians? Not at all. The initial and primary obligation is theirs, for the simple reason that it is they who have been guilty of anti-Semitism for nearly twenty centuries. But unless we Jews meet initiative with response, nothing will be accomplished.

Let us be as honest with ourselves as we want Christians to be. There is a latent anti-Catholicism among Jews. We all know the historic reasons for such animosity. When the Council recommends: "This synod urges all to forget the past,"—this is easier said than done. The dark shadow of persecution and pogrom, of Inquisition and crematoria and Crusade, cannot be expunged from either memory or conscience by the mere waving of a wand. But the Catholic Church today is not the Catholic Church of medieval times, nor even the Catholic Church of Nazi Europe. Something new is stirring restlessly even in the bosom of this most stolid and conservative of organized faiths. There are tensions and conflicts and birth-pains within the church itself. We Jews may not be able quickly and completely to forget the past, but we must realistically and graciously face the future.

At a time when increasing numbers of Catholics are at least exploring the possibility of visiting the Religious Services of other denominations, when there are even a few Catholic priests who will preach from other pulpits, it is discouraging to read that some of the Orthodox Jews who were invited to meet Pope Paul in New York refused to enter the church, but sat instead in an adjoining library. Ecumenism is a two-way road or it is nothing. We Jews have our share of obligation too.

That obligation includes the pressing need to know more and care more about our own faith. The more successful the ecumenical movement becomes, the greater will be the temptation for Jews who know little or nothing about Judaism to desert their own heritage. When the outer walls of prejudice dissolve, only an inner strength of conviction can assure the meaningful survival of Judaism. As he ventures forth to meet men of other religious persuasions, to become acquainted with them as persons and with their thoughts and beliefs, the Jew owes himself and the world intimate knowledge of his own traditions. We cannot come to the world empty-handed. We must offer mankind more than just ourselves as persons. We possess a precious heritage. Only if we know it and cherish it ourselves can our lives be strengthened and civilization be enriched.

Here, then, is the Jewish Schema as the Jew sees it. We regret the fact that it has been weakened; we rejoice in the strengths it still contains; we earnestly hope its full potential for good will be realized. We call upon both Christians and Jews to fulfill their respective responsibilities toward this end. We would remind all men, in the words of the Schema itself, that neither ambiguity nor reservation can be allowed to tarnish the bright promise of the ecumenical challenge: "We cannot call on God, the Father of all, if we refuse to treat in a brotherly way any man, created as he is in the image of God. Man's relation to God the Father and his relation to men his brothers are so linked together that Scripture says: 'He who does not love does not know God.'"

27

Ground Rules for Good Will

In a very short time now Brotherhood Week will be with us again. Many of you know from former years that my attitudes toward this annual observance are ambivalent. On the one hand, no one can quarrel with the noble objectives it professes to promote. At the same time, however, some of the methods and techniques traditionally associated with Brotherhood Week are, to say the least, open to question. It is in the honest hope of distinguishing the wheat from the chaff, the genuine from the spurious, that this sermon was planned and is now being preached.

Its basic premise is that in the search for good will, unless certain preconditions are established—ground rules, I have chosen to call them—perhaps it would be better to abandon the effort at its beginning. Before proceeding to identify these rules, let me say that our concern here is with good will only in one dimension. I speak in this sermon as a Jew, addressing himself to the problem of good will between himself and a predominantly Christian population.

If, in doing so, I seem to stress primarily what the Christian world must do, this is not because we Jews are without our own responsibilities in the matter, but because good will must obviously depend more on the majority 97%

than on the minority 3%. Very well, then, with these understandings established, what are my ground rules for good will?

First, that more than pious, pretentious platitudes are needed. Here there is much blame due on both sides of the equation. We Jews on our part seem to have an uncanny aptitude for permitting the wrong people to represent us in our overtures to the non-Jewish world. Far too frequently our promoters of interfaith activity are men and women whose entire connection to Judaism is nothing but this— men and women who know nothing about our tradition, who never worship with their fellow-Jews except at an interfaith Service, who are seldom seen in the leadership of specifically Jewish organizations. In short, the whole of their Jewishness consists of begging for recognition by the Christian world; the slightest nod from that direction sends them into ecstasies of delight. Precisely because they are so deficient in self-respect, they play directly into the hands of those Christians who are, on their part, no less guilty.

Let me illustrate. Some years ago I appeared on a national telecast which emanated from the City of Washington. Sponsored jointly by the American Federation of Labor and the National Conference of Christians and Jews, the program was devoted to interfaith relations; its participants were three clergymen—a Catholic, a Protestant and myself. Had I known the identity of my colleagues before arriving at the studio, I would have rejected the invitation. The Protestant was the pastor of the then-current President of the United States. He was a prominent leader of the so-called American Friends of the Middle East, an organization whose passionate support of the Arabs and virulent antagonism to Israel were scarcely distinguishable from rank anti-Semitism. The Catholic was a member of the

faculty at Notre Dame, formerly chaplain at a large mid-
western State University. A friend of mine who happened
to have been director of the Hillel Foundation at the same
University described this priest as "a scoundrel." Now I
submit to you: to parade such personalities as these before
the public as advocates of good will is to prostitute the
whole meaning of the term. Yet this kind of thing has been
done with deplorable frequency.

A similar example comes from our own community of
Greater Boston. A few years back the local branch of an
important national Jewish philanthropic organization sponsored a testimonial dinner in honor of a prominent Christian journalist. The man whom this Jewish group chose to
honor had publicly supported Father Coughlin in his time
and Senator Joseph McCarthy in his. He had vigorously
approved the McCarran-Walter Immigration Act, with its
ominous overtones of anti-Semitism. In his diatribes against
labor leaders he had repeatedly referred to the late Sidney
Hillman as the son of a rabbi. He had come as close as he
comfortably could to defending Joseph Kamp, a notorious
anti-Semite. Yet this man was honored—in the name of
good will!—by reputable representatives of our Boston
Jewish community. Need I continue with additional examples of the same thing? The first ground rule for good will
is that we on our part and Christians on theirs must shun
hypocrisy and avoid pious platitudes like the plague.

The second is that all who really seek good will must
eschew any claim to a monopoly on truth. Anyone who
believes that he or his group alone has access to divine
revelation is constitutionally incapable of achieving genuine
good will; what he can offer, at best, is condescension. Are
we Jews ever guilty of such arrogation? Yes, if truth be
told, sometimes we are. When some among us misinterpret

the doctrine of the Chosen People to mean—as it never did
in authentic Judaism—that we are the recipients of special
favors from God or that we possess a relationship to God
which is limited only to Jews, then we make good will
difficult if not impossible. When some of us speak, however
facetiously, of a "goyish kopf" as if Jewish intelligence
were somehow innately superior to any other kind, we put
the attainment of good will in jeopardy. Yes, we can be
guilty too.

The classic example of this kind, however, comes from
the Catholic Church. In April of 1945 *Civilta Cattolica*,
official organ of the Jesuit order in Rome, published the
following: "The Roman Catholic Church, convinced
through its divine prerogatives of being the only true
Church, must demand the right of freedom for herself
alone, because such a right can only be possessed by truth,
never by error . . . Consequently, in a state where the
majority of people are Catholic, the Church will require
that legal existence be denied to error, and that if religious minorities actually exist, they shall have only a *de
facto* existence, without opportunity to spread their beliefs . . ."*

It would be unfair to cite this passage, or others of similar
nature, without immediately adding that since 1945 the
beginning of a new spirit has appeared within the Catholic
Church. It will take time yet to determine just how far that
new spirit will go. Even so vigorous and eloquent a spokesman of ecumenicity as Pope Paul VI, in projecting the
future relationship of his faith to others in his 1963 Corona-
tion Sermon, said that his church would be "respectful,
understanding, patient but cordially inviting" to all those

* Leo Pfeffer: Creeds in Competition, p. 37. Harper and Brothers,
1958.

who—and here are the key words—"are not yet its faithful sons." I hope I am being neither cynical nor captious in saying that this last phrase—especially the word "yet"—bothers me. If the purpose of the patience and cordiality and respect the Pope promises is to help others accept in the future, the truth which he believes only he is capable of fully understanding in the present, this most assuredly will not lead to good will.

I would like to believe that the new breeze blowing through the Vatican is authentic and fresh. That, without surrendering an iota of those beliefs which are precious to themselves in their search for truth, Catholic theologians will encourage their followers to respect without reservation the same search on the part of others. Only if they do this, is good will possible. Only if all of us recognize that no human being or group can know anything like the whole of truth, that the word and will of God are necessarily refracted to us through human minds which are fallible, that what we fervently believe to be true today may be demonstrated to be false tomorrow—only if all of us operate on some such basis as this, can we achieve the good will we seek.

This brings us to the third of our ground rules. If Christians are serious about improving the relationship between us and themselves, they must stop pretending that Judaism is today only the religion of the Hebrew Bible, or, as they would prefer to put it, of the Old Testament. Since this point was made earlier, there should be no need to elaborate at length here. Let me add only that the very term *Old Testament* is offensive to Jews. It implies that there is something inferior and incomplete about our Bible which requires that it be supplanted by a New Testament.

This is in fact what Christianity has taught. That the old Covenant between God and the Jewish people has been replaced by a new Covenant between God and Christians. Dr. Rosemary Ruether, a Roman Catholic Visiting Lecturer in Theology at Howard University has expressed this historic truth with impeccable honesty: "Built into the treatment of the Jewish and Christian Bibles as Old and New Testaments respectively is the idea of Judaism as a superseded and obsolete religion, superseded not simply historically but theologically, superseded in terms of the Covenant of God with Israel itself.*

Dr. Ruether has performed an invaluable service in exposing to the light of day an obstacle to good will which has too often in the past lurked in dark unventilated corners. Interfaith amity will be possible only if Judaism and Christianity are seen as valid *contemporary* alternatives, not as one faith which is antiquated and another which is dynamic and alive. This is our third ground rule for good will.

The fourth follows ineluctably from the third and, like it, was briefly raised at an earlier point. It is an open and honest recognition of the truth that Christianity is not the fulfillment of Jduaism. The reason so many Christians have insisted that Judaism stopped growing nineteen centuries ago is precisely in order that their faith may be made out to be the logical and legitimate successor to the faith of the Hebrew Bible. To them, Christianity is a continuation of the faith founded by Abraham and Moses; they see today's Judaism as a stunted offshoot which has departed from the spirit and meaning of its own origins. Hence it is imperative

---

* R. Ruether: Theological Anti-Semitism in the New Testament, The Christian Century, 2/14/68.

—if good will is to be attained—to insist that not only has Judaism continued to develop during the Common Era, but it has developed as the fulfillment and realization of itself.

Yes, Christianity is founded on ancient Judaism. Yes, it has adopted some of the insights of ancient Judaism. But that is only half the truth. The rest is that Christianity has abandoned or perverted just as many ancient Jewish emphases as it has retained. All of which means to say: it is Christianity which is a deviant of biblical Judaism. Judaism today is the legitimate product of its own past.

Is it necessary to illustrate or to prove? Very well, then: Judaism insisted in ancient times and still does today that man is potentially good; Christianity holds that he is inherently, congenitally evil, having been contaminated from the moment of conception by Original Sin. Judaism proclaims that God is not only One but Unique—that no other creature in the universe may be compared to Him—that man at his very best is but a dim reflection of God. Christianity speaks of God becoming flesh and walking the earth in human form. Do these two examples, of the many that could be given sound as if Christianity is the continuation or fulfillment of Judaism?

Let me not overstate the case, lest I be accused of spiritual myopia. There are elements shared by Judaism and Christianity. There is a common heritage which binds us together. But there are also differences. It is not my purpose to argue these differences, to persuade non-Jews that Judaism is the superior faith. Of course I believe it to be superior for me. But I have neither desire or need to sell Judaism to others. My deep need—if genuine good will is not to be rendered impossible—is to establish as ground rule number four that the various branches of contemporary Judaism all grow legitimately from the trunk of ancient and medieval

Judaism, that Christianity is a separate tree, even if it be the fruit of seed which fell centuries ago from Judaism.

A fifth and final prerequisite for good will is that Christians, when comparing the Hebrew Bible and the New Testament, must stop matching the first at its worst to the second at its best. True, our Bible speaks of God's punishing the third and fourth generation of those who disobey Him, while the New Testament says that "God is love; and he that abideth in love abideth in God." True, the Hebrew Bible describes God as ordering that the enemy be slain "both man and woman, infant and suckling," while the New Testament quotes it as God's will that "not one of these little ones shall perish." But it is equally true that the New Testament says, "Fear Him who is able to destroy both body and soul in Gehenna," while the Hebrew Bible pictures God as "slow to anger and plenteous in mercy." The New Testament harshly threatens, "Whosoever speaks against the Holy Spirit, there is no forgiveness for him whether in this world or the next," while our Bible confidently assures us that "The Lord is good to all, and near to all who call upon Him."

You see how easy it is to prove anything one wants by juxtaposing quotations from the two Testaments. But whichever way one plays the game, it makes no sense. There are crude and noble sentiments in both. There are primitive and civilized concepts in both. There is a progression of thought covering something like fifteen centuries reflected in our Hebrew Bible. The surprising thing is not that occasionally one finds in it a crudity emanating from earlier periods, but that such crudities are also found in the Christian Bible, all of which was composed later than the most recent portions of ours.

Here, then, are our ground rules. First, platitudes and

hypocrisies must be shunned. Second, all claims to exclusive possession of truth must be foreclosed. Third, Judaism must not be restricted to the teachings of the Bible. Fourth, there must be no pretense that Christianity is the legitimate heir and Judaism only the bastard descendant of the Mosaic faith. And fifth, when the literatures of early Judaism and early Christianity are compared, this must be done with a decent regard for accuracy and truth.

Any project or plan aimed at good will, any commemoration or observance of Brotherhood Week which violates or ignores these ground rules is a fraud. Any proposal which encompasses them is valid. Rabbi Robert Gordis has understood this truth with uncommon perceptivity and expressed it with rare eloquence: ". . . the dialogue can be fruitful only if it is fair. It is true that if we reckon with the full dimensions of Judaism and Christianity, the substance of the dialogue between the two faiths is immeasurably complicated. Yet without such an understanding the enterprise is stultifying. Men were not promised that the truth would be simple—only that the truth would make them free."*

* R. Gordis: The Root and the Branch, p. 65, The University of Chicago Press, 1962.

'F